WARBURTON'S WAR

WARBURTON'S WAR

The Life of Maverick Ace Adrian Warburton
(DSO, DFC, DFC (USA))

Tony Spooner
DSO, DFC

A Goodall paperback
from
Crécy Publishing Limited

Printed by
Interprint

A Goodall paperback
published by

Crécy Publishing Limited
1a Ringway Trading Estate, Shadowmoss Road, Manchester M22 5LH

To the long serving airmen who serviced the planes in Malta 1940-1943. Although their airfields were bombed incessantly, unlike the pilots they served they received no decorations. For them, there was no 'operational rest' nor any hope of leaving the island unless by some miracle the siege could be relieved. They were the real heroes of the battle for Malta. None realised their worth more than Wing Commander Warburton and it is only right that this book be dedicated to them.

General Werner Von Fritsch of the German High Command, 1938:

'The military organization with the best aerial photo-reconnaissance will win the next war.'

Captured German Divisional Order, 1944:

'Enemy aerial reconnaissance detects our every movement, every concentration, every weapon and, immediately after detection, smashes every one of these objectives.'

CONTENTS

ACKNOWLEDGEMENTS

ACKNOWLEDGEMENTS

This biography will, I hope, introduce to a wider public a young RAF pilot known as 'Warby of Malta'. It could never have been written but for a quite astonishing amount of material most generously given by nearly 150 complete strangers.

In expressing my thanks, I am faced with the difficulty of correctly identifying them by their rightful rank and honours. The events took place over 40 years ago and virtually all the young persons who then were fighting the war alongside Warby have since risen in status. To give one example, the young CO of 682 Squadron was, when first meeting Warby, Squadron Leader Freddy Ball; when he last knew Warby he was Wing Commander Freddy Ball. He is now Sir Frederick Ball, a retired air marshal with a string of honours after his name.

To avoid a host of footnotes updating individual's ranks (and during the war, those who survived in the RAF were often rapidly promoted), I have adhered to the rank which the individual held at the time when he knew Warby. Where ranks changed while in Malta, I have omitted them. Likewise, no attempt has been made to append the many DSOs, DFCs, DFMs and other well earned medals which so many of those who fought alongside Warby richly earned. Almost all who came within his orbit seem to have been 'gonged'.

I have also made no attempt in the list which follows to differentiate between the various ranks held by the airmen. Whether LAC, AC1, AC2 etc, I have simply referred to them as 'Airman'. As the dedication shows, they all deserve the highest accolade. They too mostly rose to higher ranks as the war progressed.

I must also apologise for not being able to use *all* the fascinating details provided by my many correspondents and new acquaintances. The wealth of material provided would have filled half a dozen books. This leads me to acknowledge most sincerely my publishers who had the task of reducing the material to manageable length. Amy Myers of Kimber & Co. Ltd. successfully accomplished this task and, in a way, this is now her book almost as much as my own. Fortunately Amy became another Warby fan.

If I have missed a name or two in the long list that follows, I can only apologise and offer the lame excuse that, although my task was to research the life of an individual who disappeared without trace in mysterious fashion over 40 years ago, I found myself overwhelmed by those who remembered their Warby. Over 150 photographs were also sent and the pity, once again, is that not all can be reproduced here. Nonetheless again my heartfelt thanks to those who supplied them.

My sincere thanks go to:

John Agius, a Maltese citizen who served the RAF in wartime and subsequently.

Lt Sandy Arkin, USAF, Allied Photo-Reconnaissance (PR) pilot who knew Warby in Malta and Tunisia.

Squadron Leader Freddy Ball, fellow PR Squadron Commander who also knew Warby in Tunisia.

Lieutenant Charles Barry, SAAF, one of the several South African pilots serving in Warby's PR North African Wing.

Squadron Leader Tony Bartley, CO of 111 Fighter Squadron, on whom Warby literally 'dropped out of the sky' at Bône, Algeria.

Sergeant Frank Bastard, who flew many memorable missions alongside Warby from a Malta under fire and was decorated accordingly.

Hubert Beales, a friend of the Warburton family.

Flying Officer David Beaty, a post-war successful author who knew Warby in Malta and who has given me great encouragement to write his story.

Councillor Reginald Biggs of Bury St. Edmunds.

Mr J D Blackwood of the Ministry of Defence Gloucester, likewise Mr Hayson of the same department.

Flight Lieutenant Johnny Bloxam, a pilot colleague of Warby's when with 69 Squadron in Luqa, Malta.

Dr Charles Boffa, another loyal and helpful Maltese citizen.

Captain Bond of St Edward's School, Oxford.

Major Usher Brierley, a SAAF squadron commander who took Warby to his heart and served him well.

George A Brown, who otherwise wishes to remain unidentified. His assistance was invaluable. Without the material he gathered and freely gave, this pen portrait of a great RAF pilot would have been much less accurate and detailed.

Squadron Leader M R 'Mac' Brown RCAF. Mac flew alongside Warby in both Egypt and Malta. He also became his friend and confidant.

Squadron Leader Roy Buchanan, another PR pilot who rose to command.

Squadron Leader George Burges, a Malta colleague and one of the Faith, Hope and Charity pilots who defended Malta in its hour of need.

John Butterworth, a captain of games and prefect at St Edward's School, Oxford.

Dudley Caine, another South African who admired Warby.

Tony Carlisle, himself later an RAF 'ace', who knew Warby as well as anyone could at St Edward's School, Oxford.

Pilot Officer Bill Carr, a young PR pilot happy to be accepted by Warby in Malta. Later a Canadian General.

Major Gil Catton, SAAF another 69 Squadron pilot fascinated by his CO, during Warby's period in command of that unit.

Marion Childs (Nee Gould), a girl 'plotter' in Ops Room with memories of both Warby and Christina.

Flight Lieutenant Harry Coldbeck, another Malta PR pilot with a distinguished record and sharp memories of Warburton. Warrant Officer Philip Cole, of Luqa, Malta.

Flying Officer Les Colquhoun, who became an 'ace' pilot in his own right; duly inspired by Warby in Malta.

Flight Lieutenant Syd Collins, an understanding Luqa adjutant and confidant.

Mr H Crawford, a distant fan of the charismatic Warby.

Pat Crump and GR Cooper, both fellow schoolboys with Warby at St Edward's School, Oxford.

Captain Peter Daphne and Major Glynn Davies, two more South African pilots who came under Warby's spell, as well as under his command, in N Africa.

Florian Devatz, a Swiss air historian who provided valuable details about the flight of 12 April 1944.

Flying Officer 'Paddy' Devine, a navigating pilot whose early war career almost paralleled that of Warby's in both England and Malta.

Mr Angus Duncain of Scotland

Pilot Officer Keith Durbidge, another remarkable PR pilot who earned himself much glory by emulating his beloved CO of 683 Squadron in Malta.

Michael J. Edwards, the UK air historian.

Airman Alan Elliott of Luqa, Malta.

Airman G D Ellis of Luqa, Malta.

Airman E J Ellison, who knew Warby in the UK in the early days of and who assisted with his family background.

William Emerson of New York city, who helped me to find Elliott Roosevelt.

Corporal photographer Ken Fielder, who worked closely with his admired hero in Malta.

Geoffrey Fisher who assisted generously with RAF research.

Sergeant Pilot Ken Forbes who trained alongside Warby pre-war RAF.

Group Captain Terry Flanaghan, RAF Historical Branch.

Norman Franks, an air historian who gave generously his own Warby research material and who assisted in other ways.

Major James Fuglesang British Army Intelligence, Malta.

Sergeant Pilot Bill Gabbutt, another PR pilot inspired by Warby.

Francis Galea, a most helpful Maltese citizen.

Dr R C R Gethen, an associate of the Warburton family.

Flight Lieutenant Gerry Glaister, pilot of 2 PRU, Egypt when Warby was there.

Captain Leon Gray USAF, a much decorated American PR pilot.

John B Harper another St Edward's School contemporary.

Flying Officer Peter Hartley, another Faith, Hope and Charity pilot of Malta's early days of the war.

Captain W Heinemann a German air historian.

Robin Higham Aerospace Historian of Kansas State University who worked tirelessly on various Warby stories.

Flight Lieutenant Mike Hodsman, a photo-interpreter.

Major John Hoover USAF another renowned American PR pilot.

Pilot Officer Edward Homby, an early PR pilot.

Corporal O M Howell, RAF Fitter, Luqa, Malta.

Captain Ken Hunter, SAAF another South African PR air gunner.

Harry Hutson an experienced RAF researcher.

Corporal Kenneth Iles, of 2 PRU Egypt when Warby was there.

Bill Jackson of Toot Baldon, Oxford for information about Mount Farm Airfield UK and the Amercians who flew from it.

Flight Lieutenant Norman Jackson-Smith who shared a room with Warby in a North African nunnery.

Wing Commander Carter Jonas an early Luqa Station Commander.

Margaret Jones, a young RAF plotter in Malta alongside Christina.

Squadron Leader Phil Kelley, a flight commander of 683 Squadron under Warby: also a previous Malta survivor.

L B Kendall a friend and relative of the Warburtons in the UK.

Air Gunner 'Duke' Kent who saw Warby as a folk hero of Malta.

Corporal Harry 'Scoop' Kirk, another devoted RAF photographer, Luqa.

Flight Lieutenant Paul Lamboit, a senior photographic Officer of 2 PRU, Middle East and a friend of Warby's there.

Colonel George Lawson, USAF, a PR pilot and a most helpful unit commander at Mount Farm, the UK 1944.

Peter Lillywhite another Malta RAF officer.

Lieutenant Jim Little RN of Malta early in the war.

Pilot Officer M Llewellyn-Thomas who trained alongside Warby at two RAF establishments pre-war 1939.

Wing Commander P B 'Laddie' Lucas of Fighter Command fame in both the UK and Malta.

Flight Lieutenant Ed Maloney RCAF another Canadian who worked closely and successfully with Warby and his 683 Squadron, Malta.

Francis Marguerat a Maltese citizen with fond memories of both Warby and Christina.

Air Chief Marshal Sir Nigel Maynard whose father commanded in Malta during its early war days.

Airman H E W McDonald of Luqa, Malta.

Colonel Peter McGregor SAAF a pilot and South African air historian.

Corporal Jim McNeil another RAF photographer, Malta and Middle East, who 'thought the world' of Warby.

Group Captain 'Pop' Mitchie, Commander Luqa at a time when Warby was there.

Harold Mitchell and his aunt *Grace* who together provided a vital link to events in Warby's early life.

Sergeant Pax (Paddy) Moren, the remarkable air gunner who shared over 100 epic flights with Warby and who played an important role in his evolution as an outstanding RAF Ace.

Sam Morrison a US citizen who supplied technical details of the Lockheed P38 aircraft.

John Moreton another contemporary at St Edward's' School, Oxford.

Mrs Barbara Moss, the daughter of the talented *Tich Whiteley*, the Australian pilot and commander who in Malta groomed Warby for stardom.

Lieutenant Claude Murray USAF, who supplied some essential material regarding the flight of 12 April 1944.

Dr A A Oddie, another St Edward's School contemporary.

Wing Commander Hugh O'Neill who escorted Warby on some of his most dangerous missions from Malta.

Vincent Orange of New Zealand.

Squadron Leader Alan Orbell with tales to tell of Warby off-duty in Tunisia.

Mrs Pam Osborn Warby's cousin who remembers the young Adrian with affection: as does also her cousin Sheila [Logan] whom she kindly contacted.

Len Paris who studied accountancy with Warby pre-war.

Squadron Leader Stanley Pearce of 2 PRU Egypt when Warby was there.

Flight Lieutenant Bob Pearson. 140 Squadron, Benson.

Nigel Perry of Bedford.

Lt Robin Pittard SAAF, another South African pilot with fond memories.

Flight Lieutenant Tony Powner who met Warby in M E and the UK.

F H Pritchard, Hon Secretary St Edward's School Society.

Norman Prowting, exceptionally helpful with post war research.

Gordon Puttick, some of whose own material collected about Warby was freely given. He, too, was a RAF pilot fascinated by 'The Man'.

Jeffrey Quill, the well known Spitfire Test Pilot, for data on the Spitfire.

Sidney Ricketts of Horsham.

Corporal Ken Rogers, a rigger who devoted much of his time at Luqa to looking after Warby and keeping his Spitfire in A1 condition.

Colonel Elliott Roosevelt, the son of the great President who came to admire, respect and assist Warby in many diverse ways.

Sergeant Conyers Rutter another of the ground crew heroes of Luqa and one who served Warby's squadrons well.

M W J Saulbutts of North End, Portsmouth who supplies a vital missing link to an early Warby adventure.

Marquis Jose Juan Scicluna of the proud and loyal Maltese family.

Hazel Scott an acquaintance of Warby's in North Africa. She led me to Warby's cousin Mrs Osborn.

Sergeant John Shephard, played an important role with 69 Squadron, Malta.

Corporal Norman Shirley, one of the two unique corporals who were decorated for flights with Warby. With his humane outlook Norman instinctively touched the personality that Warby kept hidden.

Flight Sergeant Pilot Fred Simpson, another fine PR pilot of Warby's 683 Squadron, Luqa.

Major Lester Sliter, who with his assistants *Robert Slight*, *M/Sgt James* and *Mickey Russell* unearthed much good material from USAF wartime records, Maxwell AFB Alabama, Historical Research Centre.

Airman John Snook of Malta, a teenager who also contributed movingly about Warby.

Airman Jim Sommerville of Ta Kali and Luqa, Malta.

Flight Lieutenant Henry Sowerbutts of PRU Benson and Malta.

Phil and Mark Spooner, close relatives who assisted research in both the UK and South Africa.

Alan Stewart of Malta.

Les Stuart of Australia, a friend of the Whiteleys.

Airman John Tanker another gallant Luqa fitter who came under Warby's spell.

Sergeant Pilot Mick Tardif a young PR pilot inspired by Warby in Malta.

Jack Tate, archivist of St Edward's School, Oxford, without whose tireless help so much of Warby's school days would never have been discovered.

Tet Tetley (now Walston), a PR pilot who knew Warby in Tunisia and who helped greatly to unearth other colleagues of Malta.

Lieutenant Joseph Terrett USAF, another American PR pilot with fond memories of Warby in Malta and Tunisia.

Douglas Thomson, a close contemporary at St Edward's School, Oxford.

Emanuel Tonna, a Maltese citizen who still remembers the dashing Warby with his long golden hair.

Squadron Leader Trotter of Luqa, Malta.

Wing Commander Geoffrey Tuttle, the pilot and commander who did much to develop PRU as a major war winning force.

Philip Vella, Hon Secretary of the National War Museum Association, Valetta, Malta. Philip has done much to keep Warby's memory alive. He also assisted in a dozen important ways. His book *Malta Blitzed But Not Beaten*, Progress Press, Valetta, is a masterpiece.

Lieutenant Howard Vestal USAF, another American PR pilot with vivid memories of the Great Warby in Malta and North Africa.

Martin Warburton of Oxford, a cousin.

Squadron Leader R J M 'Johnny' Walker, a pilot who flew alongside Warby in both Middle East and Malta.

Airman J K Waters of Luqa, Malta.

Flight Lieutenant John Weaver, who was in at the birth of PRU in 1939.

Marion Wells of Enfield, who provided family details.

Corporal Cyrd Wood whose personal recollections of Malta would fill a book and who is among Warby's greatest admirers. A dedicated groundcrew mechanic who appreciated Warby's contribution to Malta's morale.

Airman Gerry Wilson, another fitter who served Malta and Warby well.

Helen Wright of Enfield who recalls the teenage Warby with affection.

Airman X from Rhyl, Clwyd who still recalls the Xmas booze that Warby unofficially flew in from Egypt.

In addition to the above 145 persons who provided the information which has enabled me to bring the Warby story 'back from the dead', I would also much like to express my appreciation to the Solo Syndication and Literary Agency for permission to quote from the excellent articles by Roy Nash written for the now defunct London newspaper *The Star*. Roy Nash, almost alone, seems to have appreciated what Warby did to help to win the war. As with the case of George Brown mentioned earlier, the story would have been a less complete one were it not for these 1958 articles, especially as they were written at a time when others, now dead, were able to contribute first hand accounts of the man who variously has been called 'The King of the Mediterranean', the 'Lawrence of Malta', the 'Pilot who knew no fear' and 'The most valuable pilot in the RAF'.

Most sincere thanks must also be given to the two principal women in the life of Adrian Warburton. Both remain ageless and charming but wish to remain semi-anonymous. Special thanks, therefore, are given to: 'Betty of the Bush' and Christina.

Each in their own way is a remarkable person and it is my personal plea that one day Christina, who writes with a feeling and fluency that I can only envy, will complete her own account of those terrible days when Malta was under almost constant aerial bombardment. Individually and together, Warby and Christina were symbolic of the heroic resistance of Malta and those who suffered there. They represented the spirit of a people who refused to be beaten by apparently overwhelming odds. Malta will always remember them.

It is significant that almost every one of the persons who remember Warby so clearly after all these years, has volunteered the remark. of: 'Why hasn't this story before been told?' It is a sentiment with which I can only agree. I came into contact with Adrian Warburton in Malta 1941–42. It was an experience I shall never forget. Hence this book which in a small way is my tribute to a truly remarkable man whose many sided character really defied description.

TONY SPOONER

ADDENDUM TO SECOND EDITION

Since this book was first published in 1987 further information about the remarkable Adrian Warburton has been received. One delightful but typical story is that, when in Malta, Warby discovered an unexploded bomb alongside his aircraft. He thereupon borrowed a spanner from an airman and went forward to defuse it.

"Mind what you do with that spanner", called out the airman "its on my charge!"

Further details have come in about Warby's operations as an air gunner in Wellingtons. These, like other unofficial operations, do not appear in his pilot's Log Books. They make it almost certain that in all Warby must have flown over 400 operational trips.

Sadly, Christina Ratcliffe has died. She was still living in Malta. I was delighted that the Sunday Times of Malta on January 22, 1989 printed in full my obituary notice about her. Thanks to finding relatives of her in the UK, Christina was lately reburied in an appropriate cemetery with a headstone which mentions her well earned BEM.

In response to requests from some Malta, UK, Australian and New Zealand members of the George Cross Island Association (GCIA)†, the Malta Government kindly agreed to issue a 50th Anniversary Commemorative Medal to all uniformed persons who helped to supply or defend the island between dates in 1940 and 1943.

HM the Queen, who like her father, takes a personal interest in all Malta matters, has uniquely declared that this Malta medal can be worn on line with British medals.

Also, thanks to the active participation of the GCIA (hon) President, Admiral of the Fleet the Lord Lewin KG, CBE, LVO, DSC, with generous support from HRH Prince Philip, GCIA, members and the Malta Government a unique 'living' monument to honour all those who lost their lives in the supply/defence of Malta during WWII, has been erected. It takes the shape of a huge bell, tastefully mounted within a cupola with a bronze figure of a reclining warrior alongside. It is strategically mounted on a promontory overlooking Grand Harbour, Valletta. The bell is rung on special occasions. An illuminated Book of Remembrance has also been produced with the names of all who fell during the WWII siege and Blitz. This is kept in the Valletta War Museum and, in a short ceremony, a page is turned each day.

The name of Adrian Warburton does not appear in the illuminated Book of Remembrance, as he was lost elsewhere. However when the (USAF) 7th Photo Recon Group Association came to the UK for a reunion, they put up

†The author is a (hon) Vice-President.

a monument of honour to all those who had lost their lives during WWII when operating out of Mount Farm. The Association has also placed a plaque in the village church. This mentions Wing Commander Warburton by name. At the dedication of the monument, I was invited to lay a Warburton wreath. The monument and plaque are at Berinsfield, near Oxford, as the airfield nearby at Mount Farm, no longer exists.

From other US sources, it is positively confirmed that Col 'Kit' Carson in a P-51 of the 357 Fighter Group of the 8th USAF did link up over Lake Constance with Warby on that fateful 12 April, 1944. After this, Col Carson returned direct to the UK, as planned. When last seen Warby was heading Southwards. This was as expected as Carl and he had been briefed to land in Sardinia. Carl duly arrived there but he saw nothing of Warby en route.

If Warby was heading direct for Malta (and Christina?), he may have been piloting the P38F5 that was sighted by the crew of a B17 of the 9th USAF which was returning from a bombing raid over southern Europe. They reported sighting a lone P38F5 descending towards the Adriatic, apparently out of control with the pilot either dead or unconscious. Efforts to ascertain whether or not this happened on 12 April 1944 have, so far, been unproductive.

The most sad post-production news comes from S/Ldr George Lerwill, a DFC Blenheim leader who knew Warby when both were stationed at Luqa. He happened to run into Warby 'sometime in the Spring of 1944' at Shepherds or the RAF club in Piccadilly. After a prelunch 'session' and a liquid lunch, as they parted, Warby confessed to George that he had lost his nerve and never wanted to fly again. George is not certain of the date but he remembers that within a few days he was reading about Warby's disappearance.

Could it be that, like the Greek Gods of yore – the same ones who had inspired the schoolboy Warburton, Warby's renowned reputation as a pilot placed him in an impossible position on top of a pedestal from which he was unable to climb down after his friend and mentor Elliott Roosevelt had gone to such lengths to arrange a special trip for him and Carl?

Personally, I like to think of Warby up on Mount Olympus alongside the fabled Gods who lived similar colourful lives. I somehow can not picture him, now in his seventies, tottering along to the nearest subpost office clutching a pension book.

As David Beaty has so rightly written: "He wasn't real".

Tony Spooner, 1994

ADDENDUM TO THIRD EDITION

Tony Spooner sadly passed away early in 2002, unaware that, because of events later that same year, there would be a Third Edition to his book on his friend Warby.

Late in 2002, the wreckage of an American Lockheed Lightning was excavated from a field near Egling in southern Germany. The excavation indicated that the aircraft that had crashed there was not a P-38 fighter version but in fact a photo-reconnaissance F-5 Lightning and that according to captured German records, this aircraft had crashed at about 1145 hours on 12 April 1944. Furthermore, amongst the wreckage was evidence that the pilot of this aircraft had sadly failed to bale out.

After 58 years, it was at last accepted that Warby had been found and eventually, on 14 May 2003 his remains were laid to rest with full military honours at the Commonwealth War Graves Commission cemetery at Durnbach, close to where he crashed.

Tony Spooner in his Addendum to the Second Edition says of Warby:

Personally, I like to think of Warby up on Mount Olympus alongside fabled Gods who lived similar colourful lives. I somehow cannot picture him now in his seventies tottering along to the nearest sub-post office, clutching his pension book...

There are those now who might think that Tony, an equally brave and highly decorated wartime pilot, and 'Warby' are both together on Mount Olympus looking down as I write, what will hopefully be the final story about 'Warby's' life and especially his death; I only hope that both of them approve as it is an honour for me to be allowed to write this.

In preparing the postscript to this Third Edition, there are a number of people I would like to thank. First and foremost, Frank Dorber without whose determination Warby's remains would have never been found. I would also like to thank Sue Raftree and colleagues from RAF Personnel and Training Command – an unsung, occasionally maligned team dedicated to the sad and sometimes painful and upsetting work of tracing relatives of missing aircrew. Also, I would like to thank Cpl Heidi Cox of External Communications also at Personnel and Training Command for photographs of Warby's funeral. In Germany, I would like to thank Flt Sgt Vince Taylor of the British Embassy Berlin, Dr Anton Huber for his story about the recovery of Warby's F-5 and Bernd Rauchbach for helping me contact the latter. Finally, I would like to thank Graham Day of the Air Historical Branch for his usual (and patient!) help.

Chris Goss, Marlow, September 2003

INTRODUCTION

This is the story of a boy whose favourite book was Sir George Cox's *Tales of Ancient Greece* and who was to transform his childhood dreams into reality by becoming one of the most highly decorated pilots of the war. Under the same Mediterranean skies where the legendary Greek gods lived out their fabled lives, the dreamer became a legend in his own, all too brief, lifetime, but operating in a very real war.

This is the story of a restless young man; a loner who had become an unwanted misfit: an RAF pilot who had few friends and who, during the dramatic first year of the war when Britain stood in her most dire peril, had achieved precisely nothing. By late 1940, he seemed destined to be a pilot who would never hit the headlines.

Abruptly pitchforked into Malta the hottest spot of the war, under circumstances that did him no credit, the loner rapidly found his true self. Fate found him a flight commander who recognized his worth and who groomed him for stardom. In Malta, Warburton also found a woman's love. Warmed by such experiences, the introvert emerged from the shadows into which he had withdrawn. Within months he had become, in the opinion of many, the most daring and valuable pilot of the entire RAF and for three years he continued to blaze his name across Malta's skies.

For as long as 'Six Medal' Warburton remained in bombed and beleaguered Malta, he proved to be as invulnerable as any Greek hero protected by divine powers. Operating in an environment that destroyed many, he flourished as never before.

Like many a Greek fable, the story has its tragic end. When, at last, Warburton was separated from Malta he sank back into oblivion. He became a pilot dogged by bad luck and one who was soon to disappear in circumstances that have never been satisfactorily explained: however a possible explanation is now offered.

War made Warburton and then destroyed him. How tragic that so soon after learning how to live, he was destined to die.

STRANGE BEGINNINGS

Adrian Warburton's life took a most unusual twist almost immediately after his birth: and one which was later reflected in his future. His father, one of six brothers all of whom are reputed to have displayed occasional idiosyncrasies of character, decided to have his only son christened inside a submarine. Later he was fond of declaring that he knew of no other lad who had been christened in such surroundings.

The submarine was at Malta. Adrian's birth had taken place at Middlesborough on 10th March 1918, when the First World War still had eight months to run. Geoffrey Warburton was a young brilliant submarine commander who had been awarded the prestigious Distinguished Service Order.

Christenings seem to have fascinated Commander Geoffrey Warburton. There is no evidence that he was in any way a religious man yet, during the height of the Second World War, he managed to get a phial of Jordan water transported from Haifa, where he was based, to England for the christening of his first grandchild. This unusual action was taken although he had so disapproved of his daughter's marriage (on totally unreasonable grounds that the husband was only a medical student, not yet actually qualified) that he had refused to attend the wedding or hold it from his house. Commander Warburton's other claim to fame (as he liked to call it) was that his submarine *J6* was sunk by a ship of his own British navy and that when rescued from the water, he was still wearing his captain's hat!

Warburtons at war never seemed to live normal lives. For one thing, DSO's were fairly commonplace in the family. One of Geoffrey Warburton's brothers had earned one with the Army and it is thought that a generation before another Warburton had also been so decorated. Adrian himself was to collect two of these distinguished awards, and according to one of his relatives, Captain Warburton-Lee, the first officer to be awarded the Victoria Cross in WWII, was a cousin. In times of war, Warburtons shone. What little is known of young Adrian's earliest days points to a disjointed childhood. His mother, Muriel, was the daughter of a distinguished Colonial Police Officer and a person who attached great importance to social graces and what was then termed 'good breeding'. She was a very pretty and attractive lady but, so a friend of the family has advised: 'Underneath that aristocratic and presentable exterior lay a woman of very limited intelligence.'

Possibly because of her excellent social connections, Geoffrey

Warburton after the war found himself appointed to a number of not over-arduous and pleasant appointments overseas in an official naval capacity in some distant corners of the then far flung British Empire. In one of the excellent articles written about Adrian Warburton for the London evening paper The *Star* in 1958, Roy Nash refers to a journey that the family took to Australia at a time when Adrian was only a toddler.

Adrian always had the finest of fine blond hair. It was something his mother was very proud of. Possibly it was inherited from her? As described in an interview between Muriel Warburton and Roy Nash:

> When Adrian was about two we went to Australia. In those days little boys wore their hair long, like little girls, until they were above five. Adrian had long curls. On the way out he slipped away from his governess, toddled into the ship's barber and had them cut off. They were beautiful curls. It broke my heart.

In the same article, Muriel Warburton describes a 'ten-bob flip' which she and her prep school son later took at Bournemouth. The pilot had asked if they 'wanted the works?' Without comprehending, she had assented. As a result the pilot looped and rolled the light plane all over the sky. Muriel didn't like it a bit but Adrian was thrilled.

As was the custom of those days, the children of officials of the British Empire serving overseas, would be educated back in England with the parents only occasionally seeing them during spells of 'Home Leave'. This left Alison, Adrian's sister, and Adrian to be brought up by whomever could be so persuaded to undertake the task. In some other family, the daughter Alison, five years older than Adrian, might have early become a substitute mother to the young Adrian but this was not Alison's bent. The two were always good friends but seem to have seen little of one another. Both went to local schools in Bournemouth where their grandparents lived. Alison to Fontainebleau and Adrian to Sangeen until aged about 13–14. In both institutions they were probably boarders.

For their holidays, Adrian and Alison lived with their grandmother at Branksome Park, Bournemouth. Dr Gethen, the medical man who married Alison (initially it was against her father's wishes but later, when both men were in the navy, they became good friends) has provided a description of the household at Bournemouth. The grandmother was a diminutive woman 'well under five feet' but one who ruled over her household with a firm hand. Her husband was a retired medical man given to sudden bouts of depression, during which he would stay in his room for days on end. The tiny grandmother had quite a retinue of staff in her large Bournemouth home almost overlooking Meyrick Park. Adrian could scarcely have known his grandfather since he died in 1922.

Dr Gethen recalls that the grandmother was clearly a woman of intelligence. She used to breakfast in her room but on some days, by the time that she would appear to give the staff their day's instructions, she would have already completed *The Times* crossword puzzle. Yet it may have been a household lacking in human warmth, not one where over-fond grandparents delighted in spoiling the grandchildren entrusted to them.

A boy left so much on his own, with his head full of Cox's *Tales of Ancient Greece* (his favourite book, according to his mother) and with a war hero as a father might easily indulge in heroic day-dreams. 'He didn't make many friends,' said his mother, and 'never minded being by himself'. Yet Adrian was not just a dreamer. He was a fine swimmer and a good shot: also like most English boys, he was extremely fond of his animals. He was also 'all boy' in his love of climbing trees. He knew no fear.

Life for all the Warburton family became greatly altered when, at some mid-point between the wars, owing to defence cuts Commander Geoffrey Warburton found himself axed from the Royal Navy. In some respects, the commander was more fortunate than most. He obtained a good position with Gaumont British and was soon appointed as manager of the Empire Cinema at Shepherd's Bush, London. It was a large cinema and it was at an age when the cinema dominated the lives of millions, much as TV does today. To be reasonably close to his place of work, the family settled down in a pleasant residential part of Enfield. Number 142 Park Avenue was a good address in the eyes of most but Muriel Warburton did not regard herself as 'most'.

It appears that Muriel Warburton took the axing of her husband from the Royal Navy and his employment as a cinema manager as a retrograde step. Commerce was much frowned upon by those who regarded themselves as 'upper class'. In truth it was a far cry from the life style to which she had grown accustomed. In Enfield even the English weather seemed to lack the brilliance of those Eastern skies. Above all else, to become the wife of a local cinema manger rather than of a Senior Naval Officer was a social comedown. It may have been an additional blow that Muriel Warburton seemed unable to assimilate. It may have been then that she started to drink: the curse that was ultimately to ruin her and all her pretty ways.

Two cousins, Mrs Pam Osborn and her cousin Sheila Logan, have clear contrasting recollections of Adrian as a child. It appears that Adrian's parents did not get on well together. It also appears that there were two sides to the conflict. Mrs Osborn recalls that the marriage between Geoffrey and Muriel was a far from happy one and adds that in those days, 'It was rather frowned upon to walk out, so Muriel Warburton [known to both cousins as Aunt Babs] was persuaded to stay.' Geoffrey Warburton she describes as: 'A very difficult and unpopular man, who went his own way.' Very significantly, Mrs Osborn adds: 'Adrian never got on with his father. I think Adrian's character was much influenced by his unhappy home life

entirely due to his father's attitude towards his mother, who adored him.'
She recalls Adrian, her favourite cousin, as 'always lots of fun'.

On the other hand Sheila remembers her Uncle Geoffrey as a very kind
man who provided her with free cinema seats and chocolates! She also
considers that Muriel Warburton looked upon and loved Adrian almost as
a toy and 'tried to smother him with the affection that she probably didn't
get from her husband Geoffrey'. In view of Adrian's later period when he
was regarded as a loner it is interesting that both girls saw him as a normal
friendly young boy.

Dr Gethen recounts that Adrian once ran away from school but was
brought back. Since this does not seem to have occurred at his public
school, the assumption is that it took place earlier.

Scholastically, Adrian was at least a good average. When aged nearly
14, he was sent to the excellent classical school of St Edward's, Oxford –
a boarding school of some 600 pupils. The choice was in all probability
made by Muriel Warburton because the headmaster (called the Warden)
was Henry Kendall, a cousin of Muriel's.

Warburton A, arrived at St Edward's in January 1932. That term
twelve new boys arrived. Mostly they were placed, according to the
marks which they had obtained at the Common Entrance Examination, in
the school's III or Lower IV class. However Adrian and one other, were
integrated in the Upper IV. He was appointed to Sing's House, along with
another new boy, Thomson.

By and large young Warburton was regarded as a misfit. G R Cooper
recalls that, 'He was often in trouble with authority.' Douglas Thomson
writes: 'I didn't like him … I seem to recall him as a loner, a difficult
personality with few real cronies among other boys.' John Moreton and Pat
Crump also remember him as a loner.

A common interest in aeroplanes led Adrian to become an acquaintance
of another boy of much the same age, Tony Carlisle. It was, however, the
only interest they shared in common. Tony also became an RAF ace and
before war's end had been awarded three DFC's (one an American one).
Adrian and he were often in the same class so he saw a lot of him. He frankly
regarded Adrian with horror. He confirms what both Thompson (Sing's) and
his mother have stated, namely, 'that he neither needed nor wanted friends.'
True or not, one wonders? In nearly all respects young Warburton seemed
bent on displaying characteristics that were almost the direct opposite of
those that good schools like St Edward's liked to promote. He would have
nothing to do with any team game. He regarded exercise as something to
avoid. He would spend his money on chocolate bars. Facially he had
inherited a slight sneer from his father and employed this gesture to most of
those activities of which the school was most proud. He took delight in the
fact that although he eschewed every form of exercise, he was by far the

most outstanding swimmer of the school for his age. John Butterworth who was captain of swimming, found him no trouble at all.

With the advent of puberty, he found great delight in self-abuse and quite openly boasted about how many times he could satisfy himself. This attitude shocked some of his companions who believed wholeheartedly in the maxim of: 'mens sana in corpore sano'. What both surprised and amazed them was that, despite his unhealthy habit, his refusal to train in any way, and his only average size he was not only a far faster swimmer than they were but he possessed unusual physical strength.

In the habit of all schoolboys, wrestles and ragfights occurred between them. He was so strong that none would attempt to indulge in horseplay with him more than once. Tony Carlisle mentions that when engaged in a fight with an opponent, his pale blue eyes would harden, his biceps bulged and regardless of any weight or age he was giving away, his opponents suffered.

Years later, the author can vouch for this. Once in Malta during the war, Warburton and he became embroiled in what was no more than a harmless rag. In no time the author found himself pinned to the floor in a vice-like grip with those blue eyes, suddenly turned darker, boring into him. He deemed it prudent to 'surrender' with what little 'face' he could get out of the encounter. Others were present and it seemed that it was of vital importance to Adrian that he be seen to come out best.

Yet for all this prowess in the swimming bath and at schoolboy wrestling, Warburton was never robust. He was of average height or even a little above but slim. He had the perfect build for swimming with broad shoulders but slim hips. Tony Carlisle remembers that he seemed off balance when he walked; half on his toes. Adrian Warburton was also a first class shot.

Another boy who arrived at much the same time as Warburton was Gibson. His experiences at St Edward's were even less noteworthy than Adrian's. He was neither a swift swimmer nor a crack shot. He was 'just another boy' never backward nor brilliant and would never have been recalled by anyone except he became a household name – Group Captain Guy Gibson VC, DSO, DFC. It was he who led the epic 'Dam Busters' raid of Bomber Command. A fellow schoolmate John Harper recalled: 'Guy Gibson … was by comparison (with Adrian) a retiring introspective type who did not appear to show any of the powers of leadership and qualities which so distinguished him in the war.'

Another St Edward's friend Geoffrey Fisher, has produced an interesting comparison between the two boys, Warburton and Gibson:

Warburton	Gibson
Individualist.	Team Man.
Non-Conformist.	Establishment figure.
Charismatic, in the sense of inspiring but probably very much his own man.	Nice guy, nice wife, pet dog. Did all the right things.
Highly decorated but little publicity. Was he not good material?	Wide recognition and publicity then and now.
Almost forgotten by the service.	Memorial Window at St Edward's presented by Air Council.
Relatively unknown at St Edward's.	Widow still honoured at official functions.
Strikingly handsome, attractive to women.	Pleasant good-looking fellow.
Relaxed attitude to uniform and Service minutiae, but not scruffy.	Completely orthodox in attitude and appearance.

As Douglas Bader had also been a pupil at St Edward's some years previously, this classical school, originally founded as a place of learning for the sons of clergymen – and set down in its fine buildings in the very heart of scholastic Oxford, can surely have no equal in the number of top RAF aces it turned out for World War II.

Adrian Warburton's interest in aviation was heightened by two matters. Close to the school's playing fields was a flying ground which had been used as a RFC training aerodrome way back in the early days of the first war. Port Meadows was still capable of being used as such and the Barnard Air Circus flew in there. The boys were not allowed to visit this but one of the rowing coaches, A K Emmet, had his own Bristol Fighter and occasionally used to land it there.

Tony Carlisle also recalls the great England to Australia Air Race of 1934 and the interest it generated among the 'aeroplane group' to which he and Adrian Warburton belonged. Both had guesses as to what the secret De Havilland Comet aircraft would look like and were delighted when it won with ease. Apart from this one group, Adrian took no part in any of the several societies at the school: science, drama, art, choir, engineering, literary etc.

Adrian Warburton left school a term or two earlier than was normal. No reason is known. He would not have been superannuated for lack of scholastic ability. He always seems to have kept up with others or even to have kept his place ahead of his contemporaries. He was definitely good at Maths, as Jack Tate has deduced from the VI Maths form he had reached at the age of 17 when he left.

Helen Wright who was in charge of Brian's Lending Library at Enfield at the time that Adrian left St Edward's recalls that 'Adrian was one of my favourite customers: a very quiet and attractive young man with fair hair.' A similar verdict was given by Anthony Oddie, another St Edward's contemporary, who knew him less well than some and remembers him as a 'gentle quiet-spoken boy.'

For the next two to three years, almost nothing is known about the growing young man. Dr Gethen has, however, contributed one story which speaks volumes for his general teenage restlessness. When he was about fifteen Adrian built himself a canoe from a frame of light wood covered with what was merely brown paper doped over to make it more watertight. It was probably built from instructions issued in a magazine or newspaper. Without a word to his parents, he strapped his new creation on his back and cycled off. Nothing was heard of him until nearly a day later when he was rescued from the sea near Frinton. Assuming that he launched the canoe into the Thames from close to where the family was living at Enfield, he would have travelled quite a good distance. What was he running from? Where was he heading?

Commander Warburton had made arrangements for his son to be articled to a well established Cheapside firm of accountants, Messrs Nicholson, Beechcroft & Co. There is a suggestion that the family's finances were not all that good and that the commander may have commuted part of his Navy pension in order to raise the necessary fairly stiff lump sum for this kind of apprenticeship. But Mrs Osborn, Adrian's cousin, recalls a clash between Adrian and his father when he vetoed Adrian's desire to join the RAF.

The period was 1938. Len Paris was a contemporary and had also been articled to the same firm. He recalls that the firm was a good one but *very* traditional. Len found Adrian to be excellent company but, in his opinion, unsuited to a lifetime of accountancy. The firm tended to share this view, too! The two lads became friends and when he took Adrian home for a meal, his father, also a retired naval commander, took a good view of him. His mother, perhaps struck by his good handsome looks, thought him a charming boy. Women of all ages inevitably fell for this beautiful boy with his flaxen hair and blue eyes.

At the accountants, Adrian was apt to do whatever came into his head. This made Len feel a little uneasy at times. The partners didn't approve of his offbeat antics although the junior staff were happy to have 'things livened up a bit'. One particular antic has remained with Len Paris. Adrian, returning from lunch one day, saw the managing partner's door open and decided to use his private wash-room which lay beyond. There he was caught and given a pretty rough dressing down. Adrian went back to the general office, one or two floors above, got out of the window over Cheapside, climbed down the outside and went back into the managing partner's private wash-room via an open window. He then proceeded to walk past the managing partner at his desk. The old man, thought he was seeing things!

One of the partners was almost in his nineties and, apart from Adrian's antics, life for both young men was extremely dull and in short time both left for more exciting occupations. Len left to take up an appointment in West Africa. When he went back to the 'Old Firm' to say a fond farewell to his former friend, he learnt that Adrian's articles had been terminated by mutual consent and that he had left with the intentions of joining the RAF.

Len speculates that Adrian's father might not have been pleased to see so much money thrown down the drain. It could hardly have helped to breach the gap between father and son which Pam Osborn, his cousin, had noted. However things were to change. It was at his father's warning in 1938 that 'War was coming soon and he had better get himself ready for it', that Adrian volunteered and was accepted by the local Army Territorial Unit. This was the 22nd London Armoured Car Company and he became a part time soldier No 7888844, a private. However his sights were still set on the RAF and his application to join was accepted later that year.

WARBURTON JOINS THE RAF

Late in 1938 Adrian Warburton was granted a short-service commission with the RAF and began his flying training (being at that time only in the RAF on probation) at No 10 E & R FTS at Prestwick. Acting Pilot Officer Warburton, Service No 41635, remained there from 31 October 1938 until 14 January 1939 and, having proved an ability to fly, had his RAF entry confirmed and was posted to a Regular RAF Training School, No 8 FTS at Hullavington, Wilts.

All this was normal. In order to expand the RAF rapidly in the face of a much larger German air force, Britain, thanks in part to the campaign of an out-of-office politician, by name Winston Churchill, had instigated a new Short Service Commission scheme. Under the terms of this young men were taken by the RAF to serve as aircrew for up to five years. They were merely given commissions, taught to fly the RAF's latest machines and then dismissed with a nice gratuity after having served their five years. To sort out the sheep from the goats and do so without incurring any responsibilities (and to save money), the initial training was farmed out by contract to established private flying clubs and the like. These E & R FTS schools were run on military lines. The instructors were all RAF pilots or reservists and part of the scheme was that after their five years, the officers would form a reserve of pilots trained to fly the latest types of military planes.

Adrian was no natural pilot. He never achieved a rating higher than average and, when given wings at Hullavington in May 1939, he was assessed as 'below average'. There was no lower rating. Any worse and he would have been thrown out.

During his seven months at Hullavington, Warburton was trained to fly his first real RAF machines. Prior to going there, he had only flown in the standard RAF ab initio training biplane of the time, the well known DH82 generally referred to as the Tiger Moth, an excellent trainer because it was not all that easy to master. It was small, with an engine of only 120hp.

At Hullavington, Warburton was at once introduced to the Hawker Hart trainer. This was also a biplane but one with a Rolls Royce engine of several hundred horse power. Every pilot who flew the Hart soon came to love it. It handled well. It had a lively performance for a training aircraft and it led to pupils also being allowed to fly the similar but still better performing Hawker Fury which between the wars had been an RAF first line biplane fighter.

At Hullavington, Warburton also experienced night flying in a plane similar to the Hart. This was the Hawker Audax. A fellow officer pupil, 'Tom' M Llewellyn-Thomas, recalls that Warburton, like himself, was slated for single engine types only. He vividly recalls watching Warburton hold off far too high on coming in to land and spreading the undercarriage of his biplane all over the grass. With regard to his general nature he writes:

> He was always ebullient and took nothing seriously, verging on the eccentric. The two of us later attended the No 2A Torpedo Training Course at Gosport September – October 1939, arriving there to 'celebrate' the outbreak of war between Britain and Germany (3 September 1939). One evening we set forth for a beer at the Queen's Hotel, Southsea, and I noticed that Warby was getting stared at by the people on the bus. He was wearing his forage cap back to front and completely unaware of it. I alerted him, whereon he said: 'Bugger them, I'm not one of the crowd' and left his cap that way round for the rest of the evening.
>
> At Gosport, the two of us mucked around in the station's Flight Tutor – a small plane similar to a Tiger Moth, and he nearly killed us both by aiming between the masts of one of the giant Queen lines anchored in the Solent, oblivious to the array of wires. My screech of terror dissuaded him.
>
> Later in the war, I met him and his ex-navigator (? Johnny Spires) in the Wings Club in London. By then he was a wing commander with a blinding display of medals. We had a night of it, then parted. Shortly thereafter he was killed.
>
> He was a great fellow and I am proud to have been a passing friend.

Llewellyn-Thomas, who later became a squadron leader, also remembers that he and Warby had earlier met at Uxbridge: 'We had to write a written exam and I remember this slender rather patrician blond fellow kicking me and whispering: "What the hell is a parallelogram?"'

Another pilot officer at the same Gosport Torpedo Training Unit (TTU) was Paddy Devine. Paddy remembers Adrian as a 'dark horse and bit of a loner'. They used to go into Portsmouth pubs together. Paddy recalls that:

> One evening Warby, a naval sub-lieutenant and I were in a room with two or three girls when Warby, showing off his revolver, accidentally let off a shot. It ricocheted around all four walls but none of us was hurt. Warby was not a popular junior officer. He was a line-shooter and an egoist but his later wartime glory blinded everyone to his previous unpopularity.

It would appear that Warby was both wildly irresponsible and determined to attract attention to himself: the mark of a man who was not sure of himself? Not being able to attract attention as a brilliant pilot, he seems to have resorted to highly flamboyant gestures.

The fact that Warburton and Llewellyn-Thomas had been sent to the TTU at Gosport shows that they had been selected to join Coastal Command which alone trained pilots to drop torpedoes. It is also an indication that, whatever shortcomings Warburton may have had as a pilot, he must have displayed some ability as a navigator. Here his aptitude for maths would have made him pick up the rudiments of navigation more easily than most. Only those who showed some aptitude at this study were eligible for either Coastal or Bomber Command.

Llewellyn-Thomas was posted to one of Coastal Command's Vildebeeste Torpedo Bomber Squadrons, No 42, while Warburton was posted to the only other such unit, No 22 Squadron. At the outbreak of war, Coastal Command was envisioned as a force which would be working alongside the Navy. At that time, 'Cinderella Coastal' was very much secondary to her sister Bomber and Fighter Commands. However, neither the RAF nor the Navy possessed modern torpedo-carrying planes worthy of such a name. All that the RAF could provide were the ancient Vickers Vildebeeste biplanes. This was a single-engined plane and one that would not have looked out of place in the First World War. It is the same type as the schoolboy Warburton had cut out and pasted into a scrap book at St Edward's before trading it for Mars Bars to Tony Carlisle who has preserved it.

Coastal Command in general, and 22 Squadron in particular, used this period of phoney war from September 1939 to April 1940, to prepare better for the real war that surely would hit Britain in the future. The ancient Vildebeestes were being replaced by the Bristol Beauforts. These modern twin-engined torpedo bombers were far in advance of anything that the squadron had experienced. The pilots had little or no experience of flying twin-engined aircraft. Moreover the take-off and landing speeds of the Beauforts were considerably higher and the Coastal Command airfields were not all that large. The Beauforts also introduced the pilots to flaps, retractable undercarriages, a new set of instruments and far more complicated propeller and engine controls. Quite a few pilots found the many changes more than they could manage and accidents, according to the squadron records, were all too frequent. In part, this was due to the Beauforts' engines. They were of a revolutionary kind which had rotating sleeve-valves instead of the normal cylinder head inlet and outlet valves. This was almost the first engine to have such an innovation and at first it worked far from well. To have to battle against engine failure on top of all else that had to be learnt, was asking almost too much.

Warburton had arrived at 22 Squadron at Thorney Island, near Portsmouth, along with two other pilot officers – Willis and Chave-Jones.

The squadron operational records show that very little flying was done by anyone during October 1939, or in the months that followed. The only reference to any hostile activity is clouded behind references to 'cucumbers being laid'. The 'cucumber' was a long cylindrical mine designed to fit into an aircraft's bomb bay. They were laid outside enemy-held ports.

Pilot Officer Warburton was sent on a course, details unspecified, at Thornaby on 20 November and was away until 21 December. As he never seems to have been detailed to fly in anger in either the Vildebeeste or the Beaufort, his presence could hardly have been missed.

Adrian's log-book for October shows that he was rapidly converted to flying the Vildebeestes. He took part in the squadron training activities such as dive-bombing practice, formation flying and some low level practice bombing runs. In January he was given a few circuits and bumps in a twin-engined Blenheim and flew it himself for half-an-hour bringing his total twin-engine time to 35 minutes. He then for whatever reason had a four month lay-off from all flying from January to May 1940.

The relative calm of the 'phoney' war of 1939 and early 1940 was shattered in April 1940 when the Germans began their conquest of most of Europe by the rapid seizure of Norway and the capitulation, without a shot being fired, of Denmark. On 8 April, 22 Squadron moved from near Portsmouth to North Coates airfield facing the North Sea. Real war had begun. Minelaying and bombing at night of enemy ports in Beauforts began in earnest but not until 24 April were the aircraft dispersed around the airfield. Until then neat rows of planes had been the order of the day: a glorious target for any marauding enemy plane and an indication of the placid state of mind which existed during the phoney war.

On 26 May, the squadron lost its CO when Wing Commander Mellor failed to return from a sortie. Three days later, by which time Holland (in five days), Belgium and virtually the whole of Northern France had been conquered by an offensive which only began on 10 May, the squadron for the first time assayed a daylight bombing attack. The enemy-held port of Ymuiden was the target. Wing Commander F St J or 'Joss' Braithwaite, a flight commander who had earlier been injured in one of the many Beaufort crashes, had by then been appointed the new CO. Flight Lieutenant E A 'Tich' Whiteley, an Australian, had taken over C Flight. Both these officers were soon to play a leading role in the events which were to shape the career of Pilot Officer Warburton.

Where was Adrian while these momentous events were shaking the free world? He was once again soon to be sent on yet another course. In many units there are apt to be personnel who, for some reason or another, don't seem to fit in with the accepted pattern. Warburton could well have been one such. Although he was, on paper, a member of 22 Squadron for the best part of a year, he spent up to half his time on courses elsewhere and never once is mentioned in any operational record sheet. He is mentioned just once in squadron records: an appointment to go to the dentists! He was never converted to flying the Beauforts which were now all that the squadron possessed. Yet he had been carefully and leisurely trained as a pilot in pre-war days in sharp contrast to the hasty training given to the rush of wartime pilots who had answered the call upon mobilisation and who were, as the author can attest only too well, being rushed through their training in indecent haste.

When after his four month lay-off Warburton resumed flying in May it was not to fly Beauforts but the old Hawker single-engine biplane, the Audax. Against every entry in his log book is written 'Drogue Towing' – an exercise to give air gunners air to air experience of firing at moving targets. It was not the kind of task assigned to good pilots.

The course that Warburton was to attend from June to September 1940, while the Battle of Britain raged overhead, was a lengthy navigation course at Squire's Gate, an airfield rushed into being from a racecourse at the south end of Blackpool: where the trams stopped. It was more than a normal navigation course as it involved some photography and the training of pilots to work with naval units far out to sea. It was the No 2 School of General Reconnaissance (School of GR). It so happens that the author was a young junior pilot-navigator instructor at this same school, first as a sergeant pilot but commissioned as a pilot officer RAFVR in June 1940. However he had no recollections of ever seeing, or hearing about, any Pilot Officer Warburton. A small number of pupils were assigned to each instructor and they were generally the only ones that the instructor met. The instructors did all the flying and the aircraft used were the docile Ansons. The pupils did no flying as pilots. For this task the Avro Ansons were almost ideal since they had commodious fuselages for several pupils and all their equipment. Also they were painfully slow and the effect of drift the great enemy of accurate track keeping over the seas, was most marked. Wind causes drift and there is plenty of that in breezy Blackpool.

Another event which was to shape Warburton's future destiny was that on 10 June, confident that Hitler had all but won the war, the Italian dictator, Benito Mussolini, entered the war and declared war on Britain. He immediately cast his eyes at the nearest, and supposedly easiest, piece of Britain he could seize. This was Malta, only sixty miles south of Sicily, a British colony.

Malta, against most expectations, showed no signs of giving in. Although the war had been in progress for nine months, the island was chronically ill prepared to meet the Italian challenge. Yet it did so and the initial heroic defence by three obsolescent biplane Sea Gladiators, christened Faith, Hope and Charity has passed into history.

By August 1940, with Malta holding firm, the cry went forth for some swift modern aircraft to be based there so that reconnaissance flights to the nearby Italian naval bases could be made to give early warning that Mussolini's modern and powerful fleet was about to set forth to challenge the British Navy. The task fell upon 22 Squadron. It was given three or four American-built Glenn Martin Marylands – a type completely new to the RAF – and told to train a few crews as fast as they could and get them to Malta without delay.

It was a big challenge since nobody knew what the Maryland could do and there were no American pilots to demonstrate. The controls and electrics in this US aircraft were entirely different. There was also the problem of how to get the aircraft, which were in Britain, to Malta, especially as at that time, there was no real aerodrome at Gibraltar other than a converted racetrack. For security reasons and with Spain, pro-German but officially neutral, overlooking it, the policy was that Gibraltar was not, to be used by aircraft destined for the Middle East. Such aircraft were crated and shipped by sea: a journey of several weeks or months and one of uncertainty in wartime.

Joss Braithwaite was faced with an almost impossible task. Fortunately he was a man of great resource. 22 Squadron also had a talented flight commander in Tich Whiteley. Between them they set about tackling this additional assignment. Braithwaite must have been loath to lose such a valuable flight commander as Tich but he informed him that he would be taking the Marylands to Malta. There they would be known as 431 Flight and no longer part of 22 Squadron. Braithwaite decided to test one of the new aircraft himself to see what it could do. After an early flight he sensibly took one to the nearest Fighter Command station to show them what it looked like as he had deduced that with the Battle of Britain raging at its fiercest the 'fighter boys' would be more likely to shoot down any unidentified aircraft sighted in the skies. While there he arranged for some fighter affiliation to see how the new plane handled under (mock) attack. He came back impressed. By using maximum boost, he had managed to out-run the Hurricanes! American planes were fitted with manual control over the engine boosters. In all probability Braithwaite had overboosted the engines. He had no guide to tell him and the calibrations were in units quite foreign to him. Having satisfied himself, he then handed the rest of the evaluation to Tich Whiteley and the other two pilots whom he had assigned to the new 431 Flight.

Tich's major anxiety was how to get the aircraft across the 1,350 miles of occupied Europe that separated Britain from Malta. In order to check upon this fuel consumption he arranged for three aircraft to carry out five hour endurance flights at different levels, 8,000 to 16,000 feet. He had earlier made the decision that the best hope of being able to reach Malta unscathed would be to cross Europe at night. He could only hope that the aircraft had sufficient range for the flight.

On an early night flying practice session, an enemy air raid came over. All landing lights at North Coates and other UK aerodromes were promptly doused. Tich spent almost the whole night over the North Sea. Whenever he attempted to get back to friendly territory, he found himself the attention of searchlights and anti-aircraft fire. He sat it out until first light by when he had already been posted as 'Missing on Active Service'. It had been a long night.

Thereafter arrangements were made to complete the training at Aldergrove in Northern Ireland where the war was more remote and where the fighter boys and the ground defences were less trigger-happy. The aircraft was not an easy one to master and one aircraft with its crew perished in Ireland when it hit a hangar. However a replacement aircraft was found.

Another problem was that the squadron had few specialist navigators. Accordingly, pilots with navigational training had to be detailed to carry out this demanding part of the forthcoming flight across Europe. Whether Warburton was a natural choice to be detailed to navigate will never be known. He was still completing his GR Course at Blackpool while the testing of the Marylands was in progress elsewhere. He probably was a good natural navigator, more certainly he had a dubious reputation as a natural pilot, he may therefore well have been an obvious choice on these grounds. However other factors were involved.

The author, by then a squadron leader, served under Joss Braithwaite in 1943/44 and, upon discovering that he had been Adrian's CO during the early days of the war, and already being intrigued by his own knowledge of what Warburton had achieved in Malta, he took every opportunity to quiz Joss about Warby's early days of wartime. Joss would not go beyond saying that he 'had to get Warby out of the country quick, before the law caught up with him'.Although the author returned to this subject whenever he could, all he got from his station commander, as Joss then was, was that it was 'something to do with money, women and the law' and 'It killed two birds with one stone, to assign Warburton as a navigator of one of the Marylands being rushed to Malta.' Tich Whiteley has put it on record (in a letter written in 1956 that 'My CO [Braithwaite] asked me whether I would take Warburton with me to Malta where he could have hopefully a fresh start, pay his debts and rehabilitate himself' – a typical kindly thought from an excellent RAF commander.

What then were the reasons why Warburton had to be got out of the country? For explanation it is necessary to go back to 1939 and Adrian Warburton's posting to 2 TTU in Gosport in September. One of the pubs that the young officers used to visit was the up-market Bush. Here there was a particularly lovely barmaid known as Betty (although that was not her real name). She had been a Beauty Queen aspirant and as her picture shows she was in the parlance of the day, a 'smasher'. After only the briefest of courtships during which Adrian occasionally entertained her outside working hours, they were married on 28 October 1939.

Their motives were in all probability very different. Betty was the daughter of a 'Chargehand of Shipwrights HM Dockyard', to quote from the marriage certificate. Betty came from good working stock but from early years had been seeking the wider world which she knew to exist outside the Portsmouth North End where her family lived. She was five or six years older than the 21-year-old Adrian and had already ventured beyond the relatively narrow confines of her background. At the early age of 17, much against her father's wishes, she had married a saxophone player by whom she had a daughter, who was being brought up by her parents. Betty had been trained as a hairdresser, but after her divorce also served at the Bush, where she had become known as 'Betty of the Bush'. She was greatly attracted by Adrian's good looks and his off-beat personality. He was definitely different from the other young gentlemen who frequented her blacked-out crowded bar in those first dramatic weeks of the war.

Everyone was expecting Britain to be bombed to bits by the dreaded Luftwaffe and an air of 'live for today for tomorrow we may die' prevailed. Betty was the apple of her father's eye according to her brother, and her father would not even attend the hasty Registry Office ceremony.

For the uncertain-of-himself Warburton, the marriage may have seemed a possible way out of the loneliness with which he had surrounded himself for so many years. Adrian was, it is thought, very inexperienced with girls. They invariably were attracted to him but he hadn't seemed able to respond. His habit of self-abuse at St Edward's may have become ingrained? Irresponsibility sums up nearly all his actions at that time. This was almost the supreme example. He never told his parents about the marriage. His mother, with her social inclinations, would most certainly have been aghast. Betty, with her bubbly sense of humour, recalls that Adrian always referred to his mother as 'the Lady Margaret'. Nor would his father, recalled to a position of Commander in the Royal Navy, have been pleased at his only son marrying the daughter of a chargehand at HM Docks. Snobbery ruled in 1939.

Whatever motives Adrian might have had, he almost at once had second thoughts. A few days before the marriage he had been posted from Gosport to 22 Squadron at Thorney Island, an airfield only a few miles from Portsmouth. Here he joined for the first time a real, as opposed to a training, unit. Once settled in there, he lived in Mess and almost completely ignored his new bride. He hadn't told the RAF about his marriage and continued to name his father as his next of kin. Because the RAF didn't know about the marriage, he was never given any marriage allowance. Quite early in the war, the RAF had altered its rules and did for the first time grant a marriage allowance to junior officers as well as to older and more senior ones. A pilot officer's pay was at best miserable. Young gentleman officers in 1939 were expected to have parental funds or other private means. Even with additional flying pay, a pilot officers salary came to only about 10 shillings a day. In his case Adrian could not have invoked the financial assistance of his parents since he was keeping them in ignorance about the marriage.

Betty recalls that Adrian did rent a bungalow of sorts nearby but that only on rare occasions did he come to visit her. The marriage was not turning out as Betty had hoped. Adrian made no attempts to maintain her. She 'never had a penny from him'.

Betty had never told Adrian about her previous excursion into marriage and, as far as she knows, he never knew about this nor about her nine year-old daughter. However the possibility exists that some busy-body may have alerted Adrian that he was marrying a divorcee and that he was now a step-father to a growing-up girl. If that was so, then, it might have been an additional reason for the marriage to founder almost before it had begun. However, it is hard to escape the conclusion that the marriage was yet another act of thoughtless irresponsibility by a young man who was bristling with doubts and uncertainty inside himself. Adrian had from school days onwards always wanted to become a pilot and having achieved that ambition he was only just scraping through. The advent of war promised momentarily to change things to his advantage: to demand from him the great heroics he had read about as a child but even this was turning out to be almost meaningless. The period of the 'phoney war' – with no attacks on Britain, with no great land battles being fought just across the Channel, had begun. A massive inertia had ensued with everyone keyed up to do their bit but very little actually happening.

Warburton would not have been the first man who, unable to bear the loneliness, had risked marriage instead only to find that the loneliness was within himself.

Betty has neatly summed up the situation in a few words. When being advised of the amazing feats of Warburton in Malta, she remarked, 'I never knew this man. I only knew a boy, and I hardly even knew him. I can only really recall that he was a very beautiful boy. I suppose we did consummate the event but it has left no memories.'

Fortunately Betty was both an experienced hairdresser and barmaid and thus capable of earning a living. By 1940 she was suing for divorce: then not at all easy to obtain even under favourable circumstances. By then too, 22 Squadron had been moved far away from the Portsmouth area and she was experiencing difficulty in finding out where her husband was. Moreover, it was a hard decision to make: to be suing a RAF pilot in 1940 at the time of the Battle of Britain when RAF pilots were being extolled in the Press as the saviours of the country. She had the advice of a local solicitor but still couldn't manage to serve the divorce papers upon a husband who never saw her, never maintained her, never wrote and whom she could not locate. Nor did she know his parents so could not involve them; even if she had wanted to.

Possibly because the course at Blackpool was of such a long duration, (June-September 1940) Betty discovered that he was there. Determined to see him, she took herself there and spent one night at the Palatine Hotel. They duly met, but he was not at all interested in her. They didn't spend the night together. Adrian told her that: 'He was not in a fit condition to sleep with anyone,' implying that he had some dubious sexual impediment. This could have been an excuse but also could have been true as Adrian now had an additional problem on his mind, a second reason for him to be got out of the country. Although he was not supporting his wife, he had got himself into serious debt. Could he have been spending his time and money with prostitutes? Debt for a young officer was a serious problem, too. In the eyes of the RAF, not being able to meet one's Mess bill was a crime at least the equal of busting up aircraft. Moreover the signs were that Adrian may have gone beyond this, being in arrears with his Mess account and had been writing cheques that could not be honoured. Tich Whiteley is certain that this was the case.

To the end of his life, which from then onwards was so largely spent overseas, Adrian Warburton managed to avoid having the divorce papers served on him. Thus, when he did finally take a last flight, he left behind a widow.†

Adrian Warburton must have been one of the very few who could not get on with Betty. By luck or instinct, Adrian seems to have picked himself a winner but at the time was too immature to realise it and to know what to do about it.

Marriage to Betty as if it proved anything, only proved to Adrian Warburton that he was an even bigger failure than he cared to admit. Mac Brown a Canadian pilot who later in the war knew Warby almost as well

---

† After the war, Betty went to Buckingham Palace to be presented with Warburton's medals. The press took up her case with a headline of: 'MEDALS BUT NO BREAD.' As a result, Betty received an allowance in lieu of a pension: the princely sum of £2 per week. Fortunately Betty is not a greedy or commercially minded person and accepted the ex-gratia payment.

After seeing the newspapers, Geoffrey and Muriel Warburton got in touch with Betty and persuaded her to hand over their son's medals to them. Being the genuine soul she is, Betty went to see them at Enfield and as Betty's brother recalls generously did as they requested. With her cheerful uncomplicated personality and everlasting good looks, she is now happily married again and on excellent terms with her daughter.

as anyone ever did, recalls that Warby once told him that he only got married 'to give someone a widow's pension'. He was convinced that he would soon be killed and didn't see why someone rather than no one shouldn't benefit from it. Yet foolishly he didn't bother to advise the RAF about the marriage. Irresponsibility again?

During his period with 22 Squadron at Thorney Island and North Coates Leading Aircraftman E J Ellison, an orderly room clerk, a position which amounted to the squadron adjutant's private secretary, had became friendly with Warburton. They had discovered that they came from the same district of outer London. Ellison even knew of the Warburton family. Also Warby, having masses of time on his hands, got in the habit of dropping in on him 'for a chat'. With regard to Warby's troubles Ellison recalls that he was aware that something had happened to make Braithwaite decide to get Warby out of the country quickly, but didn't know what. Les Stewart, later a friend of Tich Whiteley's, recalls being told by Tich that Warby was at one time up for court martial before leaving England, but adds that 'in Tich's opinion the whole thing should never have happened'. Tich in a long letter he wrote in 1956 doesn't go so far. He refers to Warby being demoted by 50 to 100 places in the seniority list. However even this may have been an exaggeration as the RAF authorities recently advised Betty (in April 1987) that: 'There is no indication in your husband's records that he at any time was subject to any disciplinary action whilst in the RAF.' With Joss Braithwaite now dead it seems doubtful that the full story will ever be known. It is noteworthy that Betty, despite the treatment she received, has leapt to his defence in typically admirable fashion.

Ellison makes the shrewd commitment that his frequent visitor was a: 'Young harum-scarum type of officer who wanted to do things his own way but not yet found the right niche.' He goes on to describe Warby as 'an extrovert but one whom school and service discipline had turned into a loner'. In commenting upon his appearance Ellison remarks upon 'his tight fitting cap which tried to restrain a mass of very blond hair that had not been cut in the service fashion.' He adds that, although he was in no position to judge his ability as a pilot, 'The ground crew, who always somehow knew their pilot's abilities, didn't put him among the best.'

Corporal John Shephard, a highly skilled radio-electrician who later became a tower of strength to Tich Whiteley in Malta where he had flown as an air gunner, also recalls Warby at North Coates in quite a different light. He recalls that Warby once pulled him up for not saluting him: a quite astonishing recollection to anyone who later knew Warby in Malta.

From Warby's log books it is seen that virtually the only flying that Warby did during almost a whole year with 22 Squadron was 44 hours of which about half was on Vildebeestes on such exercises as 'Dive Bombing' (in an obsolete biplane!) and half in an ancient Audax biplane target towing for gunnery practice. Attempts made to give him dual instruction on twin-engined aircraft (Anson and Blenheim) had rapidly been abandoned, implying that he had been 'given up' as a possible twin-engined Beaufort pilot.

Few pre-war trained RAF pilots (not injured) could have flown or been of less use to their service or country during the perilous period when Europe was overrun and Britain stared defeat in the face. It is also clear that Warby, having found an airman to whom he could relate, paid scant attention to the invisible barrier which the services erected between their officers and men. Having found an airman with whom he had something in common he treated him as an equal.

By far the most important event for Warby in 22 Squadron was to be brought into personal contact with Tich Whiteley, the talented Australian. Without his guiding hand, the chances are that there would never have been a Warby legend, but thanks to him this extraordinary tale of the misfit who turned into a hero was just about to begin.

Having been absent from 22 Squadron on so many courses – and having been away for the whole three months immediately prior to the establishment of 431 Flight, Whiteley could scarcely have known the young blond pilot officer given him as one of his navigators. Two others were also detailed to navigate. A Sergeant Frank Bastard, a trained navigator, and Pilot Officer Paddy Devine who had also attended No 2 School of GR. However Tich Whiteley was no ordinary flight commander. For one thing, he was in addition to being a competent pilot, also a trained ground engineer and an experienced navigator. He detailed to Warburton and Devine the responsible task of working out a flight plan of how to get the aircraft to Malta while he got on with the necessary testing of the aircraft and training of the other two pilots: Sergeant J W Bibby and Flying Officer Foxton. The Maryland required a three-man crew as it was fitted with two twin-gun rear mounted positions. Accordingly three air gunners were included in the party to be flown to Malta. Not that all three were actually air gunners per se.

All the signs are that, together with Paddy Devine, Adrian Warburton responded with alacrity and enthusiasm to the challenge. The very fact that he would soon be going back to the island where, so he had often been reminded by his father, he had been so strangely christened, must have intrigued him. More to the point, with the 'trouble with the law' hanging over his head, he was being given a chance of a new start in a new land.

According to Tich, the navigation plan submitted by Devine and Warburton was a masterly piece of work. It took into consideration all the radio aids that might have been of use, the airfields, the weather and what enemy opposition might have to be encountered.

It left no stone unturned. Whiteley was delighted with it and accepted it without change. The plan was for the three Marylands to depart from Thorney Island, near Portsmouth, to fly over enemy-occupied France at night, then to set course for Sardinia to be reached at first light. From there the planes would skirt around heavily defended Sicily, where the enemy kept hundreds of fighter planes, before heading for Malta.

None had attempted this journey before under wartime conditions, yet it was to become the standard route for hundreds of aircraft to follow: not that those which followed were as successful as the Marylands which departed one after the other around 0145 on 6 September 1940, having only arrived at Thorney Island the afternoon before.

Whiteley summed up his first impression of Warby: 'Warburton, by his navigation plan, had demonstrated to me that he was a capable reliable officer just looking for a challenge.' War, Warburton and the island that would always be associated with his name had begun their unique relationship. Between them, Braithwaite and Whiteley had set Warby on his way. He was not to let them down.

MALTA AND MARYLANDS

All three Marylands were flown from North Coates to Thorney Island, near Portsmouth on 4 September and departed on their trail-blazing journey the next night. All three duly arrived safely at Luqa airfield, Malta, early next morning the 6th. As Tich Whiteley wryly remarked in his account of the journey: 'This put the total of RAF aircraft on the island into double figures provided the count included unserviceable aircraft!'

Although Tich and his companions had had no problems on their flights: two of the three Marylands which were soon after despatched to add to the small flight were lost en route. This was to have repercussions later.

Tich Whiteley, always one to get on with whatever task was given him, arranged for the aircraft to photograph Sardinia as they crossed it in the early light of dawn. This island with its ports and airfields had not previously in the war been photographed from the air. From this moment onwards, the Maryland always flew with cameras. Photo-reconnaissance (PR) was to be their primary role.

The three Maryland skippers were Whiteley, Flying Officer James Foxton who flew with Warby as his navigator, and an all-sergeant crew composed of Bibby, Frank Bastard, navigator and Paddy Moren, WOP/AG.† It was that crew which made the fastest time: 6 hours and 47 minutes. For quite some time this stood as the unofficial record for flights to Malta from the UK. An inspired choice of Tich's was to take with him as his WOP/AG the experienced wireless and electrical mechanic, John Shephard. The Maryland had far more electric circuits than British aircraft, including an electrically operated Curtiss-Wright propeller. They required an expert hand. The virtue of this choice soon became apparent. Upon arrival at Luqa, although made most welcome by the station commander, Squadron Leader Carter 'Jonah' Jonas, Tich soon found out that the handful of men assigned to him for maintenance of his aircraft fell far short of his high standards. He, with John Shephard's expert assistance, trade-tested all nine and rejected eight. Tich, almost uniquely in the RAF, was a qualified pilot, navigator and ground engineer. He was a man of many talents and to the surprise of none had been awarded the Sword of Honour after his initial course in pre-war days when competition had been at its fiercest. Jonah and others have described Tich as a workaholic. Nothing seems to have daunted or tired him and, until such time as ground crew

†Wireless Operator/Air Gunner.

who met his standards could be found, he, with the help of his unusual WOP/AG, instructed the aircrew how to service their own aircraft. Tich also found time to overhaul Warby's complicated finances and made arrangements whereby part of his pay would be stopped in the UK and paid into an account specifically to settle his debts. Tich's abilities seem to have been almost unlimited.†

The British Navy were at the time of the arrival of 431 Flight, much concerned with the dispositions, and operational readiness, of the huge modern Italian battle fleet, which was, on paper, superior in size, speed and guns to the British fleet in the Med. Consequently one of the first tasks assigned to the flight was to see if it could obtain photographs of the Italian naval stronghold of Taranto in the heel of Italy. Tich wasted no time and within days the task had been accomplished. Tich also set about bringing his small band to a high state of efficiency. Having discovered that the adjudged misfit Warburton had responded well when given with Paddy Devine the responsible job of planning the route to Malta, Tich now appointed him both his photographic officer and his ship recognition expert. Both were essential to the tasks that lay ahead. Warby in the latter role arranged for all aircrew to have monthly checks of ship recognition: nor did he exclude his CO from these tests and, as Tich has recorded, 'He extracted penalties from me for any errors made'. He describes it as an early example of 'management participation'. Clearly a rapport was developing between the two of them.

Two of the photographic LACs or corporals were Harry ('Scoop') Kirk and Jim McNeil. Both soon became devoted to Warby who took his new assignment as photographic officer seriously; so much so that, as Jim recalls, 'He loved to help in the darkroom, and got in the way, but he really was the nicest chap I think I have ever known.' Jim later became a squadron leader. Warby's log book records that the day after their arrival in Malta, Warby was allowed to carry out under supervision a trial circuit or two as pilot of the Maryland. However, for operational sorties he continued as Foxton's navigator and as such was soon guiding his pilot to Tripoli in the south, to the Italian-held island of Pantellaria to the north-west and to Stratovathi.

---

†Another aspect of his abilities was revealed when some years after the war Tich was posted to the UK from Singapore. He claimed the cost of bringing his car home. When this was rejected, he took the RAF to court and by quoting an ancient law which had enabled an officer overseas to be allowed the cost of bringing home his charger and pointing out that a car was now the equivalent to any officer's 'charger'. He won his case too. Soon thereafter the Bristol Aero Co offered him a top job in his native Australia. He resigned from the RAF to take this. When the job folded, he joined the Australian Broadcasting Corp and ended up as its Chairman, in Victoria.

Still in September, Warburton flew as navigator to Tich on one of his invaluable Taranto reconnaissance flights. In a matter of a couple of weeks, thanks to the three Marylands, the Navy was finding itself able to keep tabs on all major enemy naval units. Henceforth Taranto, Brindisi, Palermo, Messina, Tripoli and Benghazi were never to be far from 'open books'. Italian naval bases as far north as Naples and Spezia were soon also included. The intentions of the enemy battlefleet were thus easy to deduce even though Malta was already suffering from the intense bombing which was to become its hallmark for the next two years. The enemy's principal targets in Malta were the naval bases around Grand Harbour and Sliema and the airfields.

There were three operational airfields. In the south was Halfar where the Fleet Air Arm kept its few obsolescent planes. In the centre of the island was Ta Kali. Here the island's pathetically few fighter aircraft were based. Much the biggest of the three airfields was Luqa which lay in between. There was also an emergency strip known as Safi Strip connected to Luqa by a narrow tortuous taxi track that went uphill and down dale. Eventually, Safi, Luqa and Halfar were all connected by such twisting taxi tracks. Malta is basically all rock. Bombs never penetrated deep but the fragments thrown up would be hurled far and wide. Such fragments damaged aircraft parked within range and the range was quite considerable. That September, Malta suffered 25 air raids. By 1943, the total had risen to 3,340 separate air raids. Although the Regia Aeronautica totalled some 1,800 planes, with up to 1,000 or more capable of operating from the many airfields in nearby Sicily, the presence of the handful of Hurricanes at Ta Kali had been enough to cause them great concern.

Tich's Marylands were suffering on two accounts. The type was not one that the RAF had ordered from USA. Britain had merely taken over the remains of a French order, and numbers were scarce. Others had to be assembled from parts shipped to the UK from America. Spares were in short supply.

It didn't help the situation that few in Malta knew anything about how to maintain Marylands. On top of which they were being damaged by the fragments of rock and bomb casing resulting from 'near misses' at Luqa. The loss of the two, out of three, of the replacement planes while en route was serious. Soon Tich had to scratch around for spare parts with the inevitable 'cannibalisation', to keep the unit operational. With the consent of the AOC, Air Commodore Maynard, he 'impressed', i.e waylaid, two Blenheims which had arrived in Malta to refuel en route to their destination in Middle East. This 'impressing' was to become another hallmark of Malta for the next few years. Without such pilfering of planes, the islands† could scarcely have survived.

†There are a number of islands in the Malta group. The two biggest are Gozo nearest to Sicily and the much larger Malta, it is convenient to refer to Malta in the singular.

Warburton was to make several trips as navigator in Blenheims as well as carrying on as navigator to Foxton and other Maryland pilots. One of the Blenheim captains, Flying Officer Horgan, had described Warby and his fair hair and skin in observant terms: 'Joyfully young and enthusiastic, blond with a perfect skin: not feminine but such as to suggest lovely sisters: brave, reckless, a child of the sun.'†

Warby might have carried on as a navigator on 431 Flight but for one of those quirks of fate that so often shape a man's destiny. Within a few days of the arrival of 431 Flight both Sergeant Bibby and James Foxton were laid low with diarrhoea, the dreaded 'Malta Dog' stomach trouble. Tich needed replacements. There was no alternative but to see if his navigators, Warburton and Devine, could cope. His problem was how to find out. The Maryland was not fitted with a normal dual control. Down in the nose at the navigator's station, was a partial set of retractable controls. The best that Tich could do was to take the younger men aloft with him and see how they managed with this half set. Then to let them loose on their own with fingers crossed.

In Warby's case, his total solo time on twin-engined aircraft was a bare 35 minutes. It compounded his difficulties that not since before reporting to No 2 School of GR at Blackpool, in June, had he flown any aircraft of any type. That was nearly four months before. The Maryland was American, sophisticated and not easy to fly – how would Warby cope?

During his pilot training, Warburton A, had been assessed as either 'average' or 'below average'. The accuracy of those assessments was about to be demonstrated. The unit that had described him as below average had added a remark: 'Landings and forced landings weak.' How right they were! Warby was never lacking in get up and go. The Maryland is apt to swing sharply during take-off unless treated with respect. Almost as soon as Warby had slammed the throttles wide open, the plane began to swing and career all over the airfield. Violent over-correction with rudder hardly helped. Miraculously the undercarriage withstood these gyrations and the aircraft staggered into the air. For his early attempts to fly the Maryland, Warby had been assigned the two sergeants who had flown out with the now stricken Sergeant Bibby. Frank Bastard, navigator and Paddy Moren, a WOP/AG of unusual courage and skill. Both have given hair-raising accounts of those first few circuits flown by Warby.

The 'arrivals' (to call them landings would be an overstatement) were as hair-raising as were the take-offs. On one such 'arrival' the aircraft came back trailing strands of wire from the airfield's perimeter fence.

†From 'The Unknown Air Ace' by Roy Nash, *The Star*, March 1958

This nearly put paid to Tich's attempts to get Warby operating as a pilot. The officer i/c flying at Luqa happened to be watching alongside Tich and tore into the anxious Australian for allowing such a 'hamfisted idiot' to be in charge of the plane. Tich had to plead to allow the type conversion training to continue. It didn't help Warby's cause either when Paddy Devine, a natural pilot, slipped into another Maryland and executed a perfect circuit at the first attempt.

Demands on 431 Flight were pressing. Accordingly training had to be cut to the very minimum and almost within days Tich was almost forced to send Warby out with a full load of petrol to carry out a photo-reconnaissance of Taranto. The official records show this as an abortive sortie because of 'hydraulic failure causing the aircraft to belly land.' The truth is that the hydraulics failed because for once the Maryland's undercarriage simply couldn't take Warby's savage zig-zags and one wheel had been torn off: requiring an emergency return. The crisis that was soon reached has been vividly described by Paddy Moren:

> His take-off was a clear indication that Chubby Checker was not the creator of the dancing rage, the 'twist'. Eventually he landed with the top strand of the airport's wire fence wrapped around the tail wheel ... to complete the most savage groundloop I have ever witnessed. The snag was to find a crew to fly with Warby ... however Frank [Bastard] and I were old friends, and out of sympathy for Warby we actually volunteered to be assigned to him. Initially Warby had lapses into circular take-offs and violent zig-zag landings with tail spins that would have tested the morale of any regular in the RAF. Fortunately for Warby, Frank and I were only 'temporary wartime assassins'. We shared a belief that he could not get any worse. We both quickly learnt that the flak and enemy fighters at Messina and Taranto were a 'piece of cake' compared with take-offs and landings with Warby at the controls.
>
> Finally Tich Whiteley sent for us. He was worried. I well recall him asking us, but not ordering us, to give Warby just one more chance. If we had opted out Tich would have given up Warby as a pilot. I well remember saying to Tich: 'He's almost house-trained, sir, and I think that Warby is going to be the best we've got. He's loaded with guts.'

It was he and Frank Bastard, in Paddy's opinion, who that day saved Warburton from oblivion.

Even night take-offs were on occasions carried out by the photo-recce planes of 431 Flight. By taking off in the dark a flight could arrive over the target at first light. Paddy Moren recalls one such when Warby, as he was invariably known in Malta, waltzed among the Goose-neck flares which had been laid out in order to delineate the runway. In his words: 'Paraffin was cascading in a burning flood in every direction as we mowed down the flarepath. Some was even adhering in full flame to the rudder of the plane.'

In spite of these excitements, 431 Flight, under Whiteley's benign but firm leadership, coped magnificently with every difficulty: air raids galore, inadequate ground crew (soon put right), Malta Dog, lack of replacement aircraft, no qualified navigators. In no time it rapidly built up a splendid reputation: one that it never lost.

The Navy wanted to know where every major Italian ship was and what it was doing. The Army stationed in Egypt also wanted to know what the huge Italian Army based at Tripoli and Benghazi (both Libya and Tripolitania were Italian colonies) was up to. 431 Flight kept both Services informed as excellent photographs of all major bases north and south of Malta continued to be taken almost daily in spite of the foul winter weather and the overwhelming enemy Air Force based so close at hand.

By October the Navy had become more than usually interested in what enemy units were in Taranto. Photographs showed only too clearly that the Italians had built up a massive and powerful battlefleet there. On one of Warby's first visits to this well defended stronghold, he had come back with reports that there were already 28 warships at the ready. His photographs when developed proved the accuracy of his oral report. For the immediate reporting of such information by wireless, Paddy Moren had to use morse code encyphered by the ingenious Syko machine which transposed each of the actual letters of the message into other letters by a secret card applicable only to that particular day of the month. It was a complicated procedure which was apt to baffle the RAF (and Navy which also used it) as well as the enemy.

The British Navy with its older slower battleships was prepared to contest Mussolini's boast that the Mediterranean was an Italian lake ('*mare nostrum*'). However, it had a trump card in its aircraft carriers. They were few in number but they were soon to prove their effectiveness. The Navy intended to raid the Italian battleships and cruisers right in their well protected Taranto naval base. They would move a carrier to within flight range of the ancient but honourable Swordfish aircraft that HMS *Illustrious* carried. These single-engined biplanes which looked like WWI aircraft and had performance to match, could however each carry a torpedo. The attack depended much upon the Swordfish pilots knowing exactly where each major enemy ship lay at anchor. Only 431 Flight could supply this information.

Meanwhile, without neglecting their primary role of photo-reconnaissance, Warby and Moren had started on 30 October 1940 their 'fighter score' by shooting down a Cant Z506 seaplane. It was one of Warby's first sorties in command of a Maryland. Only the day before he had been navigating a Blenheim for Flying Officer Horgan.†

Before the week was out, Warby had got the better of another encounter. This time, crewed with Johnny Spires (not Frank Bastard) and the inevitable Paddy Moren in the gun turret, they were attacked when over Taranto by a Cant Z506 and three Italian Fiat CR42 fighters. This latter type, although a biplane, was fast and highly manoeuvrable. In the ensuing fight, Warby and Moren damaged one of the fighters and shot down the seaplane. When this was seen to be still afloat on the water, they continued to attack it there. They ultimately destroyed it and wounded the pilot.

On 7 November, when operating a Taranto photo-reconnaissance flight, Warby and his crew found themselves in a running fight with four Macchi C200 fighters. These Italian planes should have been more than a match for the Maryland. The plane was a modern fighter similar to the Hurricane in performance. The aerial battle lasted for about 20 minutes. One Macchi was shot down and the Maryland returned safely. Paddy Moren has added some interesting technical details of some of the original fighting tactics that Warby employed. When finding himself being outturned by a fighter such as the Macchi C200 he would, whilst still in a tight turn, put down a few degrees of flap. This altered the plane of the turn and simultaneously slowed the Maryland down. As the enemy plane overshot, Paddy would be able to bring one of his pairs of guns into play.

The Maryland was unusual in that none of the three crew members could reach one another. The navigator was in his glass house in a lower nose compartment. The pilot was alone at his controls. Behind him was the WOP/AG with the wireless set and, uniquely, two positions for twin maxims: one on top and another beneath the plane. He sat on a collapsible seat and, if wanting to get at the underneath pair, had to fold this away and scurry to the lower position: hopefully in time. When used by the Americans, the plane carried four crew members so that both pairs of guns could be manned simultaneously. Co-operation between the three RAF crewmen was solely via their helmets and intercom.

Some idea of the size of the enemy fleet marshalled in Taranto can be gauged by Warby's report of 10 November. He had spied and

---

†Tich thought that the workers at the Burtonwood factory who were assembling Marylands from parts brought over from USA by sea, would be bucked by the news of Warby and Moren's first 'kill'. Accordingly he prepared an appropriate official signal. However, on grounds of security, the officials ruled that it could not be sent. Tich then went to an ordinary Post Office and despatched a commercial telegram that: 'Your friend Bob Martin has been engaged in a boxing match and had won by a knockout'. This was duly sent and when next Tich visited the factory during one of his flights back to UK (forever looking for spare parts,) he found his telegram pinned up. Tich himself was made most welcome at the factory where he was assured that his 'boxing match' telegram had proved to be a great morale booster.

photographed five battleships, 14 cruisers and 27 destroyers. By then he had become an expert at ship recognition and was able to identify the major ships by their class as well as type.

Sergeant Johnny Spires, a navigator who flew with Warby almost as often as did Frank Bastard, has left a dramatic account of one of his forays into this most heavily guarded of all Italian naval bases. It was a sortie carried out in appalling weather:

> 'We are going in at zero feet,' Warby had warned. 'Get yourself a sharp pencil and plenty of paper. If we can't photograph the ships, you'll have to plot their position on the harbour map.' Paddy Moren was the WOP/AG and he was assigned the task of reading the ships' names as they flashed by. It wasn't much encouragement that the Maryland in which they planned to enter the enemy's most defended basin was the one in which they had been shot up in the air and holed by bomb splinters on the ground at Luqa. Among the crew she was known as the 'Sardine Tin' or 'Whistler's Mother', from the noise of the air whistling through its many holes.

Warby flew straight to Taranto. The weather was so bad that Spires maintains that even the birds were walking. The Italians were not expecting aircraft to be flying in such conditions. Their balloon barrage had not been raised. Once their initial surprise had worn off, the Italians started shooting with every gun they had. Warby attempted camera shots, Spires scribbled away. Moren did his best to read the names of the ships.

They escaped unscathed. Most fortunately the hail of flak had missed. When clear they compared notes. By then Warby knew Taranto like his home town. He was surprised to learn that a *sixth* battleship had been seen. Normally there were only five. He knew that the chances were that the photographs which he had snapped at such low level were unlikely to provide the conclusive confirmation.

'We'll have to go back again,' said Warby. 'We'll count the battleships together.'

On their return to the lions' den, the flak was even fiercer. As Spires remembers; 'We flew so low that the wing tips were cutting furrows in the calm water.' Together they counted aloud the battleships over the intercom which alone connected them. Five. That was all. An Italian cruiser had earlier been mistaken for a battleship.

They arrived back with a souvenir. An aerial from an enemy ship was caught in their tail wheel. This incident was recorded in print by a RAF cartoonist. It is one of several featuring Warby or his crew which were widely widely distributed among the RAF personnel in Malta.

During the night of 10 November HMS *Illustrious*, one of Britain's latest aircraft carriers, moved stealthily towards Taranto. Whiteley himself had carried out the final pre-strike photo-recce that same day and came back with clear pictures of both the inner and outer harbours, and all that they contained. The defence booms etc, had been well pin-pointed beforehand by earlier photographs. The Swordfish, armed with Tich's updated plan of the enemy, which had been relayed to *Illustrious* flew in undetected and launched their deadly 'tin-fish'.

It was as well that the enemy was caught by surprise. The cruising speed of the Swordfish is a bare 85 knots. The pilots reported strikes but couldn't hang about to check their results. Warby was detailed to fly in immediately in order to report on the results. He issued only an initial guarded statement, transmitted by radio using the Syko machine, that considerable damage appeared to have been inflicted. His photographs however were more illuminating. They showed a number of Italian capital ships sitting on the bottom, with massive oil leaks spreading from others.

Within days, those Italian ships which could move under their own power had withdrawn to safer harbours far distant from Malta. It took quite a few reconnaissance flights by 431 Flight to discover where they had gone; so far had they been removed. The Taranto attack was widely proclaimed in the British press and much of the success was due to the very accurate photo-recce flights of Tich Whiteley and Adrian Warburton. 431 Flight rightly received congratulatory messages not only from the AOC Malta but from Admiral Sir Andrew Cunningham, the Naval C-in-C in the Mediterranean.

Taranto was really Whiteley's triumph but after the legend of Warburton grew, it became a common error to attribute all the key pre and post strike recce flights to him. However it was during the six month period November 1940 – May 1941, that Warby truly came into his own. By the time that the author first arrived in Malta, in late summer 1941, Warby had already become a talking point throughout the island. The name of Whiteley, who had left for the UK in June, was unknown to him. It was the age of the film stars. They were household names but few knew the names of those who had made them stars. Thus it was with Warby and Whiteley. It seems strange that although Warby never truly mastered how to land the Maryland – or any other twin-engined plane – neatly, he possessed an astonishing ability to 'throw it around in the air', once he had managed to get it there. In his hands, this 'three place, two fan, pursuit ship' as the Americans called it, while flying on missions when aerial photography was all that was required, became an awesome fighter plane: and did so without ever neglecting the primary photo-reconnaissance (PR) role.

Much of Warby's success as an unofficial fighter pilot was due to the splendid co-operation that developed between him and his WOP/AG, Paddy Moren. Paddy was no ordinary air gunner. He had joined the RAF Volunteer Reserve before the war and had been accepted for pilot training.

However when Britain declared war on Germany the RAF were flooded with applicants to become pilots. The training schools developed waiting lists. Paddy was, in his own words, 'sold a bill of goods' and advised that if he wanted to get into action quickly, his best chance lay in transferring to train as a wireless operator/air gunner. He duly transferred. At his gunnery school at Jurby in the Isle-of-Man, he obtained a high pass mark and was assessed as above average. Later in the war, Paddy did become a pilot, and rose rapidly to squadron leader. However when told that he had flown his full quota of operational trips, and would therefore be grounded he resigned from the RAF and was accepted by a grateful Navy. He ended the war as a naval lieutenant, flying dive bombers from an aircraft carrier. No ordinary air gunner indeed!

The Marylands seldom had to penetrate deeply into enemy air space. Their PR flights were mainly to enemy ports and harbours. A sortie consisted of a quick dash in followed by an equally quick dash out. This applied also to the Sicilian airfields which they were constantly covering with their cameras. The island of Crete was likewise photographed. This had fallen to the German airborne forces and Malta had good reason to expect that a similar fate was being prepared for them. With this in mind the adjacent Sicilian airfields had to be very closely watched.

The next victim to fall to the guns of Warby and Moren (the Maryland was also fitted with four machine guns which fired forwards from the wings and were operated by the pilot) was a big Italian three-engined bomber, perhaps their most versatile and useful plane, the Savoia Marchetti SM79. This was shot down on Christmas Eve 1940 during a flight when the aircraft had been used to drop propaganda leaflets upon Naples. Earlier that month, on the 15th, Warby shot up a submarine off Augusta. It was surfaced and the crew were sunbathing; but not for long. They were quickly sent diving into the sea.

By unofficial 'arrangements' between the RAF and Regia Aeronautica there was no flying that Christmas Day. The RAF had dropped a Christmas card over Palermo wishing them a pleasant day addressed to the head of their air force and had received a similar card in return. As a result both sides 'forgot' the war for 24 hours. Generally there was little personal animosity between the two sets of pilots. Tin cans with messages used to be dropped by one air force into airfields of the other after pilots had been lost, enquiring into their fate. Replies would arrive by the same 'aerial post'. Pilots shot down were decently buried.

The propaganda leaflets were most popular in Malta: but not for their official usage. Shortages of every kind were becoming daily more evident and one annoying one was the dearth of toilet paper. Few pilots could ever see the sense of dropping propaganda leaflets upon the enemy urging them to turn on their leaders and abandon the war. At best it smacked of extreme optimism. Similar leaflets had been dropped on England by the Germans and had been treated with hoots of derision by press and populace alike. But we were chronically short of 'bumph'. Leaflets therefore mysteriously disappeared in their thousands and quite serious arguments took place at Luqa (where normal entertainments were non-existent) about the various merits of different leaflets. Although in Italian their headlines were translated and soon well known by us. Some had taken a fancy to 'Don't send your sons to Russia' while others preferred to use for toilet paper the one which began 'Women of Naples…'

Warby was once arrested in Malta. He was cycling back to Luqa one night after the strictly enforced curfew hour. He was picked up by the local regiment on guard and arrested. He was, almost as usual, rather casually dressed and this heightened the guard's suspicions. The guard, Frans Galea, had his instructions: not to let anyone approach the environs of the airfield. He contacted his officer, Lieutenant Andrew Penza, who realised that Adrian looked like an Englishman but was still rightly suspicious. He contacted Luqa and invited the duty officer to come down and collect his 'prisoner'. Lieutenant Penza was a bright officer and decided to test Warby. He suggested that while they waited, Warby might care for a drink of 'the renowned Maltese whisky'. Warby responded, 'That's rubbish, no whisky is made here.' Penza didn't comment but he knew from that moment that Adrian really was what he said he was. It is one example of how splendidly the Maltese people co-operated with their British 'visitors', whose very presence on their island was directly responsible for all the bombing which they had to endure. In addition there were large numbers of Maltese in the Army and Royal Navy and others had flocked to join the RAF.

Dr Boffa, a Maltese citizen, relates that Warby was one of the officers who gave up part of his spare time to going round the schools lecturing the eager students about the war, its aims and how they could help. It is a side of Warburton that few knew about. In these talks, Warby emphasized the risks of picking up strange objects (which were at times camouflaged anti-personnel bombs) and how to behave in the event of the expected invasion.

Events in Malta were, throughout the war, much affected by the success or otherwise of the Allied Army in the Western Desert. Almost on the day when 431 Flight first flew itself into Malta, the huge Italian Army which at the outset of their war (for Italy this was 10 June 1940) stood on the Libyan-Egyptian border, made a cautious move into Egypt. By 16 September they had advanced some 90 miles into Egypt. However a month after Warby and Paddy had destroyed their first Macchi C200, the Western Desert Force mounted a brilliant offensive which not only regained the ground lost but which swept on at a furious pace until by February 1941, it had advanced as far as Benghazi some 800 miles beyond Cairo. The almost total collapse of the Italian Colonial Army, and the loss largely by capture of over 1,000 planes of the Regia Aeronautica, were to seriously affect Malta for the next three years: *adversely* as it happened.

Hitler detailed a small force to go to the aid of his ally, Mussolini. The German Afrika Korps, under a young and then little known general, Rommel, was despatched to Tripolitania to save the face of the humiliated Italians. To support this Korps, the Germans moved into Sicily an Air Army, Fliegerkorps X, of some 800 planes. Sicily had many airfields and there was no difficulty about accommodating this Fliegerkorps. One of its main striking force was its squadrons of Junkers Ju87's, the dreaded Stuka dive bomber. It was immediately apparent to the citizens and men stationed in Malta that the Luftwaffe were a different kettle of fish to the Regia Aeronautica.

In spite of the presence in Sicily of efficient Luftwaffe planes such as the Messerschmitt 109's, Warby and his crews continued to keep watch, along with the other crews of the enlarged 431 Flight, over the Sicilian airfields. More Marylands had been found, assembled and flown into Malta. Another new pilot, Roger Drew, also began to shoot down enemy planes and for a short while was running almost neck and neck with Warby. Paddy Devine continued to fly. Foxton, a fine natural pilot, applied to be transferred to Ta Kali where he flew Hurricanes but, sadly was killed defending the island.

In Malta, officialdom seldom ruled. If a pilot thought he could do better in another active role, no obstacles would be put in his way. By the same token George Burges, a Coastal Command flying boat pilot on HQ staff in an admin capacity, when Italy had entered the war, had become the ace 'fighter boy' of the Faith Hope and Charity Gladiators period of Malta's first few months of air fighting. With those memorable planes gone, George Burges had joined 431 Flight and become another Maryland PR pilot, the next most senior to Tich.

In January 1941, 431 Flight had grown in size to be redesignated 69 Squadron with, in theory, a full quota of planes: 12 Marylands and 10 Beauforts. In practice, as one of the airmen has recorded, 'We were supposed to have 22 aircraft but due to the shortage of spares and bombing, we could only produce one serviceable.' As Tich Whiteley grimly remarked, 'This Whitehall decision to make us a squadron with a full establishment was not going to deliver aircraft or spares to Malta.'

In the same month Warby was promoted to flying officer. On 27 December he had received the DFC. It was his first award for gallantry, and far from his last. It was already becoming the custom to give special tasks to Warby. He had by February 1941 already established a reputation akin to that of the Royal Canadian Mounted police. They invariably 'got their man'. Warby invariably 'got his pictures'. A historical task assigned to Pilot Officer Warburton was to take photographs of the important Calitri viaduct in Italy, a vital link in the rail network between the factories in the North and the ports from which supplies were shipped to North Africa. These photographs were required by the Army which was planning a new type of action. A small force of Royal Welch Fusiliers were to be dropped from Whitley bombers and would plant explosive charges, to destroy the viaduct. The troops would then make their way to the coast to rendezvous with a submarine. The type of operation had never before been attempted by British troops. It if worked, or seemed feasible, then specially trained forces would be developed. At that time there was no paratroop regiment, no Special Forces nor Commandos.

Paddy Moren had recorded in his personal log book (which generally contains far more detail than Warby's own sparse entries†) that excellent photographs were taken from a height of 25 feet.

On the raid, although the troops were duly dropped and placed their charges the viaduct remained standing though obviously damaged. The troops did manage to destroy an adjacent railway bridge, but sadly they were all taken prisoner. However the potential of the sabotage exercise was realised and in due course whole regiments and divisions of the British Army would be trained for such duties.

Warby was also sent out after the raid to check upon the damage caused. Again he took first class pictures from near suicide low heights.

The fact that such close-ups could be taken was again due to Tich's initiative. The Marylands had been fitted with the excellent, if large, RAF F24 Cameras which took remarkably clear pictures from considerable height. They were mounted to take vertically. Tich soon realised the need to take oblique pictures and, during the months of appalling winter weather that plagues both Malta and Southern Italy, to have to take photographs when the clouds were almost on the deck. He experimented with his personal Leica camera and, finding that this worked, he went to AOC 'Sammy' Maynard to see what other cameras could be found. Together they went to see the Marquis Scicluna in his palace. The gallant marquis is now dead but his son, the present Marquis Jose Juan Scicluna, a British pro-patriot like his father, witnessed the meeting which left an indelible impression. AOC Maynard stressed that aircraft didn't always return and that he might never again see his expensive equipment. The marquis without demur handed over his Leica complete with expensive extras. Another example of Maltese co-operation, unreservedly given.

In March 1941 Warby was involved in another historic episode – the

†Yet Warby, throughout the war, includes in his personal log book the deaths or 'missing' of all fellow pilots of his squadrons. This is quite out of the ordinary. For example during his first period in Malta he records the death or missing of some half dozen crews. By 1943 he had recorded a total of 40 pilot friends shot down on the kind of missions he was flying.

naval victory at Matapan. On 27 March the Italian Admiral Iachino took his battlefleet to sea, under pressure from the Germans to strike a blow at the convoys sailing from Africa to Greece. His plans were known in advance to Cunningham, the naval C-in-C, through the decrypting of signals, but every effort had to be made to keep such foreknowledge secret. The need for reconnaissance pilots to confirm the sailing was vital, and it was Warby and Moren who found the enemy fleet at sea and relayed the essential information back to base: or at least tried to do so. However wireless traffic, due to the many naval ships at sea, was heavy and they could not get their Syko coded message received. In desperation, they resorted to using a high priority prefix. It happened to be one which indicated that the sender was an Air Marshal and not a junior officer! Although this did the trick they were later reprimanded. To end the story, the message in reply requested them to try to identify as many vessels as they could. Warby's way of doing this was to fly at sea level between the lines of ships and get his crew to read off their names! Low flying never seems to have worried Warby. Airman G D Ellis, one of the mechanics who serviced his planes, has recounted how one plane came back with many indentations on its lower fuselage which had been caused by stones thrown up by his propeller wash as Warby had swept low over an enemy airfield.

On another occasion when Warby and his crew were over the sea, they espied a formation of troop-carrying planes on their way to North Africa. There were, Moren recalls, seven Ju52s and three SM79s, and they were flying in loose formation, Warby followed them for an hour to determine their destination. Before parting company, he fired several long bursts into them but, surprisingly, with no visible effect. At least he made no claims. It speaks well for the Ju52's rugged construction. There is the story, recorded by David Beaty, that on one occasion Warby, who was proud of his ship recognition, came back and reported that a certain Italian major ship was in a certain harbour. The Navy didn't think this possible and said so. With a few days Warby banged down a photo on their desk. It was the ship in question; taken at such close range that its name could be read!

Spares were still a major problem and Whiteley made visits to the UK to obtain, and to bring back with him, as many spare parts as a Maryland could accommodate. On such visits he would also have a shopping list of essential 'goodies' that all in Malta by then lacked. On one such visit he brought back a supply of lipsticks and other cosmetics for the overworked nurses in the hospital. This proved to be a shrewd move. Soon thereafter the Marylands were almost grounded because the island had run out of hydraulic oil which was necessary to keep the Maryland serviceable. Tich now revealed himself as a chemist. He declared that given a supply of caster oil, he could manufacture an acceptable substitute. The snag was that there was no official supply of this commodity either. With George

Burges in tow, Tich visited the hospitals. They took with them a good supply of lipsticks and came back without them: but with enough caster oil to enable him to carry on until hydraulic oil could be officially obtained!

On one of Warby's flights south, on 20 June 1941, 69 Squadron was given a very special task by the army hard-pressed by Rommel in the desert. They wanted the entire coastal road from Benghazi to Tripoli and beyond photographed. This was the 250-mile Via Balbia, the one and only road along which all supplies to the enemy front line had to travel. It was a mammoth assignment and it was estimated that it would take half a dozen sorties spread over a week or more. The first was given, quite naturally to the squadron's top pilot, to Warby. Although four times chased out to sea by enemy fighters based at airfields alongside this vital road, he came back, thanks to his skilful use of a wider than usual camera lens, with photographs of the entire road: all in the one sortie and without any gap despite being several times interrupted by enemy fighters and having to keep in mind the exact place where he had last taken photographs. The hundreds of prints were joined up to show a complete picture of the road. The only place that could be found to lay such a continuous strip was on a series of long tables in one of the Malta palaces. With pride the RAF presented the Army with this yards-long mosaic. A very senior Army officer (not one involved with the request) gazed at the long thin strip for a while and remarked that they were wonderful clear photographs: 'a jolly good show but it was a pity about that line in the middle'. 'That line' was the coastal road: the object of the exercise!

Nor was that all that Warby and his crew accomplished on that same sortie. On an earlier flight to Tripoli, Warby, who by then knew this area as well as any, had noticed a new airstrip being used a few miles to the south of Misurata. After having accomplished the coastal road mosaic, he went to take a look at his latest discovery. As he approached, for a closer look and to count the planes, a green light was given from the airfield control. Warby responded by making as if to land. When only a few feet up, he opened up the engines and aimed the Maryland at a line of big SM79's. With front guns blazing he shot them up, leaving three in flames. Moreover he managed to get in a few quick snaps with his hand-held camera. As they sped away, Paddy Moren brought the rear guns into play to add to the confusion and damage.

Another incident involved a lighthouse keeper. Warby made use of this lighthouse as a clearly identified navigational aid but when he was flying in low, the lighthouse keeper would come out and take pot shots at his Maryland as it sped past. This annoyed Warby and especially Paddy Moren who swore vengeance. Weeks of waiting brought the opportunity and as Warby flew by at 'zero feet', Paddy chased him up an exterior ladder with a hail of bullets finally catching him at the top with a final burst.

That Warby had devised a way of obtaining photos of 250 miles of the Via Balbia in one sortie is due in part to the great interest he had taken in aerial photography ever since being made the flight's photographic officer immediately upon arrival in Malta. The camera mechanics and photographic experts could not keep him away from their closeted quarters and dark rooms. Ken Fielder, a ground photographer, recalls how he first met his hero. On his first day at Luqa he was being shown around the hangars, which were then still standing. On the oily floor of one hangar he came upon a bunch of airmen squatting and playing cards as they awaited the return of 'their' plane. (Airmen always talk with pride about 'their' plane and 'their' pilot.) As he moved around to see what cards being held, he was amazed to see that one of the players sitting on the filthy floor was wearing officer's tabs on his shoulders. That was his first glimpse of Warby.

Right from the moment when Tich had ordered the aircrew to take a hand with the servicing the Marylands, Warby had made friends with the groundcrews. To a man, they became devoted to him and in return there was nothing that Warby would not do for them. He would share his meagre cigarette ration with them. He would go down into the 'Gut'- the redlight district of Valletta and strictly out of bounds to all officers – to find them and bring them back if in trouble. He treated them as exact equals. On one occasion at Christmas, as Corporal Cyril Wood has recalled, when Warby, already an island hero, was invited to attend a champagne party with some of the top brass of the island, he turned up with Cyril and another airman. To a man they knew him as 'Warby'.

Among the many devoted airmen who helped to service the planes of 69 Squadron, was Harry ('Scoop') Kirk. He was a camera/photographic mechanic. One day he was casually chatting to Warby who was watching him at work when he asked 'what were the Camel Trains that he had heard people talk about?' Warby didn't say anything at the time but when next flying along the coast road that runs between Tripoli and Alexandria, he spotted the very thing. Back at base, Scoop found himself developing the print which appears in this book It is little wonder that airmen like Harry Kirk would do almost anything for 'his' pilot. Scoop and Warby often discussed Warby's unique idea of how to put Italy out of the war. Mount Etna, the active volcano in Sicily, was at that time continually issuing volumes of smoke. Warby's idea was to get hold of the biggest bomb possible and drop it inside the smouldering crater. 'I wonder what would happen?' he mused. He seemed to have some notion that perhaps most of Sicily would disappear. The volcano seemed to attract him 'like a candle attracts a moth' as navigator Johnny Spires confirmed in one of Roy Nash's articles.

Warby's attention to detail was considerable. He had taken the trouble to quiz the Navy about how ships would be loaded when in port. For example he had learnt that at Palermo ships that were in the process of being loaded for the run to North Africa would leave their normal berth and be tied up along the outer mole. As he had a clear picture in his head of Palermo and the ships it usually contained (he knew it so well that he would come back with reports such as 'all vessels in their usual places') he could at once detect when a certain ship was getting ready to run the gauntlet to Tripoli. This information was invaluable to the RAF and the Navy who would then make plans how to stop it. Warby even came to recognize certain merchant ships by name. The RAF and Navy Ops room in Malta, thanks to its serviceable Marylands, were receiving service beyond any that they could have hoped for.

The major problem for Malta was not the incessant bombing. The problem was how to keep the population alive. Malta needed a constant flow of supplies: food as much as arms. The first convoys got through satisfactorily but even when having only the inefficient Italian Navy as the enemy, the few merchant ships which comprised the convoys were deemed to require massive naval escorts: sufficient strength to keep Italians in their ports rather than at sea.

It was against this precarious background that Warburton continued to make a name for himself on what were supposed to be no more than reconnaissance flights. In Malta both incessant bombing and a far from perfect diet were to become his standard way of life. Yet he seemed to thrive on it and rise above such daily difficulties. He appeared perfectly at home amidst these surroundings. He was scarcely recognisable from the misfit whom Squadron Leader Braithwaite had thought necessary to 'get out of the country quick'. Moreover he had found a 'girlfriend' – Christina. She was as charismatic and adventurous as Warby. A cabaret dancer, originally from Cheshire, she was well above average intelligence. Her vivacious good looks and high spirits, and a willingness to go anywhere, had led her before the war to find engagements not just in England but in many places in Europe. She had appeared in Paris, Switzerland, Genoa and in Barcelona where she was bombed and caught up in the Spanish Civil War. She was evacuated, along with other British nationals, on a destroyer HMS *Gallant*. But the Mediterranean still held its attractions for her and she later had obtained engagements in both Algiers and Tunis.

On 10 June 1940, the day that the war came to Malta with Italy's entry, Christina was dancing in a cabaret in Valletta. She had made arrangements to go next to Tunis in order to finalize the arrangements of her marriage to a young French judge. Mussolini's Air Force raided Valletta that same night. Thereafter a curfew was imposed and all cabarets closed. Christina and other artistes were out of a job: moreover they found themselves stranded in Malta. For the next three years it was impossible for any civilians to leave. Many service personnel were similarly stranded. Just as it was next to impossible to get supplies to the island, owing to enemy ships and planes, it was equally impossible for personnel to get away from the place. Malta was besieged: cut off from the rest of the world and, until the Battle of Britain was won, left very much to its own fate.

Christina realised that the island was full of troops and that they lacked every form of entertainment; she was sharing a flat with Cecil and Babs Roche and along with other artists similarly stranded on the island, they formed themselves into a Concert Party which they called the 'Whizz Bangs'. From the very start they were a hit as they toured Army, Navy and RAF camps and Messes performing on make-shift stages. Initially, for money or food, they had to rely upon 'passing around the hat' after each performance but later the Whizz Bangs were adopted by the NAAFI and the cast assured of a more regular income.

Christina's fluency with French led her to becoming friendly with Jacques, a brave young French airman, who had made a daring escape from Tunis. In the casual way things were done in Malta Jacques was incorporated into 69 Squadron. Jacques was fond of telling Christina about an English pilot who was: *'magnifique ... formidable'.*

The inevitable soon happened. At the beginning of the New Year Jacques went out on a PR sortie and failed to return. Within a few days at a rather rowdy party, a young RAF officer whom she hadn't before met approached her. To her surprise he knew her name. 'I'm so sorry, Christina, about poor old Jacques', he began. Warby and Christina had met.

In her eyes, she says, 'with his long golden hair and his incredibly blue eyes, he looked like a Greek God'. As Warby was also slim, tallish and athletically built the analysis is apt. 'I noticed that he was wearing the new ribbon of the DFC. His mouth was full and sensitive and when he smiled a deep crease came into his left cheek'. She soon came to admire his love of adventure and his devil-may-care attitude: as well as his cool nerve. The former attributes matched her own. With two such dynamic personalities on the small island, it was inevitable that they should come together. They were drawn to each other like magnets.

It was inescapable on such a small island that others should take an interest in such an outstanding pair. As Marion Childs (née Gould), then a very young girl working for the RAF, has written: 'They were a very glamorous couple.' John Snook, an 18-year-old airman who arrived later, writes: 'Warby's exploits were a shot in the arm for every man on the island.' Frances Marguerat, a Maltese citizen, recently assured the author: 'We shall always remember our Christina.' With their personalities, zest and determination they were to become living symbols of the island's unconquerable spirit.

Ken Rogers later writes; 'Christina filled a vital part of his life. He was the squadron but she was part of it too – even to a nice clean shirt for him.

She filled an important need in his life and gave him a haven of peace and happiness in the midst of it all.' Squadron Leader Tony Trotter similarly affirms: 'They were genuinely most fond of one another.' Many of course envied Warby for monopolising the most attractive girl on an island where there were thousands of servicemen but only about 60 English girls, mainly the daughters of serving officers.

Although working hard with the 'Whizz Bangs', Christina answered a call for English girls to volunteer for work with the RAF. After a brief spell as a telephonist, she soon became (still a civilian) a plotter in the underground ops room established in some ancient catacomb-like warren underneath Valletta, generally referred to as 'the Hole'. She was later appointed Captain of D Watch and finally rose to become assistant to the Controller. Only when given this last responsibility, did she give up performing for the Whizz Bangs. For over two years she doubled her two quite different roles. She was as indefatigable and tireless as Warby. She matched him in energy and spirit. To this day, as the author recently discovered, when men meet in the cafes of Malta to while away the time by discussing those never to be forgotten days when Malta was literally 'under fire' the name of Christina still crops up. Even the London Imperial War Museum possesses over 50 wartime photographs of her in Malta.

Warby and Christina were not fast-living party-every-night people. As Sergeant Pilot Les Colquhoun wrote rather enviously; 'Warby kept her much under wraps … he had to!' Christina has confirmed that when they were together Warby seldom drank much and even smoked little. Surprisingly, she also added, 'He was not a very sexy person.' Both loved parties and openly enjoyed them without seemingly having to look for such occasions. At such functions they may have fallen unconsciously into the habit of appearing to live up to the glamorous life that others expected from them: he the 'ace', she the dazzling cabaret dancer. However the photograph in this book of Warby winding wool for Christina is probably more typical of their hours together.

An indication of his consideration for her has come from 'Johnny' Walker, a flight lieutenant who later was associated with Warby's Beaufighter period. Warby knew that Christina loved to be taken out to a dance. So when a dance at a club was arranged, Warby used secretly to ask Johnny to join them so that he could dance with Christina. Warby confessed to being a 'two-left-feet' dancer himself.

A story which indicates her care for him is that when his threadbare RAF cap became so worn out that it threatened to disintegrate, she managed by skill to extract matching threads from inside the seam of his uniform trousers and repair it almost invisibly. By that time not only were there no uniform replacements but the island had completely run out of sewing cotton: a reel on the black-market would fetch 15 shillings, at least £15 to-day.

Before Greece was swiftly overrun by the Germans who, as in North Africa had had to come to the rescue of the inept Italians, Christina was indirectly involved in a typical Warby incident. He secretly- arranged to allow himself to be chased by enemy fighters across the Adriatic. He would then be obliged to land in Greece. There he had friends. Once in Greece, he would stock up with bottles to bring back to Malta which was chronically short of decent drinks. In due course, on 7 March 1941, the squadron records show that Maryland AR735 with Warby i/c aided by Paddy WOP/AG and a Sergeant Bolton navigating were 'Chased by 4 Macchis; aircraft short of fuel landed at Menidi, Greece. Flight time 6hrs 20mins.'

Officially they were reported missing and Christina's friends tried to commiserate with her. She had been forewarned by Warby but had been sworn to secrecy so she tried to 'bear up with her grief as bravely as she could.' She must have enjoyed this role. The next day, Warby appeared as if from the dead with the promised seven bottles of brandy for her. Brandy and ginger ale, ('Horses Neck') was his favourite tipple and he was embarrassed at having drunk all her strictly limited supply. Paddy Moren was, naturally, also in the know. He told the author that Warby came back not just with brandy for Christina but with the Maryland loaded to the gunnels with booze for the squadron. His aim had been to bring back in all 365 bottles: one for each day of the year.

Another version of what appears to be the same story comes from the airman Cyril Wood. He describes how Warby appeared at dispersal armed to the teeth: 'He looked like a brigand. He wore the service issue holster with revolver around his waist. Tucked into each flying boot he had another revolver. With a wave of the hand, chocks were pulled away and he shouted above the roar of the engine noise that he would not be back until the following day.' Cyril, not in the know, assumed that he intended landing behind the enemy lines and that, when he reappeared a day late, he had somehow refuelled with German fuel. Almost certainly included in Warby's personal armoury was his celebrated knife. He was never without this razor sharp weapon which he would delight to fling horribly near one's head (as the author knows!) when attracting attention. When visiting an office, the first that the occupant was apt to know about his visitor was when the knife came whistling into his desk. He was very accurate with it and would practise diligently. It was usually tucked into the Army Desert Boots which he liked to wear.

Tich, while in charge of Warby, was a stickler for correct and smart attire. However circumstances changed. Soon it was impossible to get hold of either replacement clothes or of such requirements of smart dress as shoe – or button polish. Even soap disappeared. After Tich's departure in June 1941, Warby wore virtually whatever he fancied. He had got hold of an Army battledress blouse with shoulder tabs for RAF ranking stripes. He preferred a cravat to a tie. He seldom wore uniform shoes and clearly liked something more comfortable and less formal. As he became known in the island – a living legend – he used to be recognised and cheered by the local Maltese as he drove through the narrow streets in his battered old car at times dressed only in pyjamas and slippers. His battered cap was grease-stained but he loved it dearly and would put it on top of his flying helmet when in the air. He acquired a loose but comfortable pair of what looked like Oxford Bags, the casual trousers of grey flannel much liked by the students there, also a pair of sheepskin long trousers for flights into the old upper atmosphere. Comfort and practicality seemed to predominate over official regulation dress. Yet at official functions he could be as correctly attired as any.

Having proved the Maryland as a 'fighter', Warby and Paddy Moren determined to see what it could do as a bomber. To both of them it seemed wasteful to be over enemy territory and not to leave a 'visiting card' of sorts. Unofficially, though Paddy believes that Tich knew all about it, they started to experiment with bombs. They had no difficulty about scrounging bombs from the armoury. Warby was already the airmen's No 1 wonder and if he wanted bombs then ways would be found to see that he got them put on board. Also the daily bombing by the enemy was made slightly more endurable by the knowledge that someone was replying in kind.

Warby and Moren principally carried with them a supply of fairly light 25lb incendiary bombs. They found that the easiest way to launch them was for Paddy to open the lower hatch and kick them out. On one occasion, however, Warby was diving the Maryland at such a speed that the airflow caused one incendiary bomb to blow back and for a while it was blazing away inside the rear of the fuselage with Paddy yelling at his skipper to slow down. Moren's log book records: 'Plane on fire – shaky do'. In all they carried out 21 unofficial bombing raids of enemy targets as far apart as Spezia in northern Italy and their 'usual' targets in the south, Tripoli and Benghazi. However these activities were always kept secondary to their assigned primary PR role. They continued to bring back first class photographs of virtually every enemy port and airfield that menaced Malta. Naturally other crews in 69 Squadron were also doing this but with aircraft so often damaged on the ground, there was a tendency for experienced crews, such as Warby's, to 'hog' most of the flying: especially after Tich had departed to the UK.

On 25 June the Maryland of Warby and his crew was *officially* invited to try bombing. It had been learnt that a most important enemy convoy had sailed, loaded with tanks and armoured division personnel. Rommel was in great need of these reinforcements, and a joint RAF/RN plan was hatched to attack it regardless of cost. The Navy despatched a submarine and plans were made for the few Blenheims on the island to bomb it at low level.

Blenheims suffered so appallingly on low level attacks that as a diversion the Marylands of 69 Squadron (two appear to have been serviceable at the time) were ordered to try simultaneously to dive-bomb the ship from 6,000 feet and so draw the escort's fire and divert attention away from the low flying vulnerable Blenheims. It was known that the precious cargo ships were heavily defended by Italian destroyers. Obviously it would also be surrounded by German and Italian fighter planes.

It was to the surprise of none that Warby and another crew were detailed for this dive bombing offensive role. The Fleet Air Arm was also brought into the plan. Their 830 Squadron at Halfar, with torpedo-carrying Swordfish, would also try to attack at the same time as the Blenheims and Marylands. Warby, with his favourite crew of Frank Bastard and the inevitable Paddy Moren, at once set about practising dive bombing. To the south of the island is a Filfoa, a rock which for years had served as a practice bombing target. Warby was soon diving the Maryland at it and scored a direct hit with a practice bomb.

Dive bombers are specially strengthened planes. The stresses imposed are severe. The Maryland was not so stressed. In their enthusiasm to show what the plane could do, Warby had dived and pulled out with such savagery that a hatch cover had been torn off. It had hit the tail-plane but fortunately had not wrecked the aircraft. The Maryland could not however be made serviceable in time for the attack schedule.

The only other Maryland at all flyable was one that was notoriously slow with unreliable engines. Pilots did not like to fly it. The engines spluttered. This did not deter Warby. However, its slow speed and the late start resulted in Warby having to attack alone and not as part of the combined RAF/RN/FAA plan. The affair is well described by Frank Bastard:

> On 25 June 1941, the Blenheims were to carry out a low level attack on the convoy off the coast of Sicily and it was decided to send a Maryland to draw off the AA fire by dive-bombing from 12,000 to 6,000 feet. That morning we had a practice on Filfola. We managed a direct hit but lost the pilot's hatch cover which damaged the turret and tail. By the time that we had obtained a replacement aircraft and had it bombed up with 2 ? 500lbs bombs we were too late for the rendezvous and arranged interception but Warby went ahead anyhow as this was something new to him: dive bombing. We located the convoy so Warby started to dive but 'forgot' to pull out at 6,000 feet. He just carried on and it was my guess as to whether us or the bombs would hit first. Just one bomb hit and the other was within yards of the ship. The hit was later confirmed by the shadowing submarine.

Paddy Moren has supplied further details. Because of their slow speed and late start, they found themselves flying towards the enemy in formation with some German Ju88s which were being sent as fighters to guard the convoy. For some reason, they assumed that the Maryland was friendly and made no attack, possibly because it stayed with the Ju88s.

Warby and Bastard may have even been aided by the Ju88s in locating the convoy. It turned out that whereas they did find it straightaway, the main RAF and FAA strike force had to circle around to locate it and although starting earlier they all arrived after Warby and his crew. In their mass attack which followed Sergeant B P Hanson and his crew, in another Maryland, were shot down and lost.

Johnny Spires who flew as Warby's navigator about as often as did Frank Bastard tells in one of Roy Nash's *Star* articles about another unique bombing venture. They had been sent to scour the Tunisian coast to check upon the remains of a convoy which had been attacked and badly mauled in shallow waters. Its ships were thought to have been largely sunk. However they had taken on board two 500lbs bombs in case any enemy vessels had survived the attack. As Spires reported to Roy Nash:

We found the sunken ships but on counting them, we found. them one short. Possibly one has escaped the attack. So we went on a tour of (neutral) Tunisian ports to look for it. (The attack had taken place off Tunisian coastal waters and it was known that in the past enemy ships had taken refuge in Tunisian ports and that the nervous French there had not tried to impound or impede them while there as technically they, as neutral, might have done). We found the ship in Sfax – there she was. Warby was undecided what to do. Attack an enemy sheltering in a neutral port? We flew inland and held a conference over the desert. Warby finally made up his mind that we should sink the ship with our bombs and back we went to Sfax, making an approach over the harbour at nought feet.

'Up she goes,' said Warby. Flying at masthead height, we got the ship in our bombsight – an old piece of wood with three nails in it. Just as I said, 'Bombs gone', I saw a red flag fluttering below. I shouted, 'For Gawd's sake, get down on the water. It's a munition ship.'

I shall never forget the roar as that ship went up and I don't know why we were not blown to pieces. We found the edges of our wings corrugated when we got back to Malta – but I suppose it was because Warby managed to get down so quickly. Warby and Spires managed to get a picture of the vast column of smoke arising from the blown up ship. Underneath in Spires' album is written: 'There was a ship in Sfax … there was.'

Wing Commander Adrian Warburton, late summer 1943. (*Keith Durbidge*)

Adrian Warburton (second from left) at his sister's wedding to Dr Gethen.
Muriel Warburton is third from the right.

Commander Geoffrey Warburton,
DSO, OBE.

'Betty of the Bush': the lovely wife of
P/O Adrian Warburton. Not surprisingly,
Betty was a National Beauty Queen
aspirant when this picture was taken.
(From a damaged photograph).
(*Bobby Collins*)

Paddy (Pax) Moren. (*P Moren*)

Tich Whiteley

No 9 ATS course at Hullavington, Summer1939. The fair haired P/O Warburton is easily
picked out in the centre row, second from the right. (*via T Forbes*)

III

Tony Carlisle at St Edward's school swapped some chocolate for Warby's 100-page aeroplane scrapbook. Adrian Warburton flew the obsolete Vildebeeste early in the war. (*via Tony Carlisle*)

Glenn Martin Maryland of the type used for PRU. (*G Wilson*)

Warby's patched-up Maryland at Luqa. (*Ken Fielder*)

'That'll teach you to put your red nose into our squadron's war!' A cartoon of Warby's gunner, Paddy Moren, circulated at the time. (*P Moren*)

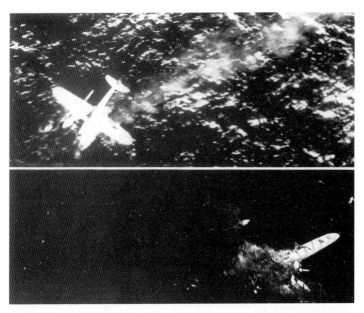

Two pictures of the Cant Z506 shot down by Warburton and crew. Both pictures show the Cant on the water, on fire and with a crewman, apparently dead, floating on the aircraft's port quarter. (*Ken Fielder*)

Warburton liked to go in low! Taken from a cartoon of the time, it shows the Maryland's three separate crew positions. (*P Moren*)

Sad remains of the Beaufighter which Warby had repaired, bombed up, armed and crashed. (*Conyers Rutter*)

Bombed-out hanger, Luqa 1941/2. An airman is salvaging spares from an engine. (*G Wilson*)

Adrian Warburton winding wool for Christina in an off-duty moment. An early Malta shot. Note no decorations and the half stripe of the pilot officer. (*Christina via Philip Vella*)

Christina, whose dance teacher had told her 'you will not get anywhere'. How wrong she was. (*Imperial War Museum*)

The Whizz Bangs, the self formed troupe which did so much to sustain morale in Malta under fire. Christina is third from the right. (*Francis Marguerat*)

Virtually everything at Luqa was destroyed by the Luftwaffe, planes, hangars and buildings including this Wellington (top) and Maryland AR733. (*Conyers Rutter*)

Building an aircraft pen from fuel cans (Imperial War Museum)

Warby found another original way of getting even with the Germans who were making life such hell for all in Malta. He had much enjoyed his attack on the three SM79s at the new landing ground which he had discovered near Misurata in Tripolitania. If he could surprise the Italians why not do likewise to the Germans in Sicily? Again the details are taken from a Roy Nash *Star* article: Johnny Spires:

> We were always on the look out for gliders. Malta was in daily anxiety about an airborne invasion. We saw the airfield, Catania, through the clouds and Warby decided to have a closer look. As we swept round, Warby found that we were on the circuit for a landing. Said Warby: 'We've got a green. I'm going in.' He then put down the wheels and made a normal circuit to approach the centre of the airfield. I was flabbergasted: 'What the hell do you think you are doing. This is Catania not Luqa.' 'I know,' Warby replied, 'now watch.' He told Paddy to get ready to strafe the Huns.
>
> There were lots of transports lined up on the tarmac, like rows of soldiers. He went straight out to sea leaving a bunch of very surprised Germans behind.

Because he did not stay around to assess the result of his daring attack, Warby made no claims but a post war report refers to one four-engined transport having been destroyed and on fire and two other planes seriously damaged.

In Malta the author once asked Warby about this well known attack. It had taken place before he had arrived in Malta. Warby could be the master of the throw-away lines. In a casual tone he explained. 'The Germans would be wondering what kind of Italian plane was coming in. The Italians would be wondering what type of German plane was arriving. When I had gathered a suitable audience, I let them have it.' As he spoke, his nose gave a disdainful wrinkle. But the author is inclined to think that it was one of Warby's carefully planned and brilliantly executed ideas which he had been carrying in his head for some time and had been waiting for the exact right opportunity. It may be significant that never again did Warby attempt to repeat this novel tactic: once in North Africa, once in Sicily only.

Warby's worst moment during his first Malta tour came on a sortie when the Maryland's canopy was shot away. As Paddy Moren recalls:

> We were attacking a Cant Z501, a three-engined plane with a rear turret and their gunner was firing back. One hit smashed through the Maryland's instrument panel, then struck Warby, penetrating his harness, which also took some of the force out of the bullet, and then entered his chest. The aircraft had sustained many hits and

was on fire in a 'right old mess'. Warby retained control of the aircraft but was in obvious difficulties.

This led to the famous conversation between Paddy and Warby. Noting his pilot's distress and curious contortions, Paddy enquired: 'Are you OK, skipper?'

'I'm all right now.'

'But what are you doing?'

'I'm extracting a bullet from my chest!'

Paddy, despite having had his upper turret blasted off, managed to get a wireless message to base that his pilot had been wounded. The plane was also on fire with one engine hit. Tich, ever resourceful, went in person to meet the aircraft climbing on the wing to be near Warby. He had thoughtfully taken a first aid kit with him. He was prepared as usual, to cope with the emergency and to display, if required, an example of yet another of his many skills. Warby indicated where he had been hit and Tich tore away his shirt. The wound seemed none too serious. Meanwhile Warby was fumbling in a trouser pocket and came up with the bullet which he had extracted while still flying. By the time the ambulance arrived both men were laughing hysterically: a great release of tension, no doubt. To complete the story, Warby insisted upon parking the aircraft before submitting himself to official first aid treatment.

Henceforth Warby had the bullet (or part of it) mounted on the wristband he wore. Tich later commented: 'I realised that day how attached to Warby I had become.'

Tich Whiteley returned to the UK at the end of June and Warby must have sadly missed the man who had groomed him for stardom, trusted him, backed him and even helped to straighten out his complicated finances. Whiteley had been a flight commander in a million. Under his guiding hand, Warby's true heroic self had emerged. But fate was to be kind to Warby. A month before Tich Whiteley returned to the UK, Air Vice-Marshal Maynard had been replaced as AOC Malta by Air Vice Marshal Hugh Pughe Lloyd. Tich had brought Warby out from the shadows, Hugh Pughe Lloyd was to give him a starring role.

In 'Hugh Pughe', generally referred to by his rhyming Christian names – Warby found another godfather. The command of 69 Squadron passed briefly to a Squadron Leader Welland, a regular officer with established views, and then to Squadron Leader Tennant, a New Zealander who fell in with Hugh Pughe's policy of allowing Adrian Warburton a very free hand to do things his own effective way. For as long as he continued to 'deliver the goods' in the form of photo-reconnaissance of the highest order, Hugh Pughe was prepared to close his eyes to the way in which he dressed, where he lived and what he did in the air in addition to bringing back the required photographs; always backed up by his remarkedly detailed oral reports of what he had observed.

In one of Roy Nash's articles for the *Star*, Hugh Pughe recalled how he, an Air Vice Marshal, and Warby, then a one ring flying officer, would go about their business:

> Warburton was the absolute king of photographic reconnaissance, the Pearl of the Mediterranean. If I wanted photographs of Naples, Tripoli or any other Axis port he would say: 'Yes sir,' and go out and get them at no matter what cost. Thanks to him and the other reconnaissance pilots, I knew every time the Germans or Italians moved a boat ... I had to reprimand him about those shot down planes but never very seriously. I might say: 'Really Adrian, it is very naughty of you to go chasing these poor Italians' and he would answer a little shamefacedly: 'Well, sir, it was too easy.' Then he would come into my office and say rather sheepishly: 'I've shot down another one.' 'You mustn't do that, Adrian', I told him: and so it would go on.

Hugh Pughe also describes two versions of how Warby would report to him. Orally, all he said was:

> 'I saw a chap down below and I got him'. When pressed for more detail he reported: 'I was entering the Bay of Naples from the south at 1,500 feet when I saw an SM79 with brown mottled camouflage ... the clouds were at 2,000 feet, in a solid attack some pieces of the tail flew off and my rounds started going into the fuselage. I closed the range and concentrated on the starboard engine which started to smoke and eventually stopped. My rear gunner (Paddy Moren) wanted to try the new turret. (Paddy was always trying to increase the fire power and managed to add guns to both the upper and lower positions. There was also a period when the Maryland was fitted with a turret from another type.) So I broke away and drew parallel to the SM79, slightly above and about 100 yards to his starboard. My rear gunner put in a burst of about 20 rounds which ignited the petrol. The SM79 burst into flames and dived into the sea from about 1,000 feet. I then carried on with my recce of Naples.

First the almost casual remark, then the very accurate detailed statement – it was typical of Warby. He was an all or nothing man. Hugh Pughe in the same article went on to explain that Rommel and his Afrika Korps were completely dependent upon supplies:

Every part (for a plane), every gun, every bayonet, every spanner had to go by sea. We spent everything we had to stop it. We needed information. You only had to explain to a man like Warburton and he realised what was required ... The whole thing was a direct business between myself and the pilots. Warburton used to breeze into my office and tell me what he thought we ought to do ... You could not fail to be impressed by his character. There was something about his fair-haired good looks that reminded you of Lawrence of Arabia. Like Lawrence, he was absolutely unorthodox and completely individualist. You had to let him do things in his own way ... He was not much of a military person to look at – nearly always carelessly dressed. When he came to see me he wore a scarf. Sometimes it was clean. Sometimes it wasn't. He was very thin. I never thought that he had enough to eat but he had a magic all his own – plus courage and flair ... If he was ten minutes late coming back from a flight, I could not stay in my office ... I would go up to the airfield to meet him ... It wasn't simply that I was eager for the information he was bringing me. You can't afford to lose a chap like that.

Paddy Moren recalls one possible explanation for Warby's thin appearance. Warby had become an aspirin addict. He would take up to 20–30 tablets *per day*. Medically this must have played hell with his stomach and affected his appetite. Food, in any case was scarce and the diet was far from being a well balanced one. In Malta one ate whatever one could find with no questions asked; just as one drank whatever was offered. Perhaps it adversely affected his libido and explains, perhaps, some of Christina's comments? Paddy has no idea when the habit was formed, for how long it had been going on nor what had started it in the first place nor when it ceased. It makes it all the more remarkable that Warby was able to take the life in Malta for so long without cracking up physically: poor food; incessant bombing; demoralising conditions; ever present danger in the air; *living on his nerves*; swallowing aspirins enough to kill and daily expecting invasion.

As the Luftwaffe stepped up their attacks, life at Luqa became more than just irregular. The airmen's barracks and the officers' Mess were flattened along with almost every other building. The officer's Mess became a huge flapping tent pitched on the site of the old building.

Officers and men simply lived wherever they could find a billet. One night when Warby had had a few drinks (and he didn't take drink too well) he loosed off shots from his much cherished revolver – upwards. Thereafter when it rained heavily we in the officers' tent had to avoid the drips that came through the holes.

The airmen built themselves many 'Mangey huts' (named after the French *Manger* = to eat). For food they relied heavily upon the 'mangey waggon' which toured the dispersal areas with whatever was on ration that day. Hence their 'Mangey Huts'. They would spend all their time out at dispersal in these. Such normal RAF regular procedures as kit inspection and parades were soon entirely dispensed with. Those who could take the bombing became pillars of strength. They would attach themselves to whatever plane or flight seemed to be in most need and they performed miracles of maintenance with very inadequate equipment. Many, but not too many, developed the rational habit of taking to the air raid shelters whenever an alert was sounded. They never were the same again. For one thing the alerts were so frequent that they spent far too many hours out of action. Much of the bombing was dive-bombing which had the advantage for the spectator of realising that 99 times out of 100, some other poor devil was catching it. Dive-bombers point at their targets and all close watchers can see what those targets are. In shelters, imagination takes over. Every bomb may be heading your way. Warby, as would be expected, was one of the many who avoided air raid shelters. Philip McConnel, a sergeant WOP/AG who occasionally flew with Warby on those rare occasions when Paddy Moren wasn't available, tells a story of how Warby reacted to being shot up on the ground:

> Three of us were walking from the sergeants' Mess when five Macchi fighters came over at nought feet machine gunning the drome. While the rest of us dived behind a heap of stones Warby who had his camera with him, just stood there – side on to a power cable pole.
>
> Each of those Macchi 200's was fitted with two machine guns. As they came over, ten guns firing at once, he took a snap. One bullet hit the base of the cable pole Warby was leaning against. He didn't turn a hair. As the Macchi's flew off and we came out from our pile of rocks, he was nonchalantly winding on the film in his camera ...
> Warburton always got his pictures. On the ground as well as in the air.

Warby was seldom in Mess. It was not known by most where exactly he lived. Some clue is given by Corporal Cyril Wood, a devoted airman of a later period, when he arrived at dispersal early one morning and Warby calmly announced after a night raid of Valletta area that: 'Some bastards blew us out of bed.' He told the Luqa adjutant Syd Collins the same tale in the same words. That flat was probably in Floriana, a suburb of Valletta, Malta's capital and principal town.

Apart from spending a fair amount of his spare time with Christina (bearing in mind that she was probably the busiest girl on a busy island), Warby spent many hours with the airmen at dispersal. For an early morning detail, he was apt to get there first and would be driving around in the battered tractor that bought up supplies; helping to prepare and supply the aircraft. He had more friends, and spent more time, among the airmen than with his brother officers; especially those who took a poor view of his informal dress and his apparent disregard for an officer's normal conventions. Fortunately his known 'chumminess' with the AOC made him proof from those senior officers who might otherwise have attempted to dress him down for various breaches of regulations.

However, as conditions became more desperate, Warby wasn't the only officer to behave much as he wished. It soon became apparent tht AOC Hugh Pughe Lloyd had regard for just one type of officer: he who could do the job best. He had, so he once told the author, joined up to fight in the First World War at aged 14 by faking his age. He became an Army motorcycle despatch rider until old enough for more official action. For one with his love of action and adventure, it was natural for him to transfer, at the first opportunity, to the Air Force. Whoever selected him for Malta under fire, knew what they were at. At heart, Hugh Pughe and Warby were as one, a couple of fearless schoolboys who had never grown up. Together they achieved miracles.

With his AOC 100% behind him and with Christina providing a haven of respite from the daily traumas of operations, Warby managed to survive mentally and physically long after his official operational rest period. Tich Whiteley, Foxton and Bibby had long gone and the several surviving pilots who later came to join 69 Squadron months after Warby had done, were one by one 'operationally rested'. They had flown their quota. Warby who had flown about three times as many trips as any other in the squadron, soldiered on. It was his wish and the AOC didn't want to lose him. Losses in the squadron were high. In March Flying Officer Boys-Stones had been shot down with all on board killed. The same month Flying Officer Ainley also 'bought it' (as was the RAF vernacular of the times). Later Terry Foxton's death is also recorded in Warby's log book. Sergeant Hanson and his crew being shot down over the enemy convoy is also mentioned. Others to fall were Sergeant Lee, Flight Sergeant Wylde and Sergeant Lawrence. Warby recorded their deaths in his log book. He also recorded that of Flight Lieutenant Williams, and several others when Williams' Maryland taxied past a bomb train and set the bombs off. These deaths seemed to affect him. It is another side of this complex man: so casual with his revolver and knife-throwing yet so concerned about his companions. As for his own life, he seemed to care for it less than most.

The shortage of Marylands persisted. One diversion for Warby was to be flown to Gibraltar. Warby and Johnny Bloxam, another experienced Maryland pilot of 69, were to bring back two French Marylands. Warby and Paddy Moren flew to Gib on 26 May in the large commercial flying boat 'Golden Horn'. Two good stories have come to light about them there. One concerning flying and the other definitely not: at least not directly.

Having located the French aircraft he was to bring back to Malta, Warby was prevented from flying it back until 8 June by a senior officer in a high position at Gibraltar. He was a 'collector' of aircraft types and wanted to add the rare Maryland to his list of types flown. Warby was not impressed. However the senior officer insisted and Warby stood aside while attempts were made to start the engines. Warby, but not the senior officer knew that the aircraft being French had to be started in a completely opposite fashion. French throttle controls are arranged to work in the opposite sense. Forward is off: back is full throttle. All other Allied aircraft were to start the other way around. After the senior officer had failed many times to start the engine, and got out frustrated, Warby got in and started up without difficulty!

In Gibraltar, which was far from the main conflict, it was recognised that Warby and those with him from Malta, had been through a tough period. It was suggested therefore that before returning to that hell-hole, they might like to sample the joys of nearby neutral Tangiers. It was however necessary to visit there in civvies. RAF uniforms could not be worn. Paddy Moren tells the tale well:

> I accompanied Warby to Tangiers in borrowed civilian clothing ...
> at a hilarious party wearing this hideous attire which made us look
> like Americans on vacation ... our talk as usual was on the subject
> of flying: while Warby was recounting his early difficulties in
> flying Marylands, the waiter arrived with a round of drinks for us.
> When we enquired who had sent them, the waiter responded that
> they had been sent over with the good wishes of the Luftwaffe, like
> ourselves, wearing borrowed civilian clothing. They were sharing
> the same night-club as us and competing for the same women! As
> a result we had a hilarious evening practising détente with our
> enemies in the middle of the war. It was the only occasion in my
> life when I found the men more interesting than the women.

Warby recorded in his log book the two valuable photo-reconnaissance flights which he carried out successfully while in Gibraltar to collect the French Maryland. The French fleet – on paper a magnificent one of modern battleships and extremely fast cruisers and destroyers – was supposed to be neutralised and immobilized but it was always the anxiety of the British Navy that it might be used by the Germans against them. Some key units were close at hand at Casablanca, Oran and at Mers El Kebir. After satisfying himself that the French Maryland was flyable, Warby carried out photo-recce flights of all these bases. He overflew

Casablanca on 3 June at only 3,000 feet in spite of being chased and harried by what he describes as Heinkel 112 fighters.† Perfect pictures were obtained. These trips were dangerous as the French, after their fleet had been attacked in North African ports, had retaliated by bombing Gib and understandably were definitely anti-British at that time.

Tich was also in Gibraltar at the time. It was the last time the two expected to meet. He could well have had a hand in arranging for Warby to carry out these missions for the Navy while there. Tich while there also delighted to see how busy Gibraltar had become as an active staging post for planes being ferried from the UK to Middle East. He had for long campaigned for the runway at Gibraltar to be so used.

Although always on the look out for more valuable Marylands – the ten Beauforts on the official establishment of 69 Squadron never seemed to appear at all, the squadron's supply was constantly dwindling. One result was that for some months, Warby flew their 'home converted' PR Hurricane painted orange as often, or more often than the Maryland. He seems to have no difficulty in handling this plane although all that he could have had training would have been to have the lay-out explained to him and then – off he would have gone.

Sadly the honourable Hurricane was by then obsolescent and one German ace Lieutenant Joachim Muncheberg of 7 Staffel Jagdgeschwader 26 is credited with destroying 26 Hurricanes during a four month stint in Sicily. Yet Warby as usual disregarded the risks. On one sortie over Taranto, always heavily defended, one engine of his Maryland failed but Warby still came back with his pictures. He did, however, add 'Shaky do' in his usual succinct log book.

On another occasion while over the sea both engines cut out. George Burges, fighter ace of the Faith, Hope and Charity era, explains that as Warby glided hopelessly towards the sea with no hope of being rescued from the drink, the engines mysteriously picked up again when only 1,000 feet remained. Most pilots would have crossed themselves and eased the plane back to Malta as gently as they could for a thorough inspection. Warby simply climbed back up again and continued as if nothing had happened. He seemed completely fearless at all times.

On one Taranto recce, one of his cameras failed. Warby feared that this might result in inferior pictures so, in spite of having to evade enemy fighters and being chased out to sea, he overflew Taranto three times in order to be sure of covering the entire port area. Warby continued to shoot down Italian planes and, miraculously, to avoid the superior German fighters. On 22 July, after a recce of Taranto he and Moren shot down yet another Cant Z506. A week later he had a 15 minute running battle with a

---

†The Heinkel 112 was never put into full production, and the handful made were flown pre-war. Possibly they were Dewoitines.

Fiat G50, a modern Italian fighter with a performance at least comparable with a Hurricane I. This was after he had photographed Palermo and left a 'visiting card' of half a dozen anti-personnel bombs kicked out by Paddy in the rear. On the same trip he later photographed the enemy airfields Caligari, Elmas and Masala using both vertical and oblique cameras. Often the low-level pictures had to be taken with the borrowed hand-held Leicas.

On 24 September, by which time he had been operating without respite for a whole year, being bombed almost daily and increasingly short of rations, he with his favourite crew of Bastard and Moren, shot down another Cant Z506. Five days later they added a confirmed Macchi C.200 fighter to their total. In his log book he added, 'One bullet in wing'. During that month his bar to his DFC was announced. Whatever their opinion of Warby personally, everyone agreed that he had thoroughly deserved it. By that time the island was breathing anew. The Russian campaign had begun and the bulk of the Luftwaffe in Sicily had been transferred to the gates of Moscow and Leningrad. The huge Italian Air Force remained but the Hurricanes, few and obsolescent as they were, could cope with this.

For a few precious months the RAF regained control over the airspace above Malta. It was pleasant not to be shot up over one's home airfield. The respite was wonderfully welcomed but it was not to last. Not that the change affected Warby. He just went and got his pictures, and backed them up with extremely accurate verbal reports, no matter what the state of the war was. Luck played a part but it was allied to much craftiness, determination and skill.

Although the Hurricane was a fighter aircraft the photo-recce ones of 69 Squadron had been stripped of guns and Warby was in no position to add to his score of enemy aircraft. Nevertheless, by the summer of 1941, this PR pilot flying the reconnaissance Maryland, ably assisted by Paddy Moren, had become the top scoring 'fighter ace' of the island.

Just as his father had been sunk in his submarine by his own navy, Warby, was almost shot out of the skies by the AA gunners of Malta. With few planes daring to depart in daylight, the Maltese gunner were apt to fire at any plane within their sights. On one occasion Warby's plane was hit and damaged. The hydraulics were shot away and the Maryland had to make a belly-landing, On another occasion, a Maltese light AA unit fired a long burst at what they believed to be an enemy bomber. Later the officer in charge received a phone call from Warby.

'Are you the chap in charge of those Lewis guns?'

When the officer assented, Warby went on:

'Let me congratulate you on the accuracy of your fire.'

'Thanks most awfully,' replied the unsuspecting lieutenant, adding, 'as a matter of fact I think I did score some hits on a Jerry tonight.' (The action had taken place in fading light.)

Warby then informed him that there were 12 bullet holes in his aircraft which had not been there when he had taken off but added: 'Not to worry, old chap. Come up to the Mess and have a drink.'

Warby so very nearly shared his father's fate again when he was attacked by a Hurricane soon after a night take-off. Warby didn't often operate at night but on occasions he would depart in the dark so as to be able to photograph a target at first light. An air raid was in process and, following prescribed procedures, Warby was orbiting the rock Filfola, a supposedly 'safe area', until the alert was over.

Although, after the first attack, Warby correctly identified himself by firing off the colours of the day, the fighter persisted. After the Maryland had been hit, Warby had had enough. He told Paddy in the rear turret to 'let him have it'. Paddy's shooting was always first class and the Hurricane was so badly shot up that the wounded pilot had difficulty in getting back to Halfar. Warby was also forced to return to inspect his plane's damage. On the ground they counted 36 bullet holes in the Maryland, an episode recorded by the local cartoonist. Warby later sent a humorous message to the pilot in hospital and relations between 69 and the Hurricane squadrons were not impaired. As Moren adds: 'There was always HQ to bláme for such cock-ups.'

During his second Malta tour Warby's Beaufighter, then a newcomer to Malta, was shot at in daylight by four Hurricanes. Although his plane was not hit, one of the sergeant pilots who had attacked him, claimed to have shot him down. Warby delighted in personally sorting out this pilot and taking him to inspect his undamaged plane, read him a lecture about the inaccuracy of his shooting and gave him a severe ticking off about the making of false claims.

Paddy Moren, after their Maryland had been shot at once again by Hurricanes and Malta gunners, exclaimed that he would soon be applying to the Luftwaffe for a medal for having survived so many attacks by the British.

Paddy seems to have known all of Warby's secrets. Whereas the officers could not understand why Warby avoided the Mess, Paddy, almost alone, knew that he was almost penniless. At the best of times flying officers were poorly paid. Even with the extra money they received for flying pay, they only received about 14 shillings a day. In Warby's case much of this was being withheld in order that his debts in the UK be settled, as arranged by Tich. However David Beaty recalls that Warby, living away from Mess, was getting an allowance. Paddy was also aware that Warby was married and that the marriage had rapidly 'come apart at the seams'.

From Paddy also has come the story of two unusual pets of 431 Flight (later 69 Squadron) – pets that Warby especially treasured:

> The first was a marmoset monkey which was carried by each of the
> pilots in their leather jackets on squadron operational trips. It even

had its own log book which was subsequently lost when the crew room was flattened, by a bomb. Regrettably Sergeant Bibby [the pilot who flew to Malta with Moren and Bastard in record time] elected to take it to his room to coincide with an early take-off and unknowingly suffocated our mascot during his sleep as the marmoset had crawled into Bibby's bed for warmth. Our second pet was a seagull which was hit on take-off by an aircraft piloted by Warby. It was rushed to the Medical Officer who determined that it had a badly damaged wing. 'Sammy' the seagull received daily medical treatment and was adopted by all. Over and above his medical treatment, Sammy was permitted to bath in an open rice-pudding bowl containing beer. The bird loved this and got as sozzled as any flight crew member. In the passage of time he gradually recovered his power of flight and took regular trips around the Mess prior to his drink supply being furnished. One day a window was left open and he was gone only to return three days later with another seagull which we all assumed was his girlfriend. The girlfriend sat on the window ledge while Sammy flew into the Mess to bath in beer while quaffing his fill. Sammy never returned again which most of us attributed to the fact that we had run out of worthwhile beer!

Warby was also fond of a mongrel and used to allow it to inhabit one of his unique long sheepskin boots. As David Beaty has so soundly remarked, 'Malta was totally unreal.' Another has put it that, 'It certainly helped to be half crazy to survive.' In our hearts we believed that we had been 'written off' as undefendable and that we were expendable but that we were expected to put up a good show before falling to the inevitable.

There is more than an element of truth about the contention that Warburton and his Maryland survived longer than most in Malta simply because he was more often in the air than anyone else. The Wellington bomber squadrons which sent flights periodically from Egypt or the UK were deemed too slow for daylight operations. They bombed Tripoli, mainly, and other targets, only at night. Thus they sat on the ground all day at dispersal. Here they were decimated by the attacking planes. Warby and his Maryland would often be airborne during these attacks. Statistically, a plane had a better chance of survival when over enemy territory and not on the ground in Malta.

No 431 Flight, later 69 Squadron, was among the first to appreciate the danger to their aircraft when on the ground. Under Tich's inspiration, huge pens had been constructed from the stone blocks, which were ever plentiful in Malta. They were built around each dispersal point and these pens were widely scattered around the airfield at Luqa. Once inside these 'fortifications' the planes were safe from all but a direct hit. Others units followed but for the most part, when the idea had become widespread and pens were being constructed on every corner of every airfield for every aircraft on the island, these later pens were built from 4 gallon petrol tins filled with rock or earth. It took about 65,000 tins† to build a pen around a Wellington but the island was not short of either men or tins. The Army and Navy also assisted. Safi strip was never, until very late in the war when Malta had been fully liberated, used as a runway. Instead it became the graveyard for the scores of aircraft, many of which were Wellingtons, which had been written off on the ground. Parked there in rows, but still looking reasonably sound, they seemed to attract the enemy bombers and fighters which wasted a large number of attacks further damaging these already written-off machines.

The greatest danger around Malta for Warby and the other pilots of 69 Squadron was during take-off and landing. Then when at their most vulnerable, they were liable to be attacked by the marauding Me109's.

Warby seems to have been well aware of his own good luck in survival. After having used the Maryland to beat up enemy airfields by pretending to be about to land, he conceived the fantastic idea of landing behind enemy lines on the long lonely desert road that ran close to the North African shore and, leaving Frank Bastard in the plane with engines running so as to be ready for a rapid departure, Paddy and he would hide and then waylay an important looking staff car, shoot it up and return to Malta with a senior German officer as prisoner on board. 'With our luck', Warby told Paddy, 'we'd probably get Rommel!' But they never carried out this imaginative idea.

'Warby's luck' became a talking point among his fellows in Malta. Yet, upon closer analysis, much of what he achieved was accomplished only after much thought and had been well worked out. Nor did he stick his neck out on the same enterprise too often. Having fooled the enemy just once in Africa and once in Sicily he had the sense to leave it at that and did not again fake a landing approach at a hostile airfield. The risks he took were often well calculated and he was never tired of talking to all at HQ in order to better understand his enemy and what they were about.

At the time many knew him as 'Mad Warby' but some who were close to him and those who flew regularly with him were inclined to disagree. None doubted his courage, his flair and the manner in which he managed to attract attention both in the air and on the ground, yet as Gerry Glaister has written:

> He was an extremely fine pilot but by no means the daredevil that some people made him out to be. He was a cool and calculating

---

†As machinery was absent, A.V.M. H.P. Lloyd likened it to 'building the pyramids'.

recce pilot who never took unnecessary risks. He once said to me 'I only take calculated risks'. He never went in at low level unless he thought it advantageous to do so and the surprise of a low level flight would ensure a very high chance of success. He had immense confidence in himself and his own abilities.

Gerry Glaister, now a well known BBC figure, flew alongside Warby at a later date in Egypt but the comment is valid for much of Warby's early Malta exploits also. But for every perceptive commentator such as Gerry Glaister, there were many who simply thought of Warburton as 'Mad Warby'; much as they cherished his memory and respected his bravery. An interesting view comes from Airman Ellis who recalls that on one occasion:

We were a bit early at dispersal so we had time for a chat. He said that even if there was no war, to succeed one must have a singleness of purpose and never waver from it.

One such example of singleness of purpose was Warby's attempts to go fighting in a Beaufighter which had crash landed en route to Egypt. The pilot was in hospital but the Beau was not seriously damaged. By then Warby had developed a taste for shooting down the enemy and for bombing his bases. Let Corporal Cyril Wood take up the tale:

After some months Warby obtained permission to have the plane repaired. With his usual enthusiasm, he got volunteers from his own ground crew to work on the Beau and, after begging, borrowing and making the various bits and pieces, the 9–10 ton Bristol built fighting machine with the fire-power of a tank was ready to fly.

Warby ran up the engines, checked the mag drop and with a wave of the hands ordered 'chocks away'. Here was the maiden flight of the rebuilt Beaufighter. At this time the Luqa long runway was little more than 1,000 yards long. At one end was the dreaded quarry, already half-filled with the carcases of burnt-out Wellingtons that had landed there or which had been destroyed by the Germans. The lower end of the runway (it had a pronounced slope to it), terminated in a wide ditch. Warby taxied to the take-off point, nosed on to the runway and got his green light. He coaxed her into the air and eventually landed back safely. He then dashed off to the AOC to get permission for a raid upon enemy aerodromes. One trip, so said Warby, was approved and the armourers loaded up the six machine guns and four 20mm cannons. The adventure was set for the following day.

The take-off was never accomplished for, as the plane thundered down the runway, try as he would, Warby couldn't lift it into the air and it finished up a crumpled pile on the edge of the 'drome. Undaunted Warby stepped out of the wreckage, grinning as usual, with the remark to his would-be rescuers: 'That's that.'

Jim McNeil, a corporal photographer attached to 69 Squadron, recalls that the permission to have the plane repaired, came not from the AOC (the author much doubts that even Hugh Pughe would have sanctioned such a dangerous mission for his most valued pilot) but from the wounded pilot languishing in hospital. Apparently Warby had plagued him with requests to 'have a shot at fixing up his Beau' until worn down he had agreed. Jim McNeil also comments that the reason why the Beau refused to rise was that one propeller was in fully fine pitch and the other in fully coarse. Warby was, of course, totally unfamiliar with the type. Not one word of this appears in Warby's official log book. Throughout he has for the most part confined his entries to official missions. This is a pity as stories about various unofficial missions are numerous. Another omission is what he was doing between 17 and 19 July when sent on temporary posting, along with Flight Lieutenant Wyle, Flying Officer Paddy Devine and Sergeant Stripp, to Egypt. It is known that they flew to Heliopolis, near Cairo, on the 17th in company with five Hurricanes. They flew there in the French Maryland which Warby had picked up at Gibraltar. He returned in another one (BJ 423) on the 19th, again accompanied by Hurricanes.

It is the author's belief that Warby realised the odds against him ever leaving Malta a free man were high and that he was determined to sell his life as expensively as possible. This is one reason why he always carried a revolver and knife with him. More than once he openly exclaimed that they would never take him alive. 'You will not be taken a prisoner', Warby once told a man detailed to fly with him. Other crews deliberately did not carry side-arms in the belief that, if shot down over enemy territory, it was better not to appear belligerent.

One of the paradoxes of Warby's character was that although he was a man who went out of his way to attract attention he was quickly embarrassed by the aura of fame which surrounded him. Paddy Moren holds the view, much as he loved and admired his skipper, that: 'Warby simply had to have admiration or sympathy.' A story from Squadron Leader 'Johnny' Walker, who at the time was Warby's senior officer of their small Beaufighter detachment, tells of this:

I remember on one occasion we were in the Club in Valletta with a bunch of submariners, one of whom was Commander Wanklyn VC DSO DSC of HMS *Upholder* who had already made a big name for himself. I remember pulling Warby into the circle and introducing him as Adrian Warburton and Wanklyn grabbing his hand and saying, 'So you're the great Warburton' and Warby blushing to the roots of his hair and being completely tongue-tied.

Johnny Walker goes on to add that, 'Yet Warby was completely in his element when dealing with the ground staff except that the respect they paid him often seemed to disconcert him a little.' Elsewhere Johnny Walker adds that, 'I always got the impression that Adrian, with a name like that, always tried to give a bit of a 'limp wrist' impression to belie or perhaps enhance, the row of gongs he carried.' To Walker, Warby once said that Malta was his idea of the perfect operational set-up and that he intended to stay there until he was kicked out:

> He operated directly under the AOC (H P Lloyd), got his targets from him, did a quick recce of them … and had Christina as a base to operate from. He would work like this for about six months, get a gong, be sent off to somewhere quieter where the food was better, have a good rest and about two months later would start a campaign to get posted back to Malta. I never went out on a party with him and never saw him take a drink. He was the complete loner.

September 1941 was to be the last month of this, Warby's first, operational tour in Malta. It was typical of him to leave the island in a blaze of glory. On his last trip, on the 29th, teamed with both Frank Bastard and Paddy Moren, they were attacked over Sardinia by Macchis and on their third attack Paddy shot down a Macchi 200. Warby recorded it as his eighth confirmed kill and it came less than a week after they had shot down yet another Cant Z506. Warby who prided himself upon his recognition of enemy ships and aircraft, identified it as a Z506 *B*.

During this month Wing Commander Dowland, the very Regular RAF CO, paid Warby his final tribute. Boldly he wrote across Warby's log book: 'As a GR and PRU Pilot … EXCEPTIONAL.'

Flying Officer Warburton had come a long way from the 'Below Average' rating given to him in May 1939 at the time he was granted his RAF wings.

AOC Hugh Pughe Lloyd, when awarding Warburton his second DFC on 9 August, made a comment reported in *The Times of Malta*. This local newspaper was a great daily booster for the troops. In spite of all the difficulties it was produced daily in English under the direction of a great Maltese lady, the Honourable Mabel Strickland OBE. The AOC referred to the crew of Warburton, Bastard and Moren as being a 'crew with a price on their heads', and advised them, after they had shot down their eighth Italian plane, that 'they had better avoid visiting Italy after the war.' There was no other crew in Malta in which both sergeants had been awarded the

DFM and their skipper a double DFC moreover the score that Warby and Moren had chalked up – 8 confirmed kills and several more damaged as well as several destroyed on the ground, made the crew by far the top scoring one in the island; including fighter pilots. This colourful phrase and the publicity given to it (it was copied elsewhere as well) was in Paddy Moren's opinion, the reason why, on posting to Egypt, the crew was broken up. Apparently the RAF didn't relish crews 'having a price on their heads'. They considered that it would have gone ill for them had they been shot down and captured.

During that September, Warby had enjoyed a spell of ten days' leave. Yet in the remaining few days he carried out eight operations in locally modified Hurricanes Mark I and II. Also during that September he had carried out five Maryland reconnaissance flights. He had completed his 155th operational trip since arriving on that battered island over a year ago. He had shot down two planes. He had also chased and shot at the seven Ju52's which he had followed almost all the way to Tripoli. He had bombed Pantellaria. He had tracked down a French ship the *Strasbourg*. He had photographed Palermo from 12,000 feet and Messina from 50 feet. He had been iced up over Tripoli and Zuara. He had ranged all over Sardinia, Italy as far north as Naples and had covered again and again the enemy airfields in Sicily. He had photographed Tripoli yet again. He had survived another 30 air raids: yet it had been his *quietest* month for almost a year.

As is now known, he was expecting to be posted home to the UK but at the last minute the orders were changed. Instead he was posted to 223 Squadron at Heliopolis as a flying instructor. But would instructing suit or satisfy him? Against all the odds and against his fatalistic beliefs, he was leaving Malta alive and well: already a hero and a living legend. How would he find life outside?

CHAPTER FOUR

EGYPT

On the first day of October 1941, the 'crew with a price on their heads' in Maryland BS761 flew themselves out of the madness that was Malta direct to Heliopolis, Cairo. By then Frank Bastard DFM had been commissioned. Paddy Moren, likewise the holder of the DFM, was still an NCO. It was to be their last flight together. They tried to make it yet another memorable one. They chased a Ju88 which they had sighted but failed to get within range. As it was, they were 5hrs 30mins in the air; almost the maximum endurance for the type.

In his quiet but always thorough way, Air Marshal Tedder, the new AOC in C Middle East, liked to know what was going on and he arranged for the crew to go to HQ so that he could talk with them: and so learn more about Malta and the conditions there. AVM Lloyd once told the author that Tedder considered Warburton 'the most valuable pilot in the RAF'. No 223 Squadron was an operational training unit rather than an operational squadron. The squadron had seen its share of fighting early in the war but was now a unit where the South African pilots of the SAAF and others who had been trained in South Africa and Rhodesia, were sent prior to taking part in operations for the first time. Seasoned crew members such as Warby, Frank and Paddy would be putting the final gloss on their training. The aircraft types used were Marylands. But these were, as ever, in short supply, and 223 Squadron had also acquired a few Blenheims. In both types, bombing, low flying (which during early training was frowned upon) navigation and other practical air exercises formed the basis of the curriculum. When passed out, the pilots and other crew men were posted straight to front line squadrons in the Western Desert.

Warby was due leave and was well over any limit of operational hours permitted. His father, called up from the Navy reserve, held an important shore appointment with the navy at Haifa. As the holder of a double DFC, Warby had little difficulty in arranging a ten day visit to his father at Haifa.

In a letter to his mother during the visit (see Appendix III) he assures her that 'I have retired from operations for a bit.' The general tone is to reassure her about both his father and himself. For instance he comments upon how 'fit and brown' he found 'Pops' and that the Jewish cooking was so good that he himself was regaining the weight he had lost in Malta. He expressed sympathy with the rough time that she in the UK seemed to be having and contrasted it with the 'lap of luxury' he was enjoying with all the parties that he was being taken to by his proud father 'who knows everybody and seems very cheerful'. He also remarked upon the good bathing.

The letter ends with 'All my love Adrian.' Throughout it is a most kind and thoughtful letter from a fond son and from one who got on well with his father.

Back in Egypt on 12 October, he immediately joined 223 Squadron at Shandur, where Paddy had become a gunnery instructor. It didn't take Warby long to realise that in his mind he could be doing better things to win the war. For the rest of that October he flew occasional flights in Marylands but without pupils. He flew around, to quote from his Log Book, 'with a few Army types' for AA gun training in the Suez area. More significantly he flew himself to Heliopolis. It was probably a most fruitful visit.

During the first week of November, he carried out just three exercises with the pupils sent to 223 Squadron. That seems to have been sufficient for him. By then he must have learnt that there was a Photo-Reconnaissance Unit (No 2 PRU) based at Heliopolis and on the 11th, he duly joined them. In Paddy Moren's words, 'Warby wangled a posting to 2 PRU but Frank and I were instructing at various places for almost a year. The fact that 2 PRU had a flamboyant CO might have been relevant.' Johnny Walker, a 2 PRU pilot, records, 'Warby arrived 9 November out of the blue. I've no idea where he came from but we soon learnt that there was precious little we could teach him.' 2 PRU had been born in unusual circumstances and had a very charismatic CO. In many respects it mirrored the original No 1 PRU, based at Benson.

Prior to the outbreak of the war on 3 September 1939, the RAF had a sound ground photographic unit but no means of bringing back aerial pictures. However a highly colourful character Sidney Cotton came to their aid. He, and a friend Bob Niven, had concealed a vertical camera underneath a small Lockheed Electra airliner (Lockheed 10). From July 1939 onwards, Cotton had been secretly photographing German military and naval bases. His cover was that he was representing his own colour film business and he soon made good friends in Germany who welcomed his visits. To take a picture he would operate a secret button under the pilot's seat. For two months they covered virtually every German port and many key military installations. From this extraordinary start the RAFs Photo-Reconnaissance Unit was formed. Originally called the Photo-Recce Development Unit (PDU), it was to prove a war winning weapon. By war's end it had grown from one aircraft to group size. Until, later in the war by when it had developed its own establishment, it was manned by most unusual types. Squadron Leader Hugh Macphail, was in charge of the second unit: No 2 PRU, Heliopolis. He was a WWI pilot who had been flying commercially for a Peruvian Airline pre-war. He was a jovial likeable type who lived well. He had served as assistant to Sidney Cotton.

When it was decided that the Middle East, as well as Benson in the UK, should have a PR Unit, Macphail was the obvious choice to command it.

He was a lively character who, like both Cotton and Warby, was adroit at getting a job done and didn't mind a damn how it was done or whose toes were trodden in the process. His motto was: 'Bullshit baffles brains'. Macphail had arrived in the Middle East with a small Lockheed airliner with cameras added. The Electra was painted a blue that made it invisible at 14,000 feet and, although Italy was not then in the war, it was used to take excellent photographs of Italian-held possessions in the Eastern Med and anything else that the Services requested. The aircraft was called Cloudy Joe. From these bizarre beginnings 2 PRU was born. It didn't take Warby long to recognize it as the kind of unit to which he ought to belong and where his talents would be appreciated.

In due course the unit became recognized and was assigned an establishment of two flights of Marylands. Then in January 1941 disaster struck. The ship carrying all its Marylands to the Middle East was sunk. 2 PRU then discovered, as had 431 Flight and 69 Squadron, that the supply of Marylands had just about dried up for good. As a stop-gap measure, 2 PRU was assigned three Hurricanes which were stripped locally of all guns and equipped with cameras having lens of 8 inches and 14 inches.

For Warby, it was almost like being back in Malta again but this time with lashings of good food and no bombs. He was again with a photo-recce unit which was having to scratch around and use initiative to find the aircraft it needed and was also under a man who did things his own way regardless of whether they were official or regular. Warburton settled down immediately and was flying one of their Hurricanes on a recce flight within four days of his last flight with pupils of 223 Squadron.

Warby arrived at Heliopolis at an interesting time. 2 PRU had realised that it could not be truly effective with its three Hurricanes and had been looking for a replacement type with greater range. It had acquired a couple of Beaufighters and, unofficially, was in the process of having them stripped of their many guns and cannons, radio equipment and even some armour plate in order to convert them into high-flying PR machines. They were painted in Macphail's special dark blue camouflage. The aircraft were being converted at Abbu Sueir and later at 7 MTU Geniofer. The officer who was looking after this 'modification' was Flight Lieutenant R G M Walker, generally known as 'Johnny' Walker. He was Macphail's No 1 and the two Beaufighters constituted 'T Flight' with Johnny Walker as flight commander.

Johnny Walker, although pleased to have been able to acquire the two Beaufighters has confessed that he was really trying to scrounge some American twin-engined B 25s – Mitchell bombers which had just started to arrive in the area. Walker, and another experienced pilot, Flight Lieutenant Whelan, had got the bugs out of the unit's highly personalized Beaufighters by the time that Warby arrived. Walker and Whelan had flown them on operations to Crete and other places. Crete was the unit's main concern. The island had been seized by the Germans on 1 May 1941, and there was great concern about a possible build up of strength there.

By late summer 1941, the Germans under Rommel had driven the Allies back to within an easy striking distance of Cairo. Only Tobruk had held firm. By then the Germans had carried all before them in Greece, Jugoslavia, Crete. On the Russian Front they were advancing towards Moscow, and were deep into the Ukraine. Inspired by such victories, Hitler, always dreaming of World dominance, conceived the ambitious plan of carrying out a vast pincer movement which would rob the Allies of its essential oil supplies from Arabia. One arm of the pincer would sweep through eastern Europe, overrun neutral Turkey and Persia (Iran) and rush on to the Persian and Gulf oil fields, while the other arm would defeat the Allies in Egypt (or bypass Cairo to the South) and would link up with the main force in the Saudi Arabian oil fields. Crete would be a vital jumping off base from which to subdue the Middle East and Turkey. If a huge build-up there could be detected by aerial photographs then the Allies would know what to expect. As it was, the only indication they had of this grandiose plan came from intercepted German intelligence reports which were being received and decoded via the Enigma machine at Bletchley Park.

It was to be able to photograph Crete that the Beaufighters had been obtained. Macphail knew that it could not be satisfactorily done with the Hurricanes. The Beaufighters were equipped with three 20-inch lens cameras. These RAF cameras are large and when the two Beaus were first modified it was not appreciated that they would also require to find space for the large camera magazines as well. Consequently, some armour plate had then to be removed as well. The author once heard Warby declare that in all they had removed a 'ton and a half' from this large and formidable twin-engined fighter.

Owing to its size, there was ample room in the Beaus for additional crew and it was decided that, for PR work, they should carry a skilled photographer. For one thing, the magazines would need to be changed in the air. It was also necessary to have the warm air diverted towards vital parts of the cameras. These operators were also invaluable as look-outs to warn of enemy fighters. A call went out for volunteers from the ground photographic staff. In response, three airmen photo-mechanics were recruited: Corporal Liebert, the senior of the small group, LAC Norman Shirley and, a little later, LAC Ron Hadden. Initially, it was Liebert who went wherever the Beaus went. The two special Beaufighters were also to become well known: T3301 and T4705.

Warby could claim that he knew all about Beaufighters. At least he had *tried* to get one airborne at Malta! Within a few days of joining 2 PRU, he and a Flight Lieutenant Davidson were trying out the Beaus and their newly installed cameras. The next day, with Liebert in the rear, Warby flew T3301 to Fuka and back. Fuka was a forward landing field close to the Allies' front line. It was closer to Crete and would be used for PR flights to that island. That was 18 November. On the 19th, satisfied that all was working well, Warby, with LAC Shirley as crew, set forth to photograph Crete.

The Beau was not designed as a high flying camera carrier. Lightened as it was, it was now capable of reaching great heights. In those rarefied atmospheres, the air is extremely cold. As a result by the time that Crete was approached, the starboard engine had failed due to the oil system being frozen and the port engine was malfunctioning. Norman Shirley has supplied a graphic account. The aircraft went into a spiral and, after recovering from this 'by grudgingly conceding every inch of altitude, we just made it to a landing strip of a South African unit. I think Warby and I talked that aeroplane back. We were slow and easy pickings for any ack-ack or fighters that were about: luckily none …' Shirley was put up in a slit trench but Warby looked after him as best he could, even to bringing him a bottle of whisky for the cold of the night. The two were to become firm friends later but as Norman Shirley has written: 'I think it was from then that I was able to look into his eyes, as men can occasionally without barriers … I felt I had earned his trust.'

It wasn't a good start but successes were soon to follow. The teething troubles were overcome and, in the hands of Warby, Walker and the other pilots of 2 PRU, the secrets of Crete were soon as much an open book as earlier, operating from Malta, the secrets of Taranto, Tripoli and Palermo and Catania etc had been. So much for Warby's well earned 'rest from operations'. He had found another niche and in Macphail, he had found another senior officer who appreciated his worth just as had Tich Whiteley and, then, Hugh Pughe Lloyd.

Compared with Malta, Warby was having a rest. He flew other less serious sorties. He flew the little Lockheed airliner AX701 and even a biplane Hart. He flew less hours than before. He was being well fed. His nights were not being disturbed by bombing. Rommel was too close for comfort but even this was soon to be changed.

The Army in the Western Desert with its new tanks and with its Air Forces reinforced by US as well as British planes, began Operation Crusader on 18 November. By 10 December, amidst great rejoicing in the UK as well as Egypt, Tobruk was relieved. The Allied 8th Army, with RAF assistance, had defeated Rommel in a desert road battle. The German troops were soon in retreat. The road to Tripoli seemed open. With Tripoli captured, that would be the end of the war in the Desert. But Rommel was no mean general. When the British forces made a few mistakes and, having received some reinforcements from Italy by sea, Rommel, the wily fox, completely turned the tables and, as 1942 commenced, it was the Afrika Korps and not the Eighth Army, which was leaping forward along that desert road in giant strides. This was to have repercussions that reached right down to T Flight of 2 PRU and the two Beaufighters which had been converted for their use. The see-saw war in the desert was to shape Warby's destiny in the months to come.

Warby was to leave Egypt under curious circumstances. At the time when it seemed that the Eighth Army was winning the see-saw Desert battle, the Allies, assuming the Desert war to be won, began to consider the future capture of Sicily among other targets. Part of the thinking behind this was that it would be a pre-emptive strike: one that would divert the Germans away from their giant pincer move to the oil fields of Arabia. It would divert their strength and delay that plan. Even if later we might be driven back out of Sicily (which would have been difficult to hold unless the Italians then caved in), it would have put paid to the scheme to grab the oil fields. Later, when America, which had only entered the war in December, had built up her strength, it would be much easier to thwart the pincer movement. Already USA supplies were flooding into Egypt: Grant tanks, Curtis fighters, Douglas and Mitchell bombers.

To prepare for a future invasion of Sicily, it was necessary first to get photographs of all possible beach landing sites. 2 PRU was the chosen instrument. Malta was the obvious place from which to carry out the important assignment. Warby was the obvious man to achieve results in the shortest possible time. Had he not, earlier, photographed that entire stretch of 250 miles of desert road between Benghazi and Tripoli in just one memorable sortie?

Accordingly, orders were given for Warby and Walker and another pilot, an Australian Flying Officer 'Benjie' White, to take the two Beaus to Malta along with the three ground photographers, volunteer flight crewmen, Liebert, Shirley and Hadden. Though Warby was an obvious choice, there were still reservations about his handling of the twin-engined Beaufighter near the ground. It remains inexplicable why such a superb pilot in the air, never seems to have learnt the rudiments of how to land twin-engined aircraft or of how to persuade them to leave the ground neatly.

Norman Shirley, who was as devoted to Warby as anyone, describes these manoeuvres as:

> His take-offs and landings … were the clumsiest I had by then experienced. He jerked the aircraft off the ground … not for him the niceties of a three point landing. He drove it on to the wheels at what seemed to me a suicidal rate … but in the air, what a difference from other pilots (he was) totally and completely at one with the aircraft … Absolutely clumsy in beginning, a total sympathy in flight and slap bang down the landing strip to finish.

Johnny Walker is less poetic. He simply stated, 'Warby was the original ham-fisted pilot' but he never flew with him so missed the symphony in flight. The author witnessed many a Beaufighter landing of Warby's in Malta and never saw one that was other than a series of small bounces down the runway. Perhaps even more strangely there are no such adverse comments about the way that he handled single-engined aircraft such as the Hurricane and the Spitfire in which he was later to enhance his reputation.

Some interesting sidelights about Warby and his Beaufighter have come from Tony Powner. He was a member of 55 Squadron, flying Blenheims which were stationed at Fuka, the normal refuelling stop for Warby when en route to photographing Crete. Tony tells that Warby's dark-blue Beau was known as 'Phoo'. Warby used to spend the night there prior to taking off for Crete and was in the habit of laying his sleeping bag in the tent shared by Tony and his navigator, Jack Sands. One night, after a heavy night's boozing in the Mess, Jack and he retired early leaving Warby to have a couple more. The wind was rising so, before going to bed they laced up the tent. When their alarm clock went off (they were on an early sortie) Warby's bed was empty and they assumed that he had slept in Mess until, with a scream of horror, Jack spotted Warby's head lying in one corner of the tent. Thoughts of Arab savagery flashed through Tony's mind ... but then it moved. His half frozen body lay outside the tent and his description of his 'friends' who had tied up the tent to keep him out was quite something to be heard but not, as Tony writes, 'to be heard by ladies or nicely brought up men!'

It is from Tony that the author learnt that, profiting from his Maryland experiences, Warby decided to take a crate of bombs with him and to have his camera operator toss them out of the side. As he was carrying out a mosaic of an ammunition dump in Greece, they tossed them out one at a time every few seconds. The result was a spectacular firework display as the dump went up. As punishment for this unauthorised act, Warby was sent again to photograph the results. He did the whole mosaic again.

Prior to Walker and Warburton taking Beaufighters T3301 and T4705 to Malta for the Sicilian landings photographs, Air Marshal Tedder who had great admiration for AVM Hugh Pughe Lloyd but nevertheless knew him for the buccaneer which he was at heart, had personally briefed Johnny Walker about not allowing Warby and his 'pal' Hugh Pughe to use the Beaufighters for other purposes. He suspected that Warby and his AOC would resume the pattern of their former operations and have the Beaus used for keeping an eye on the position of each and every Italian merchant ship or naval vessel. 'Don't be sidetracked. I want those beaches photographed.'

The interest that the HQ Middle East took in this small flight was marked. The other great RAF leader in the desert, the New Zealander Air Marshal 'Maori' (or 'Mary') Coningham also went out of his way personally to talk with Warby and it was typical of Warby's concern for all underlings who worked for him to include LAC Shirley in the technical discussion with 'Mary' Coningham about photographs and targets. This was not unusual. The two had become friends and wherever there were personal advantages for officers, Warby used to manage to have Shirley included in his Mess by instructing him to wear his flying jacket since it concealed his lowly rank markings. Few in any case would have believed that an LAC would be a crew member of the double DFC pilot and the ruse was successful. Since the Beaus could easily carry three persons, T Flight 2 PRU left Heliopolis bound for Malta on 29 December 1941 with Warby taking both Norman Shirley and his great friend LAC Ron Hadden in T4705. Johnny Walker took Flying Officer Benjie White and the third camera operator Corporal Liebert.

En route to Malta both planes stopped at Timimi, west of Tobruk, to refuel. Here they learnt that the weather ahead was poor with low cloud and almost nil visibility at Malta. Walker, who had never before been to Malta, decided to await better conditions. The Beaus had been stripped of radio and bad weather landing aids, as exist today, were not yet invented. Warby who 'knew the island and the area around it like the palm of his hand', ignored the Met reports, pressed on and successfully landed there.

Johnny Walker didn't in fact arrive until nine days later. Continual bad weather reports twice made him turn back. Then the fuel situation at Timimi became critical, compelling him to fly back and uplift at El Adem, several miles the other side of Tobruk. Malta's respite from bombing by the Luftwaffe based in Sicily had ceased. With his war machine bogged down outside Moscow and ground to a halt by the severe Russian winter weather: and with Rommel in retreat during December, Hitler vas quick to transfer another air army, this time 2 Luftflotte, to the many airfields in Sicily. With the remnants of the Tenth Air Army still there, Malta short of aircraft, ammunition, petrol and food was having a terrible time. There was scarcely a serviceable aircraft on the island and bombing and strafing of the airfields such as Luqa had become commonplace. Johnny Walker was blissfully unaware of all this. Accordingly, when he eventually did arrive on 7 January, having not seen the place before, he flew a leisurely circuit of the island to familiarize himself with landmarks.

Finally he touched down. Almost before the Beau had come to a standstill, Warby was up on the wing shouting to 'Get that bloody thing dispersed as fast as you can!' Few flight commanders could have been greeted on arrival to take command, in such terms.

Johnny Walker might have thought that he would be in charge of Warby in Malta but this was Malta and Malta was Warby's island and Warby still had Hugh Pughe Lloyd, the Air Officer Commanding, behind him. Another epic chapter in the story of Warby, Malta Ace, was already unfolding. Moreover Warby had not been idle during those nine days on his own.

MALTA AGAIN

Although Warburton was only in Malta for just over six weeks during this his second spell there, and although he almost never flew an armed plane and shot down no more of the enemy, yet it is the period when many remember him best. Apart from one sortie in a Maryland of 69 Squadron, the only plane he flew during this spell was the converted Beaufighter, T4705. This was the same plane in which he had flown to the island on 29 December 1941 with Corporal Norman Shirley and LAC Ron Hadden aboard.

By the time that Johnny Walker arrived in Malta on 9 January to 'take charge' of the small detachment, the words of advice given him by Air Marshal Tedder 'not to be sidetracked' had been overtaken by events.

AVM Hugh Pughe Lloyd fully appreciated the worth of aerial photography, and he had been briefed before he was sent to Malta to stop Rommel from being supplied. The redoubtable Afrika Korps were placed much too close for comfort to the armament factories of Italy and Germany. Compared with the long and hazardous routes between the UK and Middle East HQ in Cairo, it was child's-play to get supplies from the factories of Germany and Italy to Africa by way of Italian and Sicilian ports and thence to the Axis main African base at Tripoli. Only one thing stood in their way. Malta.

Never for one moment did Hugh Pughe cease to regard himself as on the offensive. Even at times when the island stood in the gravest danger and had scarcely a single plane or ship with which to hit back, he never ceased to plan how to destroy the enemy ships carrying their vital supplies to the Afrika Korps. With his very slender resources, it was, in his mind, absolutely essential to know exactly where those ships were, when they would be loading, to where and by what route they would be sailing. Only continuous air reconnaissance and photography could provide the answers. There was good Intelligence, too. But it needed up-to-date visual evidence. Such as only frequent PR flights could provide.

Hugh Pughe had obviously been missing Warby. 69 Squadron with the few Marylands or anything else suitable that they could 'steal' and keep serviceable, was doing all it could to keep him informed about the enemy's movements. Like the rest of the island, the squadron was having a terrible time. The arrival of Luftflotte 2 in Sicily and the failure to provide Malta with aircraft that could cope with the Me109 (or even the later Marks of the Ju88) was devastating. The Germans had won air superiority over the island. Malta was bombed throughout the war as no British place elsewhere, including London, was bombed and the bombing reached its peak during the period when Warburton arrived at the close of 1941. During the next three months, it,was raided by the Luftwaffe no less than 774 times: an average of over eight times each day. Virtually everything at Luqa was destroyed – planes, hangars, buildings. Warby's arrival with a plane which, in the pilot's opinion, could outrun anything that the Luftwaffe possessed was like manna from heaven to the AOC. It is not known if Hugh Pughe had been advised by Tedder as to their purpose in being sent to Malta. What is known is that starting from the day after Warburton's arrival, Hugh Pughe at once had Beaufighter T4705 and his favourite pilot, sent on immediate reconnaissance flights to the familiar haunts of Tripoli, Taranto, Messina, Palermo and those airfields in Sicily from which the expected airborne invasion was most likely to come: Catania, Gela, Gerbina, Trepani, Massala, Comiso, and Castel Vetrano.

By the time that Johnny Walker appeared, Warburton had carried out more than a dozen such flights! Provided the aircraft was serviceable, Warby thought nothing of covering the North African bases in the morning and then doing likewise to Taranto or Sicilian airfields in the afternoon. Almost miraculously, the dark blue Beau, often parked insolently on the airfield so as to be ready for another sortie the same day, escaped destruction from the enemy literally lurking overhead. The Sicilian beaches went unphotographed. However by early 1942 events were changing dramatically in the desert and the invasion of Sicily was no longer a considered possibility.

Johnny Walker was in an impossible position. Hugh Pughe, the AOC and Warby were in league and had established a pattern of operations which he was powerless to stop. Some idea of the strange set-up can be deduced from the official squadron records. *Both* 2 PRU in Helipolis and 69 Squadron at Luqa had reason to think that Warby was part of their set-up. Using his previous experience with 69 Squadron, Warby was having his Beau serviced with all the priority it deserved by the devoted airmen whom he had known when with 69 Squadron. He was always on good terms with Wing Commander Tennant, its new CO after Dowland was shot down and killed in January 1942, and Tennant duly signed Warby's record of each month's flying hours: as in the past. Curiously, Tennant signed January's total as 'CO 69 Sqdn' and February's total as: 'CO 2 PRU'! The author has discovered at least 25 operational flights which appear in the official records of *both* 69 Squadron and 2 PRU!

In truth, Warby, although officially in Malta as part of a detachment of 2 PRU, operated solely for the AOC when either Hugh Pughe, or Warby himself, worked out that, for the good of the island, he should do so.

The weather in Malta during winter is generally vile. Much rain, low cloud, poor visibility. In one way, this was to the island's advantage. It was probably the only reason why the Luftwaffe was not continually overhead. By then no less than 379 Hurricanes had been flown from aircraft carriers which had proceeded from Gibraltar towards Malta and 351 had arrived. But virtually all had been destroyed on the ground or in the air. More had also flown in during those periods when the Eighth Army had advanced close enough to the island from the east but had suffered the same fate. The crippling losses may have been one reason for the flow to have ceased. After the delivery from the carriers *Argus* and *Ark Royal* on 21 November 1941, when 34 out of 37 had arrived, no more were being despatched. The situation is well remembered by the author. When on one special occasion, Hugh Pughe arranged for him to take one of his rarely serviceable special Wellingtons on a sortie which, most unusually, required a daylight departure, he was promised, 'Just this once, Spooner, you will be provided with an escort of every serviceable Hurricane on the island.' One lone Hurricane was available!

The bad weather didn't make life easier for Warburton in the air. He still had to face the enemy fighters, mainly Me109's now, and the heavy AA barrages over defended bastions such as Taranto and Tripoli. He now also had to battle against ice, ever an airman's enemy in those days, snow, fog, wind and rain. He was also attacked by Hurricanes once more. Often it was only possible to get photographs by flying at wave top height and by using hand-held oblique shots with Leicas. Only one with his intimate knowledge of the enemy's landmarks and bases could have found his way to the targets under such appalling conditions. His personal navigation was superb. There is no record of his ever failing to locate whatever he had been sent to photograph.

Field Marshal Kesselring who in October 1942 took command of all the German forces in the Mediterranean, never ceased to urge his master to put Operation Herkules, the airborne invasion of Malta, into effect. He has gone on record as describing Italy's failure to capture the island immediately upon joining the war in June 1940, as the biggest tactical blunder of the whole war. Then it virtually had no air defences and the Regia Aeronautica had almost 2,000 planes within easy reach. Hitler's failure to carry out what Mussolini had initially failed to do was regarded by Kesselring as a blunder of almost equal stupidity.

The British view was that for as long as the Eighth Army could advance as far as Libya, then Malta could, just, be held. A more sober post-war view is the reverse. This is, for as long as Malta held out, then and then only, could the Allies hope to win the war in the Western Desert. The fact that Malta did hold out even during those many months when Rommel, rather than the Eighth Army, was 'on top' in the desert, was a tribute to all who were there.

Various attempts were being made to get further supplies to the beleaguered island which was, by January 1942, already desperately short of every necessity. Attempts to get supply ships to Malta from Alexandria were made. In January a lone merchantman the *Thermopylae*, made a solo attempt. It was sunk, as was the *Glengyle* which had tried to do likewise before it. Food, petrol and ammunition were especially short. In February an attempt was made to relieve the siege by a convoy escorted by one anti aircraft cruiser, seven destroyers and Admiral Vian's Force B of three cruisers and eight destroyers. But two of the merchant ships were sunk, the third was hit and limped back to Alexandria.

In March yet another attempt was made. Four cruisers and seventeen destroyers attempted to get three merchantmen, and the auxiliary *Breconshire* through the dive-bomb and torpedo-bomber alley that lay between Crete and North Africa. The *Breconshire* was crippled and on fire, but managed to stagger into Marsaxlokk Bay, Malta, being towed the last few miles, before rolling over. Blessed as she was, her oil was largely still on board and much was pumped out of her as she lay in her last resting place. She had made several brave solo trips to Malta.† The two merchantmen, the *Pampas* and *Talabot* (the third had been sunk) arrived relatively undamaged but only a very few supplies were unloaded during a murderous series of attacks by the Ju87's and Ju88's. Much of what was taken ashore was actually unloaded by airmen who, seeing that little else was going on, took it into their own hands to get their own aviation spares off those ships. The bombing was as fierce or fiercer than any that Malta and its harbour had received. The box barrage which the defenders threw up proved effective, but ammunition was one of the supplies of which the island was most short.

After Johnny Walker's arrival, Benjie White appears to have flown T3301 most of the time. Johnny Walker, no doubt also flew sorties, but Warby monopolised T4705. For a short while both Beaus lived charmed lives. However on 26 January, Warby still recording casualties in his log book, records 'F/O White shot up and wounded.' This was apt to be the usual fate of any pilot who dared to fly in daylight. Johnny Walker also recalls White being hit in the eye by a splinter. Benjie White appears to have got away with this encounter with, most probably a Me109, quite lightly. Only twelve days later, having just been promoted a flight lieutenant (as was Warby himself in late January) White was again shot up by a marauding Me109 while landing after a PR sortie. Both he and Norman Shirley, his camera crewman, were badly hit. Shirley displayed commendable bravery and cool thinking. He quenched two aircraft fires and dragged out his wounded pilot. He also thought to retrieve the magazine with the camera shots before collapsing from his own

---

†In the opinion of the author, this ship and her gallant master, Captain Hutchinson, saved Malta.

considerable wounds. He had been hit in the body dangerously near to where men with family aspirations would not wish to be hit. The Beau was a write-off and neither White nor Shirley flew again from Malta. As Johnny Walker was almost at once posted away, the result was that Warby and Beau T4705, with Corporal Liebert and LAC Hadden, was all that was left of 2 PRU in Malta.

Norman Shirley, a corporal photographer, was uniquely awarded an immediate Distinguished Flying Medal: uniquely because he had never been trained as aircrew and consequently wore no wings or half-wing badge.

A comparison between the log books of Shirley and Warby is interesting. Together before Shirley's injuries (Shirley had also been with Benjie White on his 26 January shoot-up and injury), he and Warby had flown 14 PR flights from Malta. Shirley records that on three of these occasions the aircraft was hit by fighters or AA fire. Warby only mentions one such instance. On 17 January Warby has added to his usual brief details of which targets had been photographed the words 'two dents'!

Generally Warby's log book entries are as brief and modest as could be. He does not mention, for example, that on 1 February, when flying with Shirley that the plane was on fire. This, according to Shirley, was an internal fire caused by a heating muff overheating.

Ron Hadden was the photo mechanic who most often flew with Warby. As Corporal Cyril Wood writes regarding one of these flights together:

> I remember Ron Hadden telling me: 'as we approached the harbour, the flak was intense (probably this was Taranto). Warby jinked the plane around until he was in position for his camera run. Then a terrific burst from a near-miss rocked the Beaufighter furiously. I thought we had had it. The armour plate door between Warby and me flew open. Then I saw him. He had his hat on top of his helmet: cigarette hanging from his lips; one elbow resting on the side of the cockpit, driving the plane with the other hand. His complete lack of fear and nonchalant attitude to the noise and from the flak was fantastic. Warby at his best. Fighters were chasing us, the port engine had failed but he pressed home his recce and safely returned.'

It is understandable that some of the airmen have likened him to the fictional character Biggles. Cyril Wood adds:

> In spite of his daredevil escapades, he was a completely disciplined pilot who carried out his missions regardless of the odds against him. Warby was a pilot who always completed his missions. He frequently flew at 50 feet to ensure that photographs could be taken.

Cyril Wood also makes references to the weather that Warby had to face that terrible winter of 1941–42 when 'it was most difficult to keep up spirits. There seemed to be no light at the end of the tunnel. How we yearned for Spitfires which, we figured, alone would save us from total destruction.'

The only Spitfires that the island had seen was one flown in by a young New Zealand pilot, Harry Coldbeck, who arrived about March 1942. It was en route to the Middle East and had, so the pilot imagined when he landed, only landed in Malta to refuel. Hugh Pughe changed all that. Warby was about to be posted back to 2 PRU at Heliopolis again so he promptly commandeered Coldbeck's Spit BS300 for PR work. By then the photographic team in Malta had become adept at installing cameras into aircraft. The island HQ had a couple of first-class photo interpreters Colvin and Herschel and excellent photo mechanics such as Ken Fielder, 'Scoop' Kirk, Jim McNeil, Warrant Officer Buxton and others.

Harry Coldbeck thus found himself 'shanghaied' to Malta. With no warning or training he was immediately detailed to carry out almost daily PR flights in his Spitfire. Another pilot, Phil Kelley had made at least one attempt to use this Spit in the same manner.

Phil Kelley's introduction to conditions in Malta is typical. In his own words:

> I arrived in Malta on 11 January '42 flying a Mosquito which I was to deliver to No 2 PRU Egypt … we were shot up over Pantellaria and with one engine gone, we splattered ourselves all over Luqa. I walked away but my navigator went to hospital with a broken thigh. Hugh Pughe kept me on the island to fly PR sorties … in Spitfires.

It is no direct part of the Warburton story but when eventually Phil Kelley's Mosquito was repaired, it was then used by him for PR work from Malta but almost at once this was shot down over Luqa. Phil again walked away after crash landing on Safi strip. He then was posted off the island by a transit Wellington which was being allowed to resume its assigned journey to Middle East but on take-off, the loaded Wellington on that notorious short sloping runway, ended up in the quarry at the end of the runway, on fire. Again Phil stepped out. Finally Kelley got away in a Beaufort. These events show how hazardous was life for operational pilots in Malta and give emphasis to the good fortune which enables Warby in Beau T4705 to carry out 43 operational trips, all in daylight, during this short spell on the island. Even his own log books mention various occasions when he was followed back to Malta by up to twelve Me109's. In his much lightened Beau he could outrun them at the altitudes he chose to use but when attempting the final approach and landing he and the plane were in deadly peril. All Warby mentions in his log book when chased by a dozen

Me 109s is 'dodged them'. His Beaufighter recces were taken from as low as 50 feet to as high as 30,500 feet. He invariably 'got his target'.

Details of some of the Beau's modifications have come from airman Gerry Wilson, a pre-war regular who in typical Malta fashion had attached himself to 69 Squadron and then to Warby and his personal Beau. He tells of the 'large extra fuel tanks fitted on each side inside the fuselage behind the pilot and the need to take great care when filling these to capacity, as they had a tendency to overflow by syphoning into each other and causing dangerous overspill.' It would appear from this that Warby was sitting almost surrounded by fuel. Yet we know, from Ron Hadden and others that he was prone to smoke almost continuously when aloft. However he was not alone in this. Smoking was not then known to be a serious health risk and most pilots, including the author, smoked almost non-stop when aloft as a kind of relief at getting safely airborne: whether permitted in that type of aircraft or otherwise. Habit made it seem safe.

Wilson describes Warburton as, 'a very friendly officer, fair complexion and a cheery word to groundcrew at all times.' He also recalls the hectic moments on the ground when, on landing, Warby had directed them 'to get it ready to fly again within minutes.' Wilson, referring to the other losses of 69 Squadron crews†, writes: 'It was sad for the ground crew to see these brave aircrew going out and many never coming back.' It is an indication of the excellent rapport that existed throughout the war between those who flew the planes and those who serviced them. In many respects the real heroes in Malta were those ground crew who in spite of bombing and strafing never failed to materialise when maintenance was required. Unlike aircrew who came and went from Malta and who on average probably spent less than six months in that blasted place before being grounded, killed, rested and posted away, the airmen who were there in 1940 or 1941 remained throughout the entire three year long non-stop blitz and siege. The few places which were available for leaving the island in planes or submarines, were assigned to aircrew or VIPs. The 'poor bloody erks', as they described themselves had to remain and put up with it all; including the ever decreasing scale of food rationing. Nor did they receive public acclaim as did the successful pilots.

Wilson makes a shrewd comment upon the work of the unarmed PR pilots: 'PRU pilots only had their skill, speed and the best maintenance we could give them for their ultimate survival. God bless them all.'††

†During this brief spell in Malta, Warby has listed as shot down in his log book Squadron Leader Lowry (the author witnessed this) Pilot Officer Kelley, Flight Lieutenant Williams' death on the runway, Sergeant Parker. Wing Commander Dowland was also killed on 13 June with Tennant again taking command of 69 Squadron.
††After the war, Wilson went back to Malta, found the girl he had known there and married her. They live there happily still.

Of the relatively few who knew Warby in Malta during these ten weeks when he operated Beaufighter T4705 nearly all have contributed pen portraits as well as factual information. The reason for this may lie in the fact that this was one of Malta's most depressing times and that Warburton, his feats and the conversation surrounding those feats, were almost the only things we had to cheer about. As a morale booster, his very presence was vital. The Navy, after the unfortunate demise of the superbly effective Force K (see the author's In Full Flight†) had withdrawn all serviceable surface ships. Under the continual bombing of the bases even the small force of efficient U-Class submarines of the 10th Flotilla, kept in Sliema and Larazetto Creeks, were also withdrawn during the year 1942. The RAF strike forces had been reduced to keeping a few Wellington bombers, on temporary detachment from Egypt, at Luqa for purely night operations: but these were operations that the inhabitants seldom saw. They would depart in the dead of the night using an absolute minimum of flarepath illumination and return equally unobtrusively. The Blenheim squadrons, or what little was left of them, were slaughtered almost to a man whenever attempting daylight operations. The Hurricanes were being decimated. No wonder, as Airman Snook had so ably put it: ' Warburton's exploits were a shot in the arm for every man on the island. He became a legendary figure among lesser mortals.'

Another indication of what Warby meant to those at Luqa comes from 'Duke' Kent. He was a sergeant air gunner who arrived with a Wellington unit. He didn't know Warby personally, but had heard about him from a person he describes as Warby's WOP/AG – almost certainly Paddy Moren. Duke describes Warby as being 'some sort of folk hero, beloved of all, modest, reckless and somewhat lacking in accepted discipline.' He writes that later in the war he (Kent) took a pilot's course 'much inspired by Warby's activities as he was my ideal'. He goes on to describe Warby as: 'A young flying officer with long blond hair yet commanding absolute respect and complete dedication from his crew.' He also comments that: 'Somehow Warby's exploits in the Med appear to have gone unnoticed: no books; no films; no nothing. I compare his adventures with those of Bader and Screwball Beurling. He was a modern 'Biggles' as it were ...'

Duke Kent is not entirely correct about there having been no films of Warby's exploits. The film The Malta Story was unquestionably based upon his exploits although with a quite different storyline and ending. Much of the script was provided by Christina, and Alec Guinness starred, but of course, there was no direct mention of Warby by name.

Constance Babington-Smith in her book Evidence in Camera – about photo-reconnaissance and the accomplishments of the PR units throughout

†Macdonald, 1964.

the war, remarks about Warburton:

> His achievements in his own line were quite as remarkable as those of two of RAFs most illustrious pilots. Douglas Bader and Guy Gibson who were both near contemporaries at his school St Edward's Oxford. But the name of Adrian Warburton had hardly been heard outside the circle of those who knew him, and there is no single mention of him in the official RAF history of the Second World War.

Warby was a man that attracted either hero worship or occasionally dislike. David Beaty tells the tale that when, post-war, he attended the funeral of Hugh Pughe Lloyd (both David and the author used to visit their old AOC at his super pig-farm which H P built up after having retired as an Air Chief Marshal), he there encountered two 69 Squadron pilots, whom he hadn't met before. Later when discussing Warby he learnt that one in particular definitely disliked Warby and went as far as declaring that, among his fellow officers, he was unpopular. The other was more tolerant. The former remark aligns with Paddy Devine's description. In truth it wasn't easy to like Warby, in 1941, unless you were an airman or a very senior officer. Everyone admired him, but …

Against this, Flying Officer Johnny Bloxam, who was with 69 Squadron at the time when that squadron was fighting for survival in its early days, describes him as 'one of the very best.'

David Beaty, a keen observer as befits a successful author, remarks that Warby hogged the flying – always unpopular with the other pilots and also that he drew living-out allowances for his flat. This would evoke a measure of jealousy in an almost womanless, comfortless Malta and at a station where the Mess was only a flapping tent and even officers' accommodation spartan. Beaty goes on to write:

> He was unreal. Suddenly he was there as though summoned by Drake's drum and suddenly he wasn't. A strange kind of ghost that will live in many people's memory as long as they live – definitely in mine.

Very perceptive comments about Warby at this time come from his airborne camera operator Corporal Norman Shirley. Despite the differences in their ranks and professions, an affinity grew up almost instantaneously between the two of them after that first hazardous operational trip together: the trip when the engines of the Beaufighter started to fail in the vicinity of Crete and when together they almost had 'to talk the plane back to Fuka'. Instinctively Norman understood him as a person whose childhood had left him emotionally disturbed. Norman, of course, knew nothing about his disjointed upbringing. In a post-war period, Norman became a most understanding warden of a home for deprived and disturbed children. His description of Warby and Malta can hardly be bettered. Norman who later also became a science teacher draws an analogy between Warby and a perfectly manufactured metal exactly correct for its purpose, in strength, balance, weight and flexibility. 'I think the specification of Warby was exactly right for the RAF and Malta and for the morale of everyone there, just as a alloy can be exactly right for a specific purpose, so also are men in tune, or otherwise, with a specific environment.'

Norman also recognised as did others that Warby needed to be warmed by the praise of others. By his actions Warby was always saying 'Look at me.' It was at that time as if he had something to prove to himself.

Shirley felt in tune with the man he flew with and they were able to talk not as officer and corporal, nor as pilot and crewman but simply as man to man. He describes Warby as a person who had gathered the fragments of himself together and assembled them to achieve a great goal of attainment. Both he and Ron Hadden, the other splendid camera operator who flew so often with Warby, were offered commissions. Both declined as they wished to stay with Warby. To others in Malta, the two airmen were one-off odd bods who didn't fit into any known category. Having no aircrew rank or status, they were denied every small crumb of comfort that might otherwise be going begging. They, like the many unfortunate airmen whose barracks had been destroyed, were billeted in the poor house among the lepers. Here too, they were 'different' and thus left much alone.

Norman Shirley was a skilled photographer and put up many technical suggestions that Warby accepted. It was Norman who took the hand-held close-up shots when flying too low for any other picture. It was Norman who always saw to it that, commensurate with the height and speeds involved, the cameras were always correctly set up. Norman's suggestions about adding a rear mirror camera and a forward one operated by the pilot, were later incorporated in all photographic Beaus. With such advice available and gratefully accepted by an in tune Skipper, the Beaus never failed to bring back the desired pictures. As Norman put it: 'No life was risked for blank or inadequate film.' It is little wonder that, even before Norman pulled Benjie White from a blazing Beaufighter, both Ron Hadden and Norman Shirley had been recommended, by their comprehending AOC, for the award of the Distinguished Flying Medal. The fact that they were not official aircrew didn't worry Hugh Pughe. He was, as ever, only concerned to get the job done: and done well. Those who did it got their just rewards. Shirley 'jumped the gun' and was awarded his DFM before Hadden by his action of saving his pilot but soon both airmen were in receipt of their unique medals. This was yet another Warby talking point among the hundreds of idle aircrew who were stuck in Malta with little else to talk about after the loss of their aircraft by the Luftwaffe's strafing or bombing.

Like all who flew with Warby, Norman Shirley had his adventures in the air. Fighters or flak frequently hit their aircraft. On one Taranto recce, Norman thought that he saw a cover on the sides of what appeared to be a hospital ship. 'I wished almost at once I had kept my mouth shut.' Warby's reaction was to fly up and down the harbour at zero feet examining the sides of each ship to see if Norman had been right. In the end he discovered a battleship with its usual diagonal markings covered up. Norman adds, 'There were reports that several Italian sailors lost their lives from their own side's guns as they blazed away at Warby's low flying Beau.'

On another occasion also in terrible weather the two of them flew up and down the runways of one of the main fighter bases in Sicily, Catania, taking shots with the hand held Leica or other such camera. One sequence of shots was marred by a hangar getting in the line of sight. They were that low! The Beaufighter was fired upon several times. On one such occasion when they returned safely to Luqa with bullet holes in the aircraft, Shirley started to congratulate Warby upon the exploit but Warby cut him short and with a broad grin told him, 'Better get your hair combed.' This puzzled Shirley until, upon examination he discovered by putting a hand to his helmet, that one bullet had sliced through its top. Warby then added, 'You were pretty good yourself: very good indeed.'

Another side of Warby emerges from Norman Shirley's story of how he was physically presented with his own DFM. He was still in hospital recovering from his groin and other wounds which he had received when he and Benjie White had been shot up on landing. Norman was only just out of the operating theatre recovering from a second operation for the removal of a sliver from a cannon shell which, when he had been shot up first time, had penetrated his left eye. A group of officers appeared and pinned the medal to his pyjamas. Warby remained in the background so emotionally moved that he seemed like a teenager at a party unable to find the right words.

After being discharged from hospital Norman was sent to the St Paul's Bay rest camp in a relatively unbombed part of the island. The next morning at dawn, he was almost yanked out of bed by Warby and Ron Hadden. Warby had orders to leave the island in his faithful Beau; to take it back to Heliopolis and Ron Hadden and he had come to collect Norman. They had prepared a comfortable seat at the back of the aircraft for him and had even found him a parachute. As Norman wrote: 'I could not have had two more solicitous and compassionate friends than Ron and Warby.'

So ended a brief but memorable phase in Warby's Malta career. From his log book, it is seen that he had flown nineteen sorties with Ron Hadden and another nine with Corporal Liebert as well as those with Shirley.

RETURN TO EGYPT

Just prior to leaving Malta, Flight Lieutenant Adrian Warburton was awarded the Distinguished Service Order (DSO). Within the space of a little over twelve months, the misfit who had been shipped out of 22 Squadron for reasons that concerned 'Women and the Law' to quote Braithwaite, had been decorated three times. Warby himself seems to have started the story that he intended to get a 'gong' every six months, though it was not like him to be boastful and there may have been a smile on his face when he made the remark. He may also have been delighted, rather than annoyed, at having his flippant remark taken in full seriousness. At times, he almost seems to have relished being misunderstood by his fellow officers. It is significant that the remark has been passed to the author only by officers, such as Gerry Glaister and Johnny Walker, rather than from any airman. Warby treated the two strands quite differently: to his brother officers in the Mess, he was casual and off hand, especially to those who belonged to different units. To the airmen with whom he flew – and he did not fly with any other than non-commissioned men – and to the men who serviced his planes, he was friendly and outgoing: quite oblivious of the differences of rank.

Some in the officers' Mess considered that the honour of the DSO which Warby now received did not fit Warby's unconventional behaviour. To them, however gallant he might be, the DSO seemed inappropriate. Holders of the DSO didn't normally squat on hangar floors and play cards with the airmen. Yet even those who had little time for Warby's off-duty antics, and who disliked him personally admitted that he was the bravest pilot they had known or ever likely to know. More than one have called him 'the pilot who knew no fear'.

Warby's second 'rest' period in Egypt began as the first had done. He was immediately granted well-earned leave and looked around for a way of getting himself to Haifa where his father was still stationed. By 1941 father and son were clearly on most excellent terms. Both, by then, were the holders of the DSO and both seem to have been very proud of the other: as well as being 'good pals'.

For his earlier journey to Haifa, Warby had hitch-hiked most of the way. This time he had a better idea. He borrowed the ancient Hawker Hind biplane which nominally belonged to 267 (Communication) Squadron but which 2 PRU seem to have purloined as partially for their use. During his attempt to reach Haifa in this plane, the engine failed while over the Gaza strip, and Warby crash-landed in the Desert. The plane was a write-off but Warby escaped unharmed. He was even fit enough to have walked out of the wreckage and to have reached some friendly base on foot. Thereafter in some photographs he is seen to be wearing on his left breast pocket the 'Flying Boot' emblem which was awarded, unofficially, to those who had pranged in the Desert and walked their way back to base; often from behind enemy lines.

While he was in Haifa on a staff course, Johnny Walker encountered Warby's father and describes Geoffrey Warburton as a 'Short stocky man and a great character'. His son-in-law describes him as 'rectangular' about 5feet 7inches with very square shoulders.

Warburtons in war always distinguished themselves. A ship in Haifa harbour had caught fire and was given up as almost lost. The commander, whose shore job most certainly didn't include fire-fighting on board burning ships, led a party and, for almost two days, fought the blaze. For this uncalled-for gallantry; he was awarded the OBE. Nobody was more proud than Warby. Letters were censored and he could not refer directly to an Allied ship being lost, even if not as a result of direct enemy action. In his letter home to his mother (see Appendix III) he could only refer to the incident obliquely: 'Father put (up) a most amazingly good show here, so you may be congratulating him soon.'

It is significant that in his letter home to his mother, Adrian did all that was possible to quell her anxieties. He made no reference to his Hind accident. He assures her that, 'I'm getting a rest for the moment.' As in his previous letter from Haifa, he tells her how much he would have liked to have been posted home and, again, mentions that he 'had one foot on the boat' towards that journey and that he would continue to try to get back to the UK.

Unexpected feminine touches are again evident in the letter. The references to the 'baby iris and lupins' he had seen by the roadside are much out of character with the Mad Warby image that so many in the RAF saw and admired. Was this a side of him that, perhaps, only Christina saw? The bulk of the letter is about how well his father was doing and how popular 'Pops' was in Haifa. These remarks, and the descriptions of the carefree time that the two of them were having together, must have been doubly reassuring to Muriel Warburton in a tightly-rationed England.

Much as Warby appears by his letters home to have wanted to get back to the UK, it seems doubtful that his unorthodox methods would have been fully appreciated there. Hugh Macphail, at 2 PRU and Flight Lieutenant Whelan who was soon to replace him seem to have been able to get away with a degree of Sydney Cotton's informality in their 2 PRU work, but by 1942, 1 PRU in the UK had already become highly organized upon more regular lines, and its PR Units were soon to be given squadron status. From its HQ at Benson, an airfield near Oxford, it had grown at an enormous pace and was well equipped with specially prepared Spitfires capable of great speed and of operating at heights that few if any German planes could attain. Other Spitfires were specially modified for unprecedented low level speeds.

After what appears to have been a most enjoyable, if hectic, two weeks with his father in Haifa, Warby returned to Heliopolis much refreshed mentally but almost needing another rest to get over the parties that his fond and proud father had arranged for his much decorated son! His father seems to have been particularly thrilled to have gone flying with Adrian. Warby's personal log book makes no mention of any such flight. This, regrettably, is the pattern of his entries. Many of Warby's most spectacular flights were unofficial and he was punctilious about only including in his log book officially approved flights. A pilot's personal log book is an official RAF document and has to be verified and countersigned by a squadron commander each month.

Warburton's log book shows that he continues to exhibit his unusual concern for the unfortunate pilots who didn't 'make it'. During this period there are entries such as: (June 1942) 'P/O Patrick failed to return', 'Sgt Corbett failed to return', 'Sgt Baum failed to return' etc. Generally the photo planes of 2 PRU could fly higher or faster than those of the enemy but some were occasionally caught. Then they were in serious trouble since they had been stripped of both guns and most armour. PR pilots flew alone and were far from any friendly fighter cover. In experienced hands, the pilots could generally extricate themselves from trouble. It is noticeable that those who failed to return were either young NCOs or junior officers, on their early PR sorties.

After returning to Heliopolis, Warby continued for the rest of April to carry out routine, rather than operational, flying duties: test flights; camera testing, delivery flights in the former royal Jugoslavian Lockheed Electra which 2 PRU had somehow obtained; flights to Beirut (at least one resulted in a party with both Paul Lamboit, a splendid photographer officer, and his father also taking part), to Lydda (Lod), to Nicosia in Cyprus etc. One flight of significance was a short local flight in a Spitfire. His first in this famous type. 2 PRU was at last being equipped with these planes although the original PRU at Benson had been using them for some time. (The author briefly flew them at Benson for 1 PRU as far back as December 1940.) The Spitfire was a delight to fly and it was the start of a love affair between Warby and that renowned design.

The modified Beaufighters were still the backbone of 2 PRU's operations and were the type which Warby most usually flew. They had been further modified, as Norman Shirley and Ron Hadden had both recommended in Malta, to carry forward and sideways looking cameras as well as the 24 and 36 inch vertical ones. On one detail which Warby briefly describes in his log book as 'LPF', i.e. low flying practice, Warby spotted a British staff car along a desert road. Possibly to get practice at close-up shots, with the forward looking camera he 'beat up' the car at high speed and near zero feet. However the driver spotted him coming and swerved the car off the road into a convenient ditch! Later during the same 'LPF', Warby and his crewman spotted a lone camel being ridden across a stretch of desert. Again he zoomed down at high speed. This time neither the camel nor its driver showed the slightest reaction: nor when Warby repeated the manoeuvre at even lower altitude only just missing overhead by inches.

It is significant that although Warby flew a number of 2 PRU Beaufighters, his former 'personal' one, T4705, does not again appear in the unit's records. This could be confirmation that this famous plane might have been damaged in Malta and had only been patched up sufficiently for Warby's return flight back to Heliopolis.

The original unofficial modification, carried out largely on the instructions of the unit's camera experts, Paul Lamboit and his chief, Squadron Leader R I Jones, seems to have been accepted and made official judged by the number of different PR Beaus available to 2 PRU by April 1942.

Commander Warburton seems to have taken leave, or found official duties, in the Cairo area. Even in Warby's log book, there are mentions of three flights which he made from 2 PRU airfields in April, with his father on board.

Warby was ceasing, with increasing confidence and fame, to be the loner as all at St Edward's had dubbed him. Stan Pearce, another pilot of 2 PRU, has informed the author: 'All the girls were smitten by Warby's good looks.' There are other pointers that he was acquiring a taste for variety in feminine company and parties. He was beginning to acquire a reputation of a womaniser. However, this might simply be what others would have expected of such a good looking, famous and charismatic character. There is evidence later that such affairs as he did have, were not of a serious nature.

It appears that 2 PRU was a most congenial unit: one that combined efficiency with pleasure. With Hugh Macphail in charge it could hardly have been otherwise. Paul Lamboit describes him as, 'A kindly warmhearted person and a grand chap whom I greatly admired.' 'Hugh Macphail,' another pilot, writes: 'was an amusing chap, well liked.' In June 1942, Hugh Macphail was returned to the UK and Whelan took his place. Probably the unit then became more orthodox. With Rommel drawing nearer to Cairo almost every day, the war was ceasing to be part fun. The war in the Western Desert, which seemed almost won by the Allies in December 1941, had by the summer of 1942, gone into the reverse. By June 1942 the Allies were staring defeat in the face.

Kesselring and his Fliegerkorps 2 had started it all by all but smothering Malta with bombs. As a result supplies in unprecedented quantities had reached Rommel.

One saving grace during the first months of 1942 was that the RAF, under 'Mary' (Maori) Coningham was winning the air battles over that long Desert coastal road. Another factor in the Allies' favour was that each advance lengthened Rommel's supply line, while shortening the Allies'.

Tedder and Coningham's superiority in the air prevented the long Allied Eighth Army retreat from becoming a rout. Also Rommel had been stopped short of Alexandria and Cairo. All that was needed was a general who would think alike with Tedder and Coningham. Such a man in early August was on the way. Auchinleck was about to be replaced by Monty. The see-saw war was about to take another turn. In truth much had always depended upon whether or not Malta could stop supplies to the Afrika Korps. Events in Malta were about to undergo a change too.

By May 1942, Warby regarded himself as being sufficiently rested. Also by then 2 PRU possessed a small number of Spitfire Vs modified for PRU work. From May onwards Warburton, rested from both parties and operations but still in 2 PRU, Heliopolis, started to cover the entire Middle East as he had once covered Sicily, Tripolitania and Italy. Usually he was flying a Spitfire but occasionally a Beaufighter. In short time, the coast of Greece and Crete were familiar to him. His reconnaissance flights, always taking pictures of high quality, took him to Athens, Calata, Piraeus, Salamis, Menidi to Rhodes and the Greek islands of Kos, Leros and Samos. He covered Argos and other bases in Peloponnesos. Likewise Kastelli, Kisamou and Maleme in Crete. He got to know all the airfields in friendly Palestine, Lebanon and Syria. He ranged up and down the long desert coastal road as Rommel continued to advance steadily towards Cairo.

Stan Pearce recalls one flight which was typical of his determination. When airborne, Warby discovered that his high-flying oxygen was not turned on. He had been detailed that day to roam all over Greece photographing bases from high level. Instead of turning back he completed the detail at 19,000 feet instead. Like the Mounties, Warburton liked to get his objective. June followed in much the same manner. Warby was again the PR pilot supreme. However by June Rommel advanced so dangerously close to Cairo and Alexandria, that panic set in at Cairo. Strictly against orders, with Rommel by then less than 100 miles from Alexandria, WAAFs and wives of senior officers were hastily evacuated from the area. Accordingly Warby found himself flying Beaufighters with up to six women packed like sardines into the rear fuselage. With this strange load, he flew half a dozen such loads to Lydda (Lod) in Israel: eight flights being made on 1 and 2 July. There is a story which may or may not be associated with Warby that on one such flight with women literally packed in all around him, a lower hatch was unintentionally left unfastened. As the plane gathered speed and became airborne, a vast blast of air entered the plane and almost removed all the girls' clothes.

It was almost typical of the spirit of 2 PRU officials to record such light incidents. For instance the official record of this obviously happy unit records the story of:

> F/Lt Ferguson (Hurricane engine-failure) force-landed in Sinai Desert. He had a venturesome and comfortless journey from the scene of the forced-landing to the nearest railhead on a camel. It is understood that F/Lt Ferguson is now not an enthusiastic supporter of the camel as a mode of transport.

Not all official squadron records are written in this vein. In June the unit's record mentions: 'P/O Kelley [the same pilot who had three aircraft written off under him during his short spell of being co-opted in Malta], in Spitfire BP 909, on his return presented the officers' Mess with 2 kittens on account of his engine cutting out twice.'

An unusual task for Warby during July was to accompany one of the first Liberator bombing raids and photograph the results as the bombs fell. The planes were being flown by US pilots and included a bomb-sight which was claimed to be possessed of almost incredible accuracy 'to drop a bomb into a barrel from 30,000 feet!' By more than one account the vaunted raid (Tobruk, now once more in enemy hands, was the target) was far from being an 'eye-opener' with regards to accurate bombing. The pilots were new to the task and this may be why, for once, Warby elaborates in his personal log book. Against the sortie, carried out on 19 July, Warby has written: 'Liberators bombed from 25,000 feet. Pictures OK. No damage. No opposition!!!' Perhaps the reason for this remark and the three explanation marks may lie in the story relayed by Gerry Glaister that not only did the inexperienced US pilots miss with their bombs, they also shot at Warby in his photographic Spitfire and that Warby, for once, was 'hopping mad' and took quite a bit of cooling down after landing back at Heliopolis.

The author has his most clear personal picture of Warby during this period. He was near Cairo in the Almaza transit camp awaiting a passage home. On one afternoon he went swimming at the Heliopolis Sporting Club, much used by Service officers. Warby was relaxing by practising his high diving. He was a superb diver and soon had the attention of the entire crowd in, and around, the pool. He would climb to the top board wearing what was, in those days, almost indecently brief trunks: little more than a bikini bottom of today. They were pale blue. On the top board he would stand absolutely still for what seemed ages. By then his beautiful shape and brief trunks and long very blond hair had caught everyone's eyes, especially any girls present. Eventually, he would launch himself into a graceful swallow, or jack-knife, dive entering the water with barely a splash. It was both a superb performance and, in the author's opinion, a deliberate piece of narcissism. He seemed to be demanding that all eyes looked his way. After each dive, he would swim swiftly underwater until reaching the ladder by the diving end, when he would shoot up from underneath like a performing dolphin and be up the ladder in a flash, then climb to the top board to repeat the ritual performance. It was a stunning performance from start to finish and in a short time everyone around the author was asking, 'Who on earth is he?' For one thing officers (it was an officers only club) didn't wear their hair that long. The author gained considerable kudos by just explaining that he used to know him in Malta and that he was about 'the most remarkable pilot in the Middle East, or even the whole RAF' quoting the words that Hugh Pughe had attributed originally as coming from Air Marshal Tedder.

One of Warby's well-known exploits during this period occurred when he was testing a Beaufighter with a crewman on board. He had developed a liking for low flying and zoomed his machine along a chasm in the sandy foothills to the east of Cairo. The passage closed to a width of less than the wing span of the aircraft but Warby merely banked the plane at a steep angle and went through the narrow opening sideways. As all have testified; once he had got the machine off the ground, he was its complete master until the time came to get it down again!

An airman, Corporal Iles, who was an instrument repairer at Heliopolis specializing with cameras, records that Warby once carried out a 'Victory Roll' in a PR Spitfire which succeeded in putting the amidships camera 'out of bonk', as he puts it, i.e. out of alignment. Iles is one who recalls him as 'Mad Warby' but with obvious affection. Iles was later injured during a bombing raid on 2 PRU at, probably, the airfield they often used and which was known simply as 'Kilo 8'. This shows that by July or August, life in the Cairo area had ceased to be the relatively easy going and safe area that it had been only a few months earlier. As Paul Lamboit has put it, 'The flap', as it was afterwards called, grew to such a state in HQ offices that masses of official papers were being burnt to such an extent that black cinders were flying about everywhere. Women couldn't hang out their washing because of the drifting ash. Among the men, it became known, sarcastically, as 'The Great Fire of Cairo.' Paul Lamboit and others of 2 PRU did not join in the panic and confined their evacuation activities to having papers and other key pieces of equipment ready for swift removal in case the situation really did become critical.

Norman Shirley gradually recovered from the wounds which he had received when Benjie White and he had been shot up on landing at Luqa. He was restored to flying duties – still as a volunteer, and carried out a few more operations with Warby. Meanwhile he and Ron Haddon were having a rough time of it on the ground because of the DFM ribbons which they had gained and which, according to Regulations they had to wear at all times. As neither had any aircrew badge and since this was an aircrew decoration, their predicament was understandable. They were pulled up again and again. Shirley maintains that the reason why both were offered commissions was to get them out of this particular predicament but from all that the author had heard and read, both were men of outstanding abilities and courage. Shirley and Haddon fell back upon the practical policy of not displaying their ribbons where they were not known. Among their friends in 2 PRU, they were rightly regarded as men of special merit and, prior to departing from 2 PRU, Shirley was made the guest of honour at a dinner given by a group of airmen in Cairo.

An incident which has troubled Norman Shirley ever since occurred towards the end of this period when Warby was supposedly resting in Egypt. Warby asked him to come to his Mess at Kilo 8 for a private talk. They talked for quite a while, but Shirley sensed that Warby never quite got around to the important matter that had prompted the invitation. He strongly suspects that there was something he wanted to unburden but never could quite start. One aspect of the talk worried Shirley. To keep the talk going (hoping that Warby would find the right note on which to start the serious matter on his mind), Norman asked Warby what were his plans for after the war. As Norman Shirley writes: 'I felt and hoped that I was looking at a future Marshal of the RAF: true he would have played hell with the Establishment but with maturity he was a man the country could not do without' but, with a sad look in his eyes Warby replied, 'Tea planting in Malaya, I suppose.' Shirley goes on to add:

> For the first time in my association with him, I was a little perturbed because all men have a horizon to aim for and I felt that Warby seemed to have lost sight of his ... I felt the edge had gone out of him and when we said goodbye I looked at his medal ribbons and asked if if there was to be one in front of these (only the often rumoured VC would be so placed) and he replied: 'No, Norman, there is a nasty word called "posthumous" usually associated with that one.'
> I wish that he could have lived. It would have been nice to talk or write to him on occasions, particularly on those occasions when one has to make important decisions or share one's mind.

Within days of this talk Warby was back in Malta; arriving on 11 August in a Spitfire to take over 69 Squadron. It was the most critical time of the war for Malta and in the months to come he was to accomplish his most outstanding feats of the war.

MALTA FOR THE THIRD TIME

Much had been happening in Malta during the five months that Warby had been 'resting' in Egypt. The island had suffered appallingly and was facing in August when Warby returned, almost certain starvation unless a convoy could somehow fight its way to the island.

The arrival of Fliegerkorps II at a time when the RAF had only the out-of-date Hurricanes had resulted in the grimmest of grim times. The author can recall the mood of depression that came with the realisation that the Luftwaffe could more or less do what it liked over the island's three airfields. What we wanted were Spitfires and we had perked up enormously when, earlier that year in March, a total of 31 arrived: in three lots flown from the decks of *Eagle* and *Argus*. However, their arrival had not been kept secret (almost impossible to conceal since the carriers had sailed from Gibraltar which Spain overlooked). To make matters worse, their crews were largely 'green' and inexperienced and the aircraft arrived in a state where they required essential maintenance before being fit to fight the Luftwaffe. As a result, they were nearly all written off within a week of arriving: many being strafed on the ground within 20 minutes of first touch-down and continually thereafter.

This made the situation even more depressing. We had received Spitfires but they had made no difference. What else could we hope for? The light at the end of the tunnel had become dimmed. In April 47 more arrived and received much the same immediate decimation. This time it was the US carrier *Wasp* that had brought them to within range of Malta. Although many of these Spitfires were also soon destroyed, a residue of experienced fighter pilots had accumulated. This was to prove important.

When *Wasp* and *Eagle* brought 64 more within range of Malta in May preparations for their arrival had been made in advance. Each Spitfire was met by a trained 'reception committee' which was able to have the aircraft back in the air, fully refuelled and armed with a battle-hardened pilot at the controls within less than nine minutes. It was an astonishing piece of careful planning and was brilliantly executed. When, true to form, the Luftwaffe at once flew off from the nearby Sicilian airfield to blast to smithereens yet another batch of newly arrived Spitfires, they were met in the air, before even reaching Malta: and met by ace pilots such as Laddie Lucas.† Many German planes were shot down – others flew back. That

† 'One of the war's exceptional characters' is Laddie Lucas's view of Warby. He met him on several occasions in Malta.

was 9 May. The next day they tried again in greater force only to be shot down in even greater numbers. That day is still known in Malta as the Glorious Tenth of May. Up to 63 enemy planes were destroyed or seriously damaged and never again did the Germans exert air superiority over Malta. As Corporal Cyril Wood describes it:

> Rationing of ammunition was taken off. The large minelayer *Welshman* was also in harbour having made one of its fast solo dashes to bring in 350 tons of fuel and urgent supplies. Grand Harbour was covered by a smoke screen. What a day it was! Barnham and Bailey and Flo Ziegfield had nothing on the show we saw that sunny day. Stukas diving ... Spitfires circling above the box barrage and picking them off as they flew clear. Ju88s bombing from higher levels. Eager Spitfire pilots chasing bombers right through the barrage not always coming out whole ... The sea from Malta to Sicily looked like Henley Regatta, there were so many German crews in their dinghies with rescue launches picking them up.

Fliegerkorps II had had enough. The air raids decreased from 774 during the first four months of 1942 down to 600 for the next four months (246 in May) and then to 270 for the rest of the year. The RAF had held firm. Pride had been restored.

Victory in the air did not bring food. Months went by without a convoy reaching Malta. The few supplies that did reach her were insufficient. To counter possible sabotage or theft strict orders were issued. By August the island was within weeks of having to surrender; or be starved. Yet the importance of holding Malta had, by summer of 1942, become paramount. The North African landings (Operation Torch) were being secretly planned for November. The Eighth Army was building up for the counterstroke that would send Rommel scurrying back from his position so dangerously close to Alexandria. Malta *had* to be held at all cost.

With this in mind, a tremendous effort was made to force a convoy to Malta in August. Fourteen merchant ships were loaded with supplies and set forth, from Gibraltar accompanied by the largest naval force of British ships assembled in World War II. In all Operation Pedestal, as it was called, involved the battleships *Nelson* and *Rodney*, the carriers *Victorious*, *Indomitable*, *Eagle* and *Furious*, seven cruisers and no less than 34 destroyers plus 5 corvettes, and two oilers with 9 submarines on patrol, a minesweeping flotilla, and a motor-launch flotilla. Once this large convoy and its mammoth escort group reached the area where it could be attacked by enemy planes based in Sardinia, aided by Italian motor torpedo boats and submarines, all hell was let loose. The convoy presented a prize target for the enemy.

It is sufficient to relate that between 11 and 13 August, the Navy lost the aircraft carrier *Eagle* (and another the *Indomitable* was damaged), two cruisers with two more damaged and a destroyer. Tragically nine of the fourteen merchantmen were sunk and two others, *Brisbane Star* and *Rochester Castle*, were damaged but the *Port Chalmers* and the *Melbourne Star* reached Malta unharmed as later did the two damaged ships.

The tanker *Ohio*, 'the ship which would not die', was hit by dive-bombers, torpedoed, and set on fire. She was twice abandoned, but reboarded. Sinking slowly, but held up by destroyers lashed to both sides, with another destroyer steering her by pushing from the rear, she brought her cargo of oil into Malta two days after the other ships had battled through. The inhabitants of Malta, lined the harbour, cheering and weeping. Malta could live on. The date coincided with their Santa Marija (Feast of the Assumption) and to this day the saga is known locally as 'Il Convoy fa' Santa Marija'. In an article for the Malta *Sunday Times* in 1982 Christina records her memory of that traumatic time: she was on duty as assistant to the controller in the Fighter Ops Room:

> Came a thud. A large brown-paper parcel fell into my lap. A hand gripped my shoulder tightly. Turning, I saw a handsome, bronzed face leaning over close to mine. I looked into a pair of brilliant blue eyes, laughing at me from beneath the battered peak of an old familiar cap. It was Warby ... Back, after more than five months away in Egypt.
>
> Of all the emotions I experienced during those few moments predominant was a sense of something very near to disappointment. There had been an eternity of waiting for this. All the weeks Warby had been away I had schemed and planned for his homecoming. Much of my sleeping time had been taken up with dreams of a wonderful reunion. It had certainly not been like this that he would return – unheralded, unexpected and bang in the middle of a battle.

Warburton arrived in August 1942, at the very time when Pedestal was en route. By then Hugh Pughe (who had originally been told that he couldn't possibly last as AOC for as long as six months – 'You'll be worn out before then') had been replaced by Air Marshal Keith Park of Battle of Britain fame. Park was a Fighter Command man and, with the Spitfires now 'on top' he saw to it that air supremacy remained with the RAF. Keith Park seems to have been well briefed about Warby by Hugh Pughe Lloyd and whatever he may have thought about some of Warby's more outrageous actions (and some say that at times these nearly drove him round the bend), he allowed Warby much the same free hand as had his predecessor.

Warburton now promoted to squadron leader, was given command of his old unit 69 Squadron. He wasted no time. The ships of the convoy were still struggling to reach Malta. The great fear was that the big Italian capital ships would be used to finish off the sad remains of the once huge convoy. It was essential to find out if they were still in port. Warby twice flew in PR Spitfires to Taranto on the 12th and was able to report that nothing was stirring there. The next day he again flew twice to keep watch over the nearer Italian bases of Messina and Palermo. He also carried out a search of the sea area between Sardina and Cap Bon (NE Tunisia) by then sadly the scene for so many burning ships and survivors. He operated also on the 14th and 15th.

No 69 Squadron, had in May been so decimated that Pilot Officer Foster had taken over as CO from Tennant as acting squadron leader. By August with Spitfires at Ta Kali able to provide protection for the island, the new AOC, like his predecessor had been building up the island's strike forces. 69 Squadron eventually comprised three distinct flights. 'A' Flight comprised of Glenn Martin Baltimores, a type which had been developed to replace the earlier Marylands; 'C' Flight of Wellingtons, modified to carry two torpedoes and which were used for night torpedo attacks. (The author had trained the crews at the TTU at Turnberry and the aircraft were fitted with a unique short range radar which enabled the attacks to be made in complete darkness.) There was also a sizeable 'B' Flight of PR Spitfires. This last had grown from the single Spitfire V modified as a PR Mark II which the young Harry Coldbeck had been delivering to Egypt earlier that summer.

Harry Coldbeck is one of the few pilots who hardly has a good word for Warburton. He suggests that Warby 'dressed up' his operational reports. But this seems scarcely possible, at least as regards his PR work. A fighter or bomber pilot could make claims beyond reality but can a PR pilot? The evidence is there in the camera magazines. Not everyone positively liked Warby. With his surface aloofness and frequent disappearances from Mess, brother officers were seldom close to him, Harry had another reason for annoyance. For his efforts Harry had been rapidly promoted and by the time Warby reappeared from 'out of the blue', he had become a flight lieutenant and flight commander of 69's growing Spitfire flight: duties which he took very seriously. Without warning Warby then appeared, was welcomed as a returning hero and had promptly taken over his flight – at that moment probably the only flight 69 Squadron possessed – without, so it seems, a word of thanks, praise or acknowledgement. This might have been tolerated if Warby had been a normal flight commander, but he was not. The two men were clearly not of compatible natures. One was serious, correct, reliable: the other was a flamboyant, unpredictable, genius. In Coldbeck's words, 'There has been a lot of rubbishy glamour attributed to his exploits'; he goes on to mention that 'with the demise of the fighters, we (by then Colquhoun and Dalley had joined him) were for a time the only Allied aircraft airborne over the island in daylight … leading charmed lives in the air and on the ground.' Coldbeck also writes: 'There were a lot of people working quietly away and very effectively for the common cause.' Harry Coldbeck was a team man, who had built up a team. Warburton a brilliant individualist. They were destined to clash. Harry describes how Warby's arrival had hit him:

> Suddenly about mid August 1942, Flight Lieutenant Warburton appeared with his unorthodox style and accessories, then straight away disappeared presumably to HQ or Christina. He reappeared as a squadron leader announcing he was our CO. While this was a bit startling, in effect it didn't seem to mean much at first because Warby's interpretation of his position was for him to arrive at the authorisation book area, select an aircraft and away. I was carrying on as usual and now, in addition, finding repairs for my programme caused by Warby's depredations.

Harry Coldbeck goes on to describe one day he remembers well:

> I had one leg over the side of the Spitfire (his beloved AB300) on my way to some distant place like Sardinia when Warby appeared at my elbow, with parachute etc indicating that he was now taking out the aircraft I had signed out. I was detailed to dash down alternatively and take Christina out to lunch on the *Brisbane Star* in the harbour, instead of him. So, fairly obediently, I changed my clothes again and in the heat of the day got out the bicycle and eventually found myself at Christina's residence. She was shocked at my appearance, thinking something had happened to Warby and then refused to go to lunch. Anyhow it was too late she said. We drank some tea instead laced with Scotch – a new experience for me.

Warby, thanks to his rank and reputation, was always privy to Top Brass information. He had never lost the habit of spending time at HQ the better to understand the importance of his missions aloft. But he had always operated as a 'one man band'. Harry comments on this: 'AHQ now put all the information to us through him and that's where most of it stayed; with him! None of us knew what was going on either at base or at the more distant areas of interest and concern to us.' It is not difficult to see why Coldbeck and Warburton were never on the same frequency.

Harry is, however, yet another who remembers Warby's complete disregard for his personal safety. He recalls that when he found himself standing alongside Warby during an attack on Luqa by Stukas, Warby, upon spotting a Stuka diving straight at them, simply pulled out his much loved Luger pistol and stood there firing at the pilot. Both Stuka and Warby were pointing straight at one another. As Harry comments: 'It's just as well they were both apparantly rotten shots, as the bomb also missed.'

Les Colquhoun is much more tolerant. Until commissioned sometime later, he had the *advantage* of being an NCO and soon fell under Warby's spell. Airmen and NCO's were always apt to be treated with greater respect than officers by Warby. Les is clearly a remarkable person. He is but one of that special brand who, having found that they could 'take' the appalling conditions of Malta in their stride, showed themselves to be men of sterling worth. Just as Paddy Moren had proved to be no ordinary air gunner and Norman Shirley no ordinary photographer, so did Les prove to be no ordinary sergeant pilot. By war's end he had collected both a DFM and DFC. In post war days, he became a well known jet test pilot who was awarded the rare George Medal. After quitting Vickers as a test pilot, he helped to found and manage the Hoverlloyd cross channel ferry service, a forerunner in this field. Les writes about Warby at great length and with much perceptive understanding. Like Harry Coldbeck, he was shanghaied with his PR Spitfire and detailed to operate almost daily PR sorties for which neither had been trained. Both were literally worked to near exhaustion for over nine months under horrific conditions of bombing, strafing, food shortages and, until the Glorious Tenth of May, the added ignominy of having the Me109's flaunting their superiority overhead. For a period, Les and Harry, the two young waylaid ferry pilots, *were* 69 Squadron, although by August when Warby reappeared, the squadron had expanded.

It was Harry and Les who had discovered the newly laid down glider landing strips in Sicily and alerted HQ of the probably intended invasion. As their experience grew, they would at times remain over Sicilian airfields to pin-point and count the enemy bombers taking off for raids on Malta and pass the early warning to base. Both served Malta gallantly.

Another side of Warby emerges from Les's description of how Warby recommended him for a commission and when this came through, how they planned to spend the £30 uniform allowance that was always granted. By then, there was no hope of finding an RAF officer's uniform in Malta. Accordingly, Warby suggested that the two of them should go into partnership and spend the £30 on a black-market deal. He knew one of the ship's crew well and he arranged to buy from their store for £30 all the chocolate they had. Chocolate seems to have been a Warby fascination ever since at St Edward's days. As Les writes: 'To my horror I found that £30 worth of chocolate at 1942 prices was quite a lot and with nowhere to store it also a problem. Needless to say with summer temperatures of 90° the whole project was a disaster.' Although Les became a successful businessman, it seems doubtful however that successful finance in any form was ever a part of Warby's make-up. Although 69 Squadron was growing in size and importance, Les writes:

The relationship he had with the squadron was totally informal. He decided what *he* would do and the rest of us filled in the gaps. However he set a very high standard of personal performance and expected you to do likewise. His relationship with senior officers in the AOC's HQ at Valletta also seemed to be totally informal. His comings and goings never seemed to be questioned ... Operationally he was outstanding. Whereas we would be content to take our photographs from 20–25,000 feet, Warby would sail in at much lower heights and take extreme risks that always seemed to come off ... When the Germans invaded Tunisia, Warby was flying round in formation with Ju52s landing troops at El Aouina.

Another habit of Warby's which upset some including Harry Coldbeck was his sudden disappearances to the Middle East. There he would visit ME HQ and return without any explanation. On such visits he always took the opportunity to bring back all the goodies he could cram into a Spitfire both for Christina and for his airmen devotees.

By any ordinary standards Warby was long overdue both a genuine rest and a posting back to the UK. On several unannounced visits to HQ Egypt, he was however in all likelihood, being briefed of the overall military situation. Rommel had at last been halted, at the First Battle of Alamein, which had taken place during the first three weeks of July. Later when Rommel and his Afrika Korps tried to break through to Alexandria at the end of August, he suffered what is now recognized (but scarcely was at the time) a crushing defeat at the Battle of Alam El Halfa. For those in the know, and fully aware of all the masses of planes and tanks arriving in Egypt from both the USA and the UK, the writing was on the wall for a major offensive. General Montgomery had taken command of the Eighth Army, on 13 August. It is probable that Warby was in on these plans, and those for the invasion of North Africa, planned for November 1942, and then the subsequent invasion of Sicily. For in the autumn of 1942 Warby undertook a number of what are termed 'Special Flights' from Luqa. The first of such 'Special Flights' was on 21 September after he had already paid one visit to Egypt (carrying out a long photo-sortie of the Corinth Canal and the Athens area on the way.) Fortunately, although squadron records are purposely vague about the destination of all his 'Special Flights', Warby's personal log book is more explicit. On 21 September he covered the Sicilian south coastline between Marsala and Sciacca – a distance of about 60 miles flying throughout at 500–1,000 feet. He encountered a Dornier 24 and took some shots of it. Unusually, he seems to have armed his PR Spitfire prior to departure. He claimed the Do24 as 'Damaged!'

Warby was always eager to get involved in aggressive actions. For instance, during August, soon after his arrival back in Malta, he managed to arrange to accompany Flight Lieutenant Le Mesurier on a night bombing mission of ships in the Corfu roads, listing himself as 'second pilot' of the Wellington. This brief experience of flying in a Wellington may have inspired him to organize one of his most outrageous ventures. He was acutely aware of what the airmen were suffering and had, indeed, suffered for years. Unlike aircrew who became time-expired after, on average, six months or less and were then somehow 'got off the island' on a priority basis (by submarine, or an occasional flying boat service or just crammed into a transit aircraft) the 'poor bloody airmen' were stuck in Malta indefinitely. Many served and suffered for years. Warby, ever their champion, determined to try to enliven their 1942 Christmas. The island was full of wrecked Wellingtons but one which had been 'written off', and therefore officially no longer existed on paper, seemed repairable. Warby persuaded a bunch of his most loyal airmen to give up their spare time to making this 'non-existent' aircraft come back to life. Spare parts was no problem. By 1942 there were the remains of up to 100 blitzed Wellingtons lying around: mainly at Safi Strip.

Warby took leave between 19 and 29 December and, taking off and landing back at night, he flew the Wellington which didn't exist to Egypt and brought it back full of Xmas booze. Let Cyril Wood, tell the outcome:

> The crews of 69 Squadron pooled their resources and Warby took off for Egypt in the battered Wellington which officially didn't exist. He went off to Egypt to fulfil the squadron's Christmas needs. His return was prepared for. It was to be a night landing. A Maltese driver with his lorry had been briefed to meet the aircraft. Ground crews were ready to unload the 'freight' and take it to a safe depository under lock and key.
>
> All went well. The aircraft landed and a Maltese lorry drew up alongside to take on the load. This accomplished, the lorry drove away and wasn't seen again. Two enterprising airmen had switched lorries and the one loaded was a phoney one which drove off to a secret place where the spoils were divided. Fortunately it was soon discovered that something was wrong. Investigation by Service police located the spoils above a false ceiling in the Padre's office. The offenders were quickly brought to heel and given their just desserts.

Naturally the episode increased Warby's reputation. Whether Park or the Group Captain at Luqa knew about it, is not related, though one source suggests that both were frustrated by Warby's one man war. Warby had by that time become a law unto himself. His very presence in the island had raised the morale of all. HQ were wisely cashing in on this. Warby seems ever pleased to be so used. When the remains of the August Santa Marija had staggered into Grand Harbour amidst the cheers and tears of the inhabitants, it was discovered that there were two American Naval gunners – probably brave volunteers, aboard one of the merchantships. Steps were taken to entertain them and, with full publicity, Warby and Christina took them around the island as press cameras snapped. Christina had also become a part of the island's folk lore and was likewise prepared to play her role in morale building enterprises. Warby was also used in a similar publicised manner when a Russian Lt Colonel Solodovnik visited the island as an official guest to show that Britons were also in a hot war.

Warby as CO of the squadron could have flown any of the various types the squadron was acquiring in ever increasing numbers as the attacks from the Luftwaffe eased off. Yet, apart from accompanying Flight Lieutenant Le Mesurier on a couple of bombing raids, (and his unofficial Xmas 'booze run'to Egypt) he had little to do with the Wellingtons. Warby did try his hand at flying the Baltimore alongside a flight of torpedo carrying Beauforts to photograph an attack as it was actually taking place off the Greek coast. His log book merely records that Pilot Officer Baines, Pilot Officer Hutson, Flight Lieutenant Day and Pilot Officer Bird were shot down. It was incidentally the 242nd operational trip which he had logged. But for the most part he flew the PR Spitfires on their high, or low, flying PR sorties. Attempts were made by HQ to curtail the number of operational trips he flew but he simply ignored such orders.

In October, a second bar to his DFC was awarded; it was six months since he had been awarded the DSO. For the first time Tunisian targets were now being included in his photo sorties. Few, if any, in Malta were privy to the top secret information that the Allied landings were soon to take place near Algiers and other NW African places, but it seems possible that Warby was 'in the know'. The *official* record of his first Tunisian PR flight refers only to Elmas, Cagliari and other Sardinian bases but Warby's log book shows that he later proceeded to Tunis and Bizerta. During the first part of the flight he had fought off 15 fighters over Sardinia at 15,000 feet but was undisturbed at 3,000 feet as he snapped the port and aerodromes around the Tunisian capital. He has added in what seems a joyous post-script: 'Beat up the coast!!!' It must have been a welcome change not to be shot at over neutral territory.

Another low level 'Special Tasks' sortie of Sicilian beaches followed and once again he then took himself to Heliopolis. Perhaps the story that he only took himself to Egypt to restock Christina's larder was deliberately allowed to circulate as a 'blind' for the Special Tasks, (the pseudonym which generally masked his Sicilian beaches flights) and his subsequent flights back to Egypt?

By October Beaufighters had arrived in Malta and were being used in daylight as torpedo dropping planes. On 14 October a flight of these set forth to attack shipping in the Tripoli area. Warby in a Spitfire went along to watch the attack and to report upon, and photograph, the results.†

The target was a merchantship escorted by a destroyer. The attackers were three Beaufighters. As the planes flew in, the destroyer's guns opened fire. Beaufighter 'Q' was shot down in flames and exploded in the air. All would have been killed instantaneously. Beaufighter 'Y' was hit and came down in the sea at a distance of about 5–10 miles from the convoy. Warby flew over and observed the crew of two, apparently unharmed, climb into a dinghy. There was no hope of any friendly ship ever locating them but there seemed to him no reason why the enemy should not pick them up. Life as a temporary POW in Italy was preferable to death in a dinghy in the Med. Back over the destroyer flew Warby. Surprised, but happy to respond, the ship opened fire again. Warby ignored the flak and kept circling the ship, flying alongside repeatedly and waggling his wings in an attempt to convince them that he was not hostile. For 20 minutes this strange drama was enacted until the Italians finally got the message and sped off in the direction that Warby indicated. By then six Macchi fighters had appeared on the scene from nearby Homs air base. Warby was unarmed and although four of them got on his tail he managed to use his speed and flying agility to avoid being shot down. Not until he saw the occupants of the dinghy safely aboard the destoyer did he turn for home. It was for this exploit he was awarded the second bar to his DFC.

His concern for fellow pilots shot down was never more evident yet, because (apparently) the Beaufighters did not belong to 69 Squadron (39 Squadron perhaps), he did not for once include the names of those shot down in his personal log book. They were, however, two more pilots and crews whom he had personally seen take their last flight of the war. For a pilot to see an enemy pilot shot down in flames is in a way a saddening experience because airmen respect all other airmen but to see even one colleague so killed is something not easy to erase from the mind.

Warby has recorded in his log book Harry Coldbeck as having been shot down on 11 November. Two days later he records P/O Jemmett as being 'Missing over Messina -'. The unofficial tin-can message system between the Italian Air Force and the RAF seems to have been working well because alongside the entry of 'F/Lt Coldbeck missing Augusta' he has added, 'prisoner'.

Disaster was striking at 69 Squadron but on the ground great things were happening in Egypt. The second much publicised Battle of Alamein had opened on 23 October. By early November the enemy had had enough and was in full retreat. Better still, the landings of a huge Anglo-American force in NW Africa (Operation Torch) on 7 November had taken place

† From an account in the *Star* by Roy Nash.

successfully and in short time Algiers and much of the coastal strip of French North Africa west of Tunisia was in Allied hands.

The euphoria in Malta generated by these successes was swiftly forgotten. On 15 November, when on a sortie to photograph Bizerta, the seemingly impossible happened, Squadron Leader Warburton was shot down by a flight of Me109s. It was a shock which ran round the island. All knew in their hearts that it had to happen sometime. The man was in Colquhoun's terms a 'risk taker' but, since he had lived a charmed life for so long, many had become to believe that he was, in some mysterious manner, divinely protected while operating from Malta. Had any of the inhabitants known that he had been uniquely christened in a submarine in the island, the superstitious highly religious Maltese would have been convinced that he was being spared by some all-seeing God or Christian Saint.

Almost at once the often half-suggested rumour about a Victoria Cross being awarded to the missing Warby, was again widely mooted. John Agius, a Maltese employed by the RAF for clerical duties, recalls:

A personal signal for AOC, Malta was received regarding Warburton and it was suggested that the AOC might wish to reconsider the recommendation for the award of the Victoria Cross. Apparently Park didn't see it this way. Perhaps he was finding Warburton difficult enough at times without such a prestigious award. In any event none of his Battle of Britain aces such as Bader, Tuck, Malan etc had been so honoured. The reply from Malta was that: 'If I thought that this man deserved the VC, I would have recommended it.'

Be that as it may, the island rang with rumours that Warby had ('at last' some added) been awarded the VC. The atmosphere at HQ where Christina worked was one of hushed respect. According to a young 16-year-old British girl who had also been engaged by the RAF as a Plotter in Ops Room, Marion Gould:

I do recall the day Adrian went missing. I remember we were all on edge and many of us were upset. Christina was in great distress (but was gamely carrying on) ... They were a glamorous couple: flamboyant whom most of us were interested in from the sidelines.

As a temporary measure a South African pilot, Captain Clark, was made the commanding officer of the squadron. An air of gloom hung around the place. Les Colquhoun could find no satisfaction in the fact that he, only just commissioned, was jumped immediately to flight lieutenant and put in charge of 'C' Flight. He was taking Coldbeck's place but nobody likes to step into another's shoes in such circumstances.

Meanwhile, the Allied armies in NW Africa were pressing on. A British paratroop force on 12 November had been dropped from American DC3s and had captured the airfield at Bône. By the 14 the famous 111 Fighter Squadron had flown in with their Spitfires. They were under the command of one of Fighter Command's most colourful characters: one who played as hard as he fought. Tony Bartley, while at Biggin Hill during the Battle of Britain, had the reputation of being both an ace fighter and an ace partyman.

In the air over Bizerta, Warby had run into eight Me 109's. He had completed his mission and was heading back towards Malta and when attacked was in the vicinity of Cap Bon (100 miles or so east of Bône.) The PR Spitfires were fitted with plastic blisters around the cockpit, which enabled pilots under attack to see what was hitting them from behind, provided they put their head into the blister. The cannon shells from the Me109's had ripped into Warby's Spitfire from behind and above. First they tore through the pilot's dome, then they ripped through where his head would normally have been and then into, and through, the instrument panel and thence to the Rolls Royce engine itself. Had Warby not been looking rearwards with his head in blister, he seemed certain to have lost it, literally. Although spared this, he was in great trouble. By skill he managed to elude further attacks until finding cover in the clouds. He had thrown off the Me109's but one glance at his oil pressure gauge told him the worst. The oil system had been hit and the pressure was zero.

Height was on his side and, as he later related, 'that Merlin kept partially going thanks to the quality of its bearings and Rolls' reputation.' By nursing the engine gently and only yielding height most grudgingly, he managed to half fly, half glide the crippled plane towards the most forward line of the Allied troops advancing from Algiers. He must have known or hoped that the airfield at Bône had just been seized by the Allies. Thanks to skill, and to the proverbial a 'wing and a prayer', he reached Bône and crash-landed there still in one piece. The Spitfire was a wreck and would never fly again but Warby was safe and sound. Almost by a miracle he had come to earth on recently captured Allied soil.

Tony Bartley, although a veteran of the Battle of Britain and a Fighter Command ace used to rather casual attire, was perplexed. He had never seen a pilot attired like Warby. First he noticed his almost unique row of medal ribbons: the DSO, the DFC and two bars. Warby was also dressed in his usual unique flamboyant fashion, and his blond hair hung in long locks. Fighter Command pilots such as he prided themselves upon their unconventional attire, top button always undone. But this was outrageously different.

The territorial position of the airfield that day was delicate. Technically the soil was the sovereignty of Vichy France; that of a French colony. The Germans, once over their initial surprise, had poured into Tunisia. They were somewhere close; perhaps too close for comfort. The Arabs were in evidence and prepared to sell anything or anyone to anyone. The tough British paratroops who had so recently dropped in were holding the airfield against all comers and were commandeering food, billets etc with typical decisive thoroughness! Tony Bartley was almost isolated. He had not established a communication link with any authority. 111 Squadron was having a tough time with Luftwaffe raids. They had only the barest of skeleton maintenance men and no spares. To add to their difficulties, the rain had churned the area into a sea of mud. When not ducking into ditches to avoid German strafing and bombs, Tony and his pilots were scouring the countryside for shelter, food and wine: especially in Tony's case the latter, as he relates in his book *Smoke Trails in the Sky*.

Warby decided that he had better return to civilization as quickly as possible. He got wind that the French Governor of the colonial area was in the vicinity. Somehow, he located him. Like all Frenchmen at the time, the Governor, who happened to be an Admiral, didn't quite know where he stood or what to do next. There were Darlan Frenchmen, who paid allegiance to the French Admiral Darlan. There were Giraud Frenchmen who paid allegiance to the French General Giraud. There were Vichy Frenchmen loyal to Marshal Pétain and De Gaulle Free-Frenchmen. Some French leaders welcomed the invading Americans and British Armies (with the former much more in evidence) with open arms. Others viewed the invasion of their neutral country for what it was: an invasion.

Warby soon managed to persuade the French Admiral that the best bet for his future was to throw in his lot with the Allies and get himself to Algiers so that he could make the right connections and be sure that Allied HQ knew where his sympathies lay. The difficulty was to get to Algiers. Virtually all planes of the Tunisian Colony had had their magnetos removed to ensure that they could not be flown (as had that of Jacques' in 1940) to the nearest RAF base. It had been one of the terms of the Armistice that defeated France had signed. A mail plane of sorts was eventually found and in this Caudron F-BACK, Warby, with Admiral Villeneuve and his staff, duly arrived unexpectedly in Algiers on the 17th – two days after his encounter with the Me109s over Bizerta. There had been no opportunity to let anyone know of this handy arrangement. The only local communication service of any kind was the remnants of an archaic French telephone system. Algiers Maison Blanche airport was teeming with planes; arrivals, reinforcements. It was in the hands of Americans rather than British forces. Warby and all his medal ribbons cut no ice with them. Warby was anxious to get to British soil if only to let someone know that he was still alive. He knew that signals would have been sent to his father – his nominated Next of Kin and also to his mother. The next day was the 18th and when Warby heard that a Halifax bomber flown by a Czech crew would be flying to Gibraltar, he at once sought out the captain, a Flying Officer Anderle and, using rank and charm, persuaded him to include him as an additional crew member.

Back at last on British soil, his troubles were not at an end. Gibraltar was a regular RAF station. Pilots who dressed up in fancy clothes; pilots who wore almost pretentious medal ribbons, pilots who had knives and a German pistol stuck into the Army boots they wore; pilots with long blond hair flown in unannounced by a Czech crew were suspect. They belonged to no known category. Warby was immediately arrested as a potential spy!

It took some persuasion on his part to convince the Gibraltar authorities that this highly irregularly attired person was genuine. With this hurdle overcome, Warby's next task was to find some way of getting himself back to Malta. He discovered that a Spitfire which was being delivered from the UK to where the front line was, didn't seem to have a delivery pilot. His powers of persuasion, which had within days swayed a French Admiral, a Czech flying officer, and then the Special Police at Gib, again went to work. On the 20th he took off in ER 467, a Fighter Command Spitfire, and after refuelling at Algiers, he landed back at Bône (where Tony Bartley seems to recall that before returning to Malta he flew a fighter sortie with 111 Squadron, though there is no mention of this in his log book), specifically to pick up the camera magazine from his damaged PR Spitfire. One magazine had been hit by cannon shells and was useless but the other still held his photographs of Bizerta. Warby always got his pictures. He wasn't about to let his reputation suffer just because some Messerschmitts had shot him down. After a night of enjoying Tony Bartley's excellent stock of Algerian wine and Calvados, Warby took off the next day (21 November 1942) back to Malta.

This extraordinary drama didn't end there. His route took him close to Cape Bon where the Me109s had jumped him. Almost to the spot where he had been hit six days before, his keen sight picked up a couple of Ju88s. This Spitfire was a fighter version and Warby had seen to it that it was fully armed before departing from Bône. One Ju88 went down in flames. He had hit it several times and eventually, after bursting into flames, a wing came off. He then sought out the second Junkers but after firing only a few shots his guns jammed and the Ju88 escaped him. Revenge is sweet and it must have given him considerable satisfaction to have been able to right the score over almost the same place as that where he himself had been shot from the sky.

The signal to Commander Geoffrey Warburton in Haifa advising that his son was missing is dated 16 November. The one countering this and advising that he was safe and in British hands is dated the 21st, the day when Warby returned 'back from the dead' to the astonished and happy fraternity at Luqa. As one airman describes it, 'For us it was Carnival time'. Few at Luqa had any idea he was safe. Warby positively delighted in being nonchalant. When he stepped out of the Spitfire at Luqa, as airmen, amazed but smiling, gathered around him, all he said was: 'I'm sorry to be a bit late!'

He had brought back the undamaged magazine with its pictures of Bizerta, now six days old. This he took to the photo unit in Valletta. Without a word of explanation he tossed it at the mouth-open Ken Fielder and simply requested that the film be developed. For days Ken had imagined that Warby was either dead or a POW.

During his six days' absence from Malta, promotion to wing commander had just come through. Between 15 and 21 November he had added a stripe, added to his number of kills and added to his reputation as a living legend.

As if nothing had happened, Warburton carried out another nine flights during the rest of the last week of that memorable November 1942, including yet another joust with Me109s. He had been sent to photograph, from 50–300 feet, enemy positions around Kairouan and Gafsa (inland from Sousse and Sfax, Tunisia) for Army parachutists, who were planning yet another forward drop. To escape he flew west, it must have been quite a chase by the 109s as he eventually landed up at Souk El Arba in Morocco, several 100 miles away. In his usual terse style his log book merely records, '2 Me 109s 3 holes'. On his way back he dropped in on Bone again. Perhaps it was then that he went fighting with Tony Bartley's 111 Squadron? Alternatively he might have acquired a taste for Tony's wine and Calvados!

Promotion to wing commander did not curb his flying. During the first nineteen days of December, when he also was suffering from flu, he carried out another seventeen missions. With the Allied armies now closing in on the Axis forces in Africa from both directions: and both making rapid advances almost daily, Warby was now covering the enemy in three directions. On one day he would return to his familiar airfield in Sicily or fly further north into Italy (on the 7th, he reports after a flight to Naples '3 Battleships missing': by then he knew where all the major Italian ships were normally anchored), on the next day, he might be over Sousse, Sfax and Bizerta and then on the following it might be back to Tripoli and Benghazi. The Mediterranean had become his 'canvas' and to him, was as familiar in outline and detail as his home base at Malta. Not for nothing was he being called 'King of the Mediterranean'.

He called it quits for the rest of the month concentrating thereafter on his trip to Egypt in the Wellington which did not exist to pick up the Christmas booze.

When in January, Pilot Officer Frazer 'went missing' and was believed to have ended up in the sea, Warby made a special trip to search for him or his dinghy. His concern for those who, in the parlance of the day, 'had bought it' was ever evident. His lectures to the schools about the part that they could play in assisting the Air-Sea Rescue launches may have taken place at this time.

Pilots have a fondness for a particular aircraft akin to sportsmen having a lucky bat or pair of boots. However Warby flew so often that, by the time he had finished his tour of duty with this unit, he had flown 37 different Spitfires (as well as several Baltimores and made at least one Taranto PR trip in a Beaufighter 'for old times sake' with Ron Haddon). He nonetheless had his favourite planes. For a while this was Spitfire BS 364. Warby also had his favourite maintenance team. An airframe fitter, Ken Rogers, with an engine rigger, Jack Meadows, soon came to regard Warby as part of 'their team'. His planes became 'their' planes. Warby seems to have been as fond of these two as they were of him. Ken Rogers has written warmly at length about 'his' Warby.

It was typical of the practical, if unorthodox, manner by which the RAF in Malta operated that Ken Rogers, a pre-war Regular airman came to attach himself first to 69 Squadron and then to Warby. As he tells it:

> At the time of the August 1942 convoy (the Santa Marija one), a bunch of us moved to Luqa to lend a hand and somehow or other attached ourselves to 69 Squadron. We had come from Halfar, the Fleet Air Force Station [which by then also had a few Spitfires], so we were made welcome in true Warby style. As things happened he acquired a new Spit a PR job BS 364, which was fitted with two vertical and one oblique camera … Jack Meadows and myself were duly appointed to look after it. Jack was a conscript (ex Leyland motors) with a typical Lancashire bluntness. He had been with Warby for some time. He was quite a bit older and bullied him: treated him like an errant son and rarely called him anything but 'Warby'. Warby, of course, loved it. We kept his new Spit in the pink and guarded it like a couple of Alsatians. We enjoyed a very fine relationship with this wonderful man. It extended far beyond the normal pilot/ groundcrew association. We were very proud of our part of the total picture.
>
> Warby was equally at home with the Top Brass and would then spend time with Jack and I in our little (home built) 'Mangey Hut' as though he had no worries at all – and without losing respect: on the contrary, it added to his stature.
>
> Warby's contribution to the Middle East operational scene was enormous and some of his exploits legendary but one of his most important contributions must undoubtedly have been that he made to the morale of everyone he came in contact with and his own squadron in particular. We all worshipped him. His leadership and inspiration were neglected long after his return to the UK.

Ken Rogers also tells some charming stories about Warby, Jack and himself:

Against orders, Warby smoked in the Spitfires. Jack would tell him off in no uncertain terms, 'I've told you before, Warby, stop smoking in the bleeding plane.' Not only did Warby smoke but he would push his fag ends under his 'chute, in the seat well. He would never fasten his 'chute straps either: a fact that I constantly shouted at him for – fearing for his survival. 'Stop worrying, Rogers old boy' was his usual rejoinder. Jack and I worried more about him, than he did about himself.

The story about having his head in the perspex blister when the cannon shell passed through the cockpit and instrument panel on its way to the engine, was told by Warby to Ken Rogers. 'Had he been sitting central, it would have taken his head off,' is how Rogers tells it. Jack was notorious for never removing his forage cap until lights out. When Warby was taxiing to dispersal the fighter Spit that he had brought back from Gibraltar on 21 November, in order to keep the plane steady and to help guide him around the craters in the taxi track by hand signals, Ken and Jack sat one on each wing. The speed and prop blast removed Jack's cap. At arrival in dispersal Warby was splitting himself with laughter: 'Bald as a badger and I've known him for years but had no idea.'

Jack continued to treat Warby as a naughty child. When he brought back 'their Spit' damaged he would swear at him: 'What the Hell have you been doing to the kite, Warby?' Warby would just laugh. Jack never gave up trying to persuade him to do up his shoulder straps. Warby would just grin and say: 'Stop worrying, Jack, if I had to bail out, I'd think of something.' With regards the smoking, Jack eventually had to admit defeat and built him an ashtray for the butts.

Warby thought nothing of helping the other two clean out the aircraft. He was part of the team. This was brought home at Christmas when Warby asked them both to his office prior to their special mid-day meal. They arrived to find many senior officers but Warby introduced them to all the Group Captains etc and gave them each a glass of champagne. On other occasions he got them cigarettes and alcoholic drinks which he had flown in from Egypt or Algiers.

Rogers makes the shrewd comment that 'Malta was the ideal place for Warby. In the UK, he would have been smothered.' How right he proved to be, too.

A story of a Messerschmitt 109 being 'flown into the sea' by tight turns, which had become part of the Warby legend, is attributed by Ken Rogers to a Sergeant Glubb. When picked off by a Me109 on return from a sortie, the unarmed Spitfires could only 'defend' themselves by flying tight turns. It was a battle of skill and wits versus guns and cannons. The better pilot would win the day. All the Spitfire pilot could do would be to outfly the enemy until his petrol ran short. According to Ken Rogers, Glubb went one better. He so out-twisted and out-turned the Me109 that in trying to follow it eventually spun into the sea out of control. However, many including Colonel Elliott Roosevelt, have attributed this feat, or a similar one, to Warby† but there is no such claim in his personal log book. Without doubt, Warby did have to extricate himself on several occasions from this very predicament by such skilful manoeuvering of his plane but whether or not he also lured a Me109 to destruction by such tactics remains unknown. As an airman has put it, 'It would be necessary to duck when he returned back as he would be sure to be followed by a Messerschmitt or two.'

Ken Rogers is among those who commented that, if Warby was back early from patrol, he was liable to join in a fighter patrol with some of his friends at Ta Kali, just as Bartley recalled his doing at Bône. But, apart from one particular sortie, reported by Phil Kelley and commented upon later, such extraneous trips do not appear in his official log book.

Rogers was an astute observer of the man whom he so admired. He noted that, after having been put in charge of what was now becoming a very large 69 Squadron (12 Baltimores, a dozen or more Spitfires, Wellingtons, a few remaining PR Beaufighters etc) 'His image was changing ... difficult demands were made on him. His dress was less flamboyant. He was becoming a more mature officer. He was drawing away from his earlier ways.' He considers that Flight Lieutenant M R 'Mac' Brown, and his fellow Canadian, Flying Officer Ed Maloney, may have had a part in this. Both seem to have taken it upon themselves to be Warby's 'minders'. They accompanied him everywhere: two huge men looking like bodyguards. They were excellent types but were older men and were more seriously inclined than their nonchalant CO. As Rogers writes: 'Perhaps a more serious Warby was emerging and in the process, Christina would suffer from neglect.' For one thing, Warby took up residence in the squadron's acquired Mess, in Shema, a former hotel, Meadowbank. Rogers also makes the comment that as rations got smaller and smaller -just a marmite sandwich for supper, Malta was the only place where 90% of the talk was about food, not women.' He also believes that 'they put some stuff in the tea to stop you thinking about women', since with very few exceptions, there were none to be had.

'Mac' Brown and his buddy Ed Maloney, sometimes called the 'Gold Dust twins', were Canadian pilots who had joined the RCAF on the same day and were never separated until war's end. They became close to Warby and were among his greatest admirers. Their initial meeting with Warby was however not to their liking.

---

†Gil Catton, a 69 Squadron Wellington pilot, credits this feat to Warby, but overland near Messina. Another pilot, Alan Orbell, recounts that Warby flew three Me109s into the ground by outflying them.

One behind the other Mac and Ed were delivering from the UK via Gibraltar new PRU Spitfires to 2 PRU in Egypt. Both had applied to join this after finding PRU at Benson less demanding for their love of flying, since winter weather in the UK kept them grounded too often.

A slim fair-haired squadron leader met them at Malta where they had stopped for the night to refuel and rest. He kindly found them bunks. Next morning they faced a rude awakening. The kindly fair-haired senior officer advised them that he (Warby) had commandeered their Spitfires and that they would be continuing to Egypt in a couple of clapped-out ones.

Later Warby got to hear of their keenness and ability. On one of his visits to Egypt he located Ed Maloney and told him that his pal Mac Brown had agreed to join his squadron in Malta if he, Ed, would also go along. Ed said 'fine'. Warby then sought out Mac and told him the same thing in reverse. Whereupon Mac said 'fine'. In Ed's words, 'That was one real introduction to me of the greatest of all people'. Ed also recalls that when he started to call his Malta CO 'sir', Warby advised him to cut it out. 'It sounds like 'Yes Sewer', he told him. Ed also recalls an occasion when one of the sergeants accidentally shot himself, not seriously, cleaning a gun. When HQ enquired if it was accidental, Warby informed them that it was not an accident – 'we don't post unwanted sergeants, we always shoot them.'

Mac remembers that in Egypt it was the custom in 2 PRU to indulge in some low flying antics at the completion of a high-altitude PR sortie. The excuse was that it accustomed the pilot to lower altitudes before having to land. In reality, it was joie de vivre letting off steam.

A favourite pastime was beating up Arab dhows on the Nile nearly capsizing them with air blasts. When so doing one Arab let fly at Warby with an ancient muzzle-loader and hit the aircraft with a motley collection of nuts, bolts, stones etc some of which spattered around inside the cockpit. Warby considered the incident a huge joke. He appeared completely fearless. Yet both big Canadians agree that Warby when on PR jobs was 100% professional and set an example which all in his squadron endeavoured to copy.

Warby also displayed a sympathetic understanding for those who could not reach his high standards. He got such people quietly posted elsewhere without having to have them officially tagged with the stigma LMF (Lack of Moral Fibre), the RAF's euphemism for cowardly. Warby's PR Squadron had to get results. If one pilot came back without the pictures then another was immediately despatched. He could not tolerate failures and saw to it that he had none such around.

As Mac Brown got to know Warby well in Malta, he found himself in the same situation as Johnny Walker had once been placed at dances. Mac was detailed to dance with Christina. Warby claimed that he could only dance to the tune 'Jealousy' and for his sake orchestras would play it when he appeared but even then he danced it poorly: with Christina, of course.

Both Mac and Ed describe how glamorous Christina was and how envious they were of his monopoly of her.

The two Canadian 'minders' managed to persuade Warby by pulling his leg, to get his hair-cut, wear correct uniform and generally behave like a more conventional squadron commander. Both genuinely loved and respected their CO and they became his deputies when, as was often the case, Warby continued to fly on frequent operational trips. All three shared a room in the Meadowbank Hotel. Warby responded and took his responsibilities as a squadron commander more seriously.

Yet there were occasional outbreaks by Warby, of flagrant irresponsibility. On one occasion when big Phil Kelley (well over six feet tall) was lounging on his bunk with his feet overhanging and propped against the wall Warby advised Phil that he was going to shoot off his big toe. Phil paid no attention, so Warby let fly with his much loved revolver and the bullet penetrated the wall only inches away from Phil's toe. Warby was a wonderfully accurate shot but far too prone to let off for no valid reason as the Mess tent at Luqa, locks on the doors at Meadowbank etc attested.

Mac Brown vividly recalls that when he and Warby were in Egypt on one occasion, neither could find a plane to take them back to Malta. Tripoli had recently been captured and the two 'bummed' a ride to there in a US Liberator which was flying turkeys to the American troops. Again they found themselves stuck with no transport back to Malta. Warby espied a Blenheim which had had been abandoned as useless and persuaded a couple of mechanics to work on it. He told Mac that he had flown Blenheims – an exaggeration, and got it started with Mac on board. 'Fortunately,' as Mac relates, 'the port engine cut dead *before* we got airborne or else I wouldn't now be around to tell this tale.' Warby's log book merely refers to a three minute 'flight' with three exclamation marks.

Mac also remembers an occasion when Warby accompanied a flight of day bombers on a raid on targets in Corfu and Greece. He flew above the bombers in a Baltimore and acted as fighter controller advising them of the numbers, direction and height of fighters defending the target. He was completely disregarding his own safety to ensure that others had a better chance of surviving. Mac, who also seems to have had chats with Warby about his hasty 1939 marriage and other personal matters, is convinced that Warby was a fatalist who knew that he wasn't going to survive the war and who consequently was determined to see that he did his bit and made a colourful mark before the curtains would be drawn eclipsing his life. He told Mac on more than one occasion that he only got married in October 1939 because he knew that he would be killed and he didn't see why somebody rather than nobody, shouldn't get something (a widow's pension) out of it.

Mac and Ed both appreciated the quiet manner in which, at the end of their tour of operations with Warby's squadron, Warby had arranged with help from Elliott Roosevelt for them to go to America on a publicity tour to lecture at the USA PR schools and to inspect the revolutionary new USA plane that Howard Hughes had just designed and built for future PR sorties.

By the time that Warby came into the lives of 'the Gold Dust Twins', he had lost all former aloofness and was a cheerful outgoing person, as Mac says:

> Nothing ever seemed to upset Warby: neither words nor deeds and he had the ability to react to every emergency with skill and decision. He was well disciplined within himself and highly regarded by everyone from the highest to the lowest. He had a dry sense of humour. Underneath his typically English 'What, what Old Boy' manner was a wonderful man and one who being a fatalist didn't seem to know what fear was.

Ed confirms this:

> He appeared to have it all. He just naturally treated all alike as gentlemen. It was as though he had gone full circle and discovered to his satisfaction that all men are created equal and that he was at peace with this and acted accordingly. He lived this standard. There was not a phoney bone in his body.

In February 1943 the decision was made to split the now enormous 69 Squadron into two. The large Spitfire element, B Flight, henceforth became 683 Squadron, with Wing Commander Warburton its first commanding officer. PRU (the original Photo-Recce Unit) had by then in the UK grown into an empire. The original Benson Unit (No 1 PRU) was now assigned a squadron number and status, and similar numbers were given to the other PR units. No 2 PRU, Macphail's lighthearted but efficient Heliopolis unit, now became 680 Squadron and another RAF PR unit (No 4) which was operating from the Algerian/Tunisian African front was designated 682 Squadron. In addition to which the Americans, flying modified twin-engined Lockheed P38 fighters, were also carrying out essential PR duties; over the Algerian/Tunisian battle front. The Americans were increasing in size in leaps and bounds, as was inevitable once they 'got the bit between their teeth' and had been sold on the value of PR work. They could call upon their colossal production facilities. A South African Air Force Squadron, No 60, was also in the NW Africa area operating modified Mosquitos for PR sorties.

Warby took some very well earned UK leave early in March 1943. He hadn't seen England since September 1940. It is known that he enjoyed himself with boozy parties at the Wings Club in Piccadilly which had

Frank Bastard in front of his Maryland. With Paddy Moren, he flew with Warburton when they shot down a Macchi 200 off Cagliari 29 September 1941. The AOC, Hugh Pugh Lloyd, sent a congratulatory signal reading 'My congratulations on your splendid performance this morning. You and your crew will shortly have a price on your head…' (*P Moren*)

Desert conditions – a snap from Warby's personal album.

Battleship in a Vichy-French North African port. Another PR photograph from Warby's personal album.

EXTRACT :- D.R.O's DATED 14.5.42
R.A.F. STATION, TA-KALI, MALTA

A GIBBET HAS BEEN ERECTED
ON THE CORNER OF THE ROAD
LEADING TO THE CAVES. ANY
MAN, WOMAN OR CHILD, CIVILIAN
OR SERVICE PERSONNEL, FOUND
GUILTY OF SABOTAGE, THEFT,
OR IN ANY OTHER WAY IMPEDING
THE WAR EFFORT AND SUB-
SEQUENTLY SHOT, WILL BE
HUNG FROM THIS GIBBET AS
A WARNING TO ALL OTHERS.

Warby with pet mongrel nestling inside one of his unique thigh-length sheepskin boots which he used on high altitude flights. (*Conyers Rutter*)

With invasion expected almost daily and with supplies of all kinds dwindling fast, strict orders were necessary. (*Conyers Rutter*)

Bright sunshine lends an added dignity to the bombed streets and squares of Valetta through which Christina is walking   And on her way to the shops she meets an office

CHRISTINA—OF GEORGE CROSS ISLAND

When Christina first came to Malta, she was th
dancer of a cabaret act entertaining troops i
Middle East. Then, anxious to help to avenge the
she took up important work with Fighter Control.
Christina, whom you see here enjoying a day'
earned holiday, has become one of the personalities of

Maltese newspaper feature on Christina. (*Maltese War Museum Association, Malta*)

Salvaging cargo from the Breconshire which had run the gauntlet to Malta.
(*Imperial War Museum*)

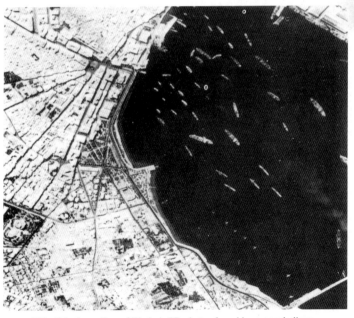

Tripoli harbour. One of Warby's PR photos from his personal album.

Squadron Leader Warburton and the Russian Lt-Colonel Solodovnik. When the Russian officer went to visit war-torn Malta, it was fitting that he be shown round by Malta's first pilot, an excellent publicity enterprise.
(*Imperial War Museum*)

Corporal Norman Shirley, DFM. A brave and sensitive camera mechanic who volunteered to serve as aircrew for Warby as well as anyone he could.
(*Norman Shirley*)

Warby and Christina show off Malta to American Sailors who had gallantly helped to bring in the few surviving ships of the August convoy by serving as ships' gunners. (*Imperial War Museum*)

A 1943 photograph of Warby, taken on the wing of a P38 F5A, and typical of his usual unconventional dress – slippers, cravat, Oxford bags and an Army battleblouse.
(*Imperial War Museum*)

Sergeant Keith Durbidge in PR Spitfire.
(*Keith Durbidge*)

The remains of US P38 F4 from which Warby was catapulted unhurt, La Marsa 6 July 1943. (*Major J Hoover*)

A neatly attired Warby with F/Lt Maloney, RCAF, F/Lt Crompton and Sgt Snowden, RAAF. (*Ken Rogers*)

Air Chief Marshal Sir Charles Portal chats with Warby on a visit to Malta, 1943. (*Imperial War Museum*)

Warby in the uniform of a junior American officer receiving instructions on how to operate a USAAF P38 F4 PR aeroplane (Lightnings in RAF language) prior to flying a sortie for the Americans in Malta. (*Imperial War Museum*)

Warby with almost a crew-cut, fills in a report while the Spit is refuelled. Note the window of oblique camera being unloaded. (*Ken Rogers*)

No 683 Squadron, Luqa, September 1943. Warby with his fair hair is easily distinguishable at centre. AT least two South African Air Force officer's caps can also be seen. (*Ken Rogers*)

become a haven and meeting place for almost the entire RAF when on home leave. The noisy boisterous throng would often end the evenings at an eating place in nearby Shepherds Market. During this leave, Warby managed to track down his old mentor Tich Whiteley and went to stay with him at his Mess. He must have appreciated all that Tich had done to make him what he was. A charming story has come to light from both Paddy Moren and also from Mrs Moss, Tich's daughter. Sadly Tich is no longer alive but his daughter has kindly sent his old papers to the author.

Warby, never a financial genius, had not bothered to check and find out what was happening to the financial arrangements that Tich had arranged for him in September 1940 so that his UK debt there could be gradually paid off. This meant that all the years that Warby had been away, some portion of his pay was being deducted at source and paid into a special 'debt settlement' account. He also learnt that because he had never bothered to take an interest in what was being deducted at source, there was by 1943 a sizeable credit balance in the special account. The rest of the story is best told by Tich Whiteley, in a letter to Paddy Moren:

> When Warby first returned from the Mediterranean, he came to see me at RAF Cranage and stayed overnight ... he was flying a Spitfire. On the Sunday before his departure, he tried to leave me with a sealed envelope addressed to me but not to be opened until after his departure. I demurred and Warby allowed me to open the envelope with him in my bedroom. The fat envelope was full of those white English £5 notes ... All his debts had been paid off and the notes in the envelope were half of the credit balance he had found in his London bank account. He wanted me to have that half!
>
> After some coffee Warby took off to return to the Mediterranean. Later a friend of mine took the envelope and redeposited the money in Warby's bank. Incidentally Warby was impeccable dressed in a new uniform. For many reasons I was proud to have him in the officers' Mess.

A few days afterwards Warby returned to Malta from this leave, bringing to his squadron a nice new Spitfire Mark IX, No EN 338. This Mark was a superior plane to the Spitfire Vs that the unit had previously had. Soon afterwards an event, which was to have a marked effect upon the rest of the life of Adrian Warburton took place. He came into contact with pilots of the American Air Force. The war in NW Africa was going well with the Americans much more in evidence than they had been in the long fought-out see-saw war in the Western Desert which was almost exclusively a British affair: although that too was going splendidly. The remnants of the Afrika Korps were being squeezed into an ever contracting bridgehead. General Montgomery and the Eighth Army had entered Tripoli on 23 January, after an astonishing advance of about 1,000 miles in two months, with the Americans advancing from the West. What remained of the German and Italian armies was packed around Tunis.

The Americans were learning fast the value of PR operations and with their eyes on the obvious next target – an invasion of Europe commencing with Sicily, sent a small detachment of one of their PR units to Malta to learn from Warby and 683 Squadron, how it could best be done. Who better to show them?

These American pilots in their P38F4 modified planes ('Lightnings' to the RAF) were not entirely green. They had worked alongside 682 Squadron (formerly 4 PRU) in Africa and had got on splendidly with Freddy Ball in charge of that squadron. In Malta at first there was a misunderstanding. The Americans seemed to think that they were simply to get familiar with an area which they had not previously overflown. Warby and 683, the 'old hands' to which the 'new boys' were attached, considered that they were there to learn how it really should be done.

An interesting account of their arrival had been provided by an airman J K Waters. He was a M/T driver and happened to be on duty when some of the planes arrived. He writes:

> Three Yank Lightnings landed on Luqa around summer 1943 [actually it was the end of March or early April] I took the pilots to Warby's HQ (hut). He had them out on the tarmac getting back in their aircraft whilst he got into his special PR (pale blue) aircraft.†
> 'Just going for a little flip around to see if these lads are any good' were his remarks. They were to follow him.
>
> On their return after about a ten minute flight, he told me to take the Yanks to the Mess. They started pumping me about Warby, but I turned the tables by saying 'Well, you've seen him fly. What do you think?' The answer I got was 'Jesus Christ man, he led us the dance of our lives; the man's a genius.' You can't have higher praise than that.

Phil Kelley was back again in Malta – the island where he had had so many crashes during his earlier period. He has supplied a very detailed account of the first few weeks of the arrival of the 'Yanks', as Waters calls them:

> The Americans who arrived in the spring of 1943 although not very experienced in the realities of war, didn't want to be told by anyone. Their early photo-recces were poor. For one thing they planned their

---

†Walters refers to a Mosquito which seems unlikely.

operations on a very conservative basis and were landing back with as much as 25% petrol in reserve. The more experienced Spitfire pilots were arriving back with as little as 10 gallons after having made the optimum use from every sortie. Even after the CO of the detachment had 'gone missing' after the very first sortie (Captain Richardson ended up in Sicily) the atmosphere was still strained.

Warby decided to show them. He announced that he would be carrying out one of their next sorties and in one of their aircraft too. Lieutenant Joe Scalpone, who had taken over from Captain Richardson as temporary CO of the visitors, naturally demurred but Warby didn't listen. 'I'm your boss here. You are under my orders'. He also threatened Scalpone that he would fly across to Africa and report him to Elliott Roosevelt, whom he had met and got on with and who was the CO of all US PR units in Africa. Elliott was also the son of the popular President and a person with considerable political 'clout'!

Joe Scalpone gave way. He gave Warby some instruction on how to start and operate his single-seat (twin-engined) plane. As can also be seen, Warby is dressed in the uniform of a junior American officer!

Warby took off and carried out an excellent PR flight. Not content with this, he mounted all the photos he had taken on a huge wall map for all to see as proof of what could be accomplished. The Americans took it well and were impressed and thereafter paid attention to Warby and all that he had to teach them.

Incidentally one of this small detachment was Lieutenant Leon Gray who later became a famous US photo-recce ace pilot.

In no time the Americans took Warby to heart. They would include him in their endless poker games and generally came to regard him as a 'good guy' and a buddy. Warby naturally responded. At heart he was really one of them, never stuffy, never too hidebound by rules and regulations, one who was prepared to be pally with the devoted ground crews and one who got on with the job with the minimum of bullshit. Also he always responded well to approbation.

Mac Brown considers that another turning point in the good relations between the visiting Yanks and 683 Squadron was the decision to go ahead with a joint booze up which had been planned for the evening of the very day when Captain Richardson was lost. The Americans wanted to cancel it but Warby, Mac and the others insisted that they all should have a good party together and so it turned out to be.

Keith Durbidge, when he arrived to be part of 683 Squadron, was a sergeant pilot but his skill and popularity with all soon convinced Warby that he ought to be commissioned. He sent for Sergeant Pilot Durbidge and

asked: 'Keith, have you ever thought about applying for a commission?'
When Durbidge replied: 'Not really', Warby told him to think about it.
Half an hour later he sent for him again: 'Well I hope you have thought
about it as you are seeing the AOC at two o'clock!' In Keith Durbidge's
opinion: 'I couldn't have had a better CO than Warby. He looked after his
men so well and had a great sense of humour.' Keith had been there when
the Americans had arrived in the spring. As he put it:

> The Americans of 3 Recce Group† had a very shaky start at Luqa.
> They arrived one afternoon with about six Lightnings and
> wrecked one immediately by taxiing too fast round Luqa's
> tortuous perimeter track. The flight commander, and presumably
> Warby also, offered to give them the low-down on operations over
> Sicily and Italy but the offer was declined – they had been given
> a briefing back at base. Their CO, Captain Richardson, crash-
> landed his Lightning on a strip in southern Sicily on the first sortie
> next day. This resulted in a mass desire on the part of the
> remainder to be briefed, as offered.

Elliott Roosevelt, son of Franklin D Roosevelt, although a navigator
rather than a pilot, had become the 'boss man' of all PR work in US and
British NW Africa. Doubtless his father's eminence helped. He seems to
have been a most helpful and unconventional character. When in Egypt and
first trying their hand at PR work, the Americans used briefly, their 4-
engined high flying bomber – the Flying Fortress – B17. Although this was
soon replaced by the much faster twin-engined P38 Lightnings, Elliott had
managed to retain one of the huge bombers as a personal transport. In this,
he brought much needed supplies official and unofficial, to the units with
which he was concerned. It is not known when his friendship with Warby
commenced, but it is known that Elliott Roosevelt thought the world of
Warby: a sentiment he never lost.

Ken Rogers recalls that it was Roosevelt who gave Warby the jeep
which Warby subsequently used in Malta. He had not seen one before and
was admiring it. Roosevelt simply said, 'There you are, son, it's all yours.'
That too had probably arrived in Elliott's B17 transport.

Phil Kelley recalls that in that B17, Roosevelt brought other much
needed extras to Malta: not just welcome food and bottles of the right
'stuff' but even items like refrigerators: very welcome during the hot
summer but quite unknown in wartime Malta.

Warby, before making a first sortie in one of the visitors' P38F4s,
sensibly carried out a couple of 'circuit and bumps' spells of local flying.
In his log book he records, underlined, 'Very nice.' The reason is not hard

†An American group was the equivalent of a RAF wing.

to deduce. All his life Warby never seems to have grasped that to take off a twin-engined aircraft, or even to a lesser degree a single-engined one, it is necessary to counter the sideways pull that the propeller gives due to engine torque. In a conventional twin-engined plane the pull is severe because both engines would be exerting the same sideways pull. But the Lockhead P38 was designed with engines pulling in different directions. It had one left-hand prop and one right-hand. The result was negative engine torque. Warby's brutal method of opening up fully on both engines did not, on this plane, cause any sideways pull.

When delivering EN338 from the UK to Malta, Warby had called in at Algiers and there are a number of occasions when he flew there during the closing stages of the Allies' campaign to capture Tunis and so finally wrap up the entire African campaign. It seems likely therefore that he was again enjoying the company of the select 'inner circle' who were planning the next major move. It also seems likely that it was during these calls at Algiers that his friendship with Elliott Roosevelt was ripening.

Major reorganisations were taking place. Tedder, now Sir Arthur and Air Chief Marshal, was reorganising the entire Allied Air Forces, both British and US in Africa. After February 1943 all the British and American air forces (including South African and Australian etc), came under his command whether operating from the Egyptian or Gibraltar side of the conflict. In virtually every case where a Britisher was placed in command of an air force unit, there would be an American deputy and vice versa. It was excellent co-operation and it worked like a charm. For all Allied PR work, Colonel Elliott Roosevelt was put in charge of what was called the Mediterranean Allied Photo Recce Wing (MAPRW) and he had a British deputy, Wing Commander Eric Fuller. This PR Wing was made a part of (now) Air Marshal Sir Hugh Pughe Lloyd's NorthWest African Coastal Airforces. That appointment would have further helped Warby sit in on the war councils which were planning the next move.

By April, Warby was playing a personal key role in those invasion plans. The Allies first planned to assault Pantellaria, the island which was so awkwardly placed, from their point of view, between Tunisia and Sicily which initially was their primary major objective in Europe. Pantellaria had high cliffs and an airfield, and was known to be a well defended rocky outpost with underground hangars for its fighter planes. It bristled with coastal and AA guns, much as Malta did.

There was a pressing need to get close-up pictures not just of every inch of its shoreline so that the best landing beaches could be selected but also of coastal guns, embedded as they were in the cliff face.

The task was assigned to 683 Squadron, and as could be imagined, Warby decided that he alone would carry out this demanding task. It was deemed so dangerous for a PR plane to fly at point blank range along the coast of this highly defended stronghold where also Italian fighters were based that, *for once*, it was decided to provide Warby with a fighter escort in case the Italian pilots decided to dispute his presence.

Warby, as usual, brought back pictures which surpassed all expectations. He had flown in so low and so close that to quote from one of his pilots Keith Durbidge: 'Warby was the only pilot I ever heard of who was fired on by AA guns from above.' In all Warby made at least four of these dangerous wave top flights under fire.

In the event, Pantellaria surrendered in June before the troops off shore in their invasion barges had even landed. It was softened up by being pounded mercilessly by both British and American planes (much as Malta had been pounded). This bombardment had such a deadly effect upon the morale of the defenders that the garrison surrendered at the first sight of the invading force. It is thought to be the first place to have surrendered, without a shot being fired, as a result of a pre-invasion warm-up aerial bombardment. This undoubtably saved many lives. The part played by Warby in disclosing so clearly every defence position, every gun etc was freely acknowledged by the Americans in particular. In all probability the brunt of the invading force would have been Americans.

With Pantellaria unexpectedly captured without a shot being fired, the Allies then turned their attention to the much more formidable task of invading Sicily. Again a vital pre-requisite was to obtain close-up pictures of the coastline so that landing beaches could be selected and defence posts and hostile guns clearly identified. Two Army intelligence officers were sent to Malta to work with 683 Squadron which had been given the demanding task of getting the required close-up pictures.

Major Fuglesang and Captain Elsworthy's arrival caused many speculations but it is likely that only Warby really knew exactly what their purpose was. Although it hardly endeared him to the other experienced and skilled pilots, Warby, as usual, decided that as before with Pantellaria he would carry out all the Sicilian beach photographs himself. He liked, as one of his pilots writes: 'To take the hairy ones'. This left the others with the more routine mundane tasks. The taking of low level obliques had become one of Warby's specialities and here again he provided the armies with all or more than they could hope for. For this outstanding work he received a personal letter of thanks from General Alexander himself†, C-in-C Middle East, and also one from Air Marshal 'Mary' Coningham. Hardly surprisingly, in July, more or less on his six monthly schedule, Wing Commander Adrian Warburton was awarded a bar to his DSO. Both Corporal Ken Rogers and Cyril Wood remark that he really appreciated these awards but whether he actually set out to gain them at six monthly intervals,

†See Appendix 1.

as some claim, seems doubtful. Openly he was casual about such honours but those who knew him best affirm that they were important to his ego. They inspired him to further effort. Mac Brown also mentions that Warby had aspirations of equalling or excelling, before the war was over, his father in rank. By 1942 they were level: Commander RN and Wing Commander.

To cover all the beaches around Sicily required a number of extremely dangerous missions. Sicily was still the base for a large number of the formidable Me109F fighters and a few of the even more deadly Focke Wulf (FW) 190 fighters had entered the fray.

For these low level missions, Warby was once again provided with a Spitfire fighter escort from Ta Kali. This was supplied by a senior pilot of 1435 Squadron, Hugh O'Neill, the CO of the squadron. He had first met Warby in Egypt when Warby had been a part of 2 PRU. Hugh had shared a flat with Macphail (which must have been quite an experience!). On these Special Tasks, Hugh in a well armed Spit flew alongside as Warby photographed the Sicilian beaches from a height of only 200 feet right under the noses of the enemy's many coastal defence guns. The pair were only a few miles from fighter airfields such as Gela containing scores of enemy fighters. In his own words:

We covered the area from Gela round to Syracuse on 27 and 28 May also 3 and 19 June. I flew about three spans out on the seaward side while he flew along with his camera whirring away. A fair amount of light flak splashed around us as we went along but this did not deter Warby who smoked a large cigar throughout.

Hugh O'Neill adds that on 3 June, he could not resist attacking an inshore schooner, although it was a diversion that took his eyes off Warby for a short while. The attack brought down the ship's rigging. Warby also noted the incident in his log book and had added '!!!!' but whether the exclamation marks were caused by the AA fire which splashed around them or Hugh O'Neill's temporary desertion of his 'charge' is not known. Hugh had difficulty getting back to Malta as his engine was running roughly. It was found to be because he had flown through a cloud of flies which had coated, and thereby unbalanced the propeller: an unusual hazard.

The cigar which Hugh O' Neill noticed undoubtedly had come from the Americans. As one US Admin Officer of 3 Recce Group wrote:

My first job was to get billets for the officers and enlisted men. The enlisted men were billeted in a large house and the cooks went to work and right away cooked up a good GI meal. Our supplies were flown in every ten days from Africa. The officers were quartered in a hotel. We travelled to and from the airdrome in an automobile and a truck. The biggest problem was securing gasoline but we didn't do badly. Our photo-lab was set up in tents on the edge of the field.

Much appreciation should go to Wing Commander Warburton who was the head of the British photo reconnaissance on the island. He and his men gave valuable information, gained from long experience, to our pilots. Everything was done to make our work and stay on Malta enjoyable.

I might add that just before I left Africa for Malta, I was fortunate enough to secure two boxes of fresh cigars and four cartons of cigarettes which came in mighty handy when I went to visit the British officials for requests – you know it's always easier to talk things over while smoking a good cigar.

Although Warby now often flew one of the Lightnings of the US detachment (they went back in June), he most often flew one of the Spitfire IX's which had arrived to replace the older Spitfire V's. An airman, Jim Somerville, who for the most part serviced at Ta Kali the Spitfires of 249 Squadron would, from time to time, also service planes at Luqa. He comments that the smoothed and carefully painted Spitfires of 683 Squadron (every effort had been made to increase their speed by polish) made our 249 Squadron Spitfires look like Tin Lizzies against a Rolls Royce. Jim was a fitter and comments upon the unorthodox chit-chat that took place between an officer like Warby and a fitter:

> Life on Malta was different. Everyone knew everyone else, especially on small Ta Kali … whether pilot, cook, fitter, armourer etc we all had a job to do and it was nothing unusual to find an airman lending a hand at work he was never trained for. It was all very informal, no 'bull-shit', no saluting, just 'make those aircraft fit to take their place in the line'. As 249 Squadron's record proved, it was a system which worked.†

Jim Sommerville had also worked for a time at Hal Far, the FAA airfield. The cameraderie and co-operation extended to all who flew whether RAF or Fleet Air Arm flyers. The Army, especially after Major General Beak VC DSO arrived as GOC, also pitched in and their men

†Some idea of how well the Malta fighter boys performed after May 1942 is given by the fact that Spitfire pilots operating from Malta produced two of the three Canadian top scorers of the war: Beurling and McElroy: the top American Spitfire scorer in the RAF, Weaver: the top Rhodesian, Plagis: the two top Australians, Yarra and Brennan: the top scoring Malayian, Schade and the second highest New Zealand Spitfire scorer, Hesselyn. These alone accounted for over 120 enemy destroyed with 'Screwball' Beurling leading the way with 26 confirmed kills.

could be seen to be servicing planes at times. The General at once fitted in with Malta's unconventional practical modus operandi.

There are many stories about Warby during the time he was CO of 683 Squadron. Sergeant Conyers 'Con' Rutter, recalls an occasion when Shem, the squadron's mongrel dog, had taken a bite at a bare-footed Maltese. Shem was a great favourite with Warby and apparently enjoyed one of his woolly flying boots as a snug home. The Maltese man wasn't such a dog lover especially after having been nipped. He had picked up a large stone and was about to throw it at the mongrel. Warby had seen the incident and had hastily come out of his office. With his much loved Luger pointing straight at the Maltese, he challenged: 'Go on, throw that stone!'

Warby at that time shared a room with an engineer officer 'Wee' 'Titch' Iddon. Although now living in Mess, Warby kept erratic hours. 'Wee' Iddon liked his sleep: and liked it not to be disturbed by Warby's comings in the middle of the night. One night, when Warby wasn't there by well past midnight, Iddon decided to lock the door in the hope that he would not be disturbed. His hopes of a peaceful night were shattered, literally, when Warby arriving home and finding the door locked, produced his revolver and shot away the locks !

Con Rutter also tells a story which reveals a very different side to Warby. The squadron didn't have enough cockpit mirrors to equip all the Spitfires. Yet these could be life-savers as they helped to tell when a fighter was roaring up from behind. One day Rutter spotted Warby about to depart in a spare aircraft which didn't have a mirror. He hastily shipped one from another plane and dashed across to give it to Warby so that he could fit it in place. Warby would have none of it: 'Give it to some less experienced bod. I don't really need it, and he might.' Rutter confirms that the de-armed Spitfires could out-run almost everything and that all armour plate had also been removed in the interest of speed and weight saving (allowing the aircraft to climb to greater height) except for just one piece immediately behind the pilot.

Rutter had been in Malta since 1941 but as he writes: 'You never really belonged to anybody in Malta.' However he, like so many other good types, seems to have fastened himself firmly to Warby's 683 Squadron. He remembers having a commissioning interview with Warby. It seems to have been carried out with reasonable normality. Was Warby changing towards conventionality?

Con Rutter confirms that Warby was always quietly spoken but that he didn't suffer fools gladly. One had to be on the look out 'When his cold blue eyes cut into you, it was almost a terrifying sight.'

The picture which emerges is that the more lowly your rank, the more likely you were able to see only the very best side of Warby: and that there was no equal to that best side. However as Warby matured with responsibility, he opened up to all and sundry, not just to his airmen pals.

A person who, although an officer, did become a close friend of Warburton's was the station adjutant at Luqa. He was a good deal older than Warby, who on occasions, took his problems to him. For instance, the adjutant, Flight Lieutenant Syd Collins, knew that Warby was married without knowing the details. He also knew that he had left the UK in debt and that, thanks to Tich Whiteley, arrangements were being made to settle the deficiency. In a way, Warby always seemed to be looking for a kind of father figure and invariably found one.

Syd Collins comments specifically upon Warburton's good sense of humour. He recalls an occasion when Warby was the guest of honour at a fairly high-ranking dinner and at which Warby turned up in *flying boots*. He also writes of another occasion:

> Jerry put on a fairly heavy raid … this started in the middle of our party. The date was 20 October which happens to be my birthday. Warby had had one or two [drinks] and the guns were making quite a noise when he suddenly goes to the phone and asks to speak to the fellow in charge of the guns. He eventually gets through to the brigadier and said: 'Would you please stop your guns from making such a bloody awful noise as they are interfering with my drinking'.

Collins also thinks that Warby's flat was demolished and recalls him saying in exactly the same words as Cyril Wood; 'The bastards blew us out of bed.'

Syd Collins (and he was in a position to know) maintains that AOC Park thought the world of Warby but others infer that, perhaps later, Park didn't quite know how to handle him. It is easy to imagine, that no matter how much one admired his operational record, there must have been times when his outbursts of outlandish behaviour hardly matched his rank and responsibility. Collins remarks upon his youthful impetuosity but still found him:

> …a most remarkable person and certainly the bravest pilot I met during my service career … yet he was without conceit about what he did. That he should lose his life so near the end of such a career was tragic. The country could do with young men like Wing Commander Adrian Warburton today.

Warby's concern for the fate of other pilots is well illustrated by the account that Sergeant Pilot Tardif gives. When he arrived in Malta a young Spitfire pilot assigned to Warby's squadron, on one of his first patrols he was detailed to take photographs of targets in Southern Italy at 22,000 feet or higher. As he ran into clouds at those levels, he descended to 16,000 feet where the photographs could be taken, popping in and out of clouds while dodging AA fire. Later that evening he learnt that the two photographic interpreters were delighted to have such clear prints; as they would have been due to having been taken from 'closer up'.

Next morning the young pilot was an early riser but was surprised to find that Warby was also up and about. Sergeant Tardif was quietly hoping for praise from his CO. To his surprise, Warby asked: 'How old are you?' '23, sir.' To this Warby enquired 'Don't you think you are a bit young to die?'

Tardif said that he didn't understand what he was talking about.

'When I want you to fly at 16,000 feet over a target, I'll tell you.' He then went on to tell Tardiff that he didn't want to spend his time writing letters to his wife advising her that she was a widow. As Tardiff explains: 'I was completely deflated.' A minute or so later, the office door opened and Warby put his face round: 'I forgot to tell they were damned good photographs, Mick, thank you very much.'

The absurdity is that Warby himself had only just turned 25 and that almost daily for the past three years he had been sticking out his neck in a far more obvious fashion.

Just before Warby left Malta for the last time (officially at any rate), there was the unfortunate accident which cost Sergeant Lewis his life. He was a young New Zealand pilot on almost his last trip. He had a young wife as well. His Spitfire collided with a Baltimore in the circuit. Warby knew that one of 'Skip' Lewis's friends was a flight sergeant pilot, 'Tet' Tetley. By the time of the accident, 'Tet' had been posted to an airfield in Tunisia. As Tet explains it: 'Warby knew of our friendship and took it upon himself to make the trip to La Marsa (Tunis) to tell me about the tragedy which he himself also felt deeply since 'Skip' was one of his pilots.' Curiously in his log book, Warby only recorded the death of 'Sergeant Lewis'. There was no mention of the loss of the Baltimore crew although they were almost certain to have been members of his (by then) old 69 Squadron. In all it would seem that the list in his log book is of only the bare minimum names of those whom Warby knew before they were killed alongside him while operating. In all he must have known of 50 or so 'lost comrades'.

Sergeant 'Tet' Tetley was impressed by Warby's habit of treating sergeants just the same as officers. 'He treated me as an equal and was the kind of person one would pick as a leader.'

John Agius, tells the story about Warby which came to him through office gossip:

> On one of Warburton's reconnaissance expeditions in a PR Spitfire, he was shot at by AA over Sicily. Naturally Warburton was very annoyed seeing he could do nothing about it. So the moment he landed in Malta, he asked for an armed Spitfire and went back to Sicily, swooped down on the gun site and gave them all he had. He was still not satisfied and went back once more, this time with his

PR Spitfire to show what he had achieved on his second expedition.

Another young pilot of 683 Squadron at that time, Bill Carr, came into Warby's life when delivering a brand new Mark XI PR blue Spitfire to 683 Squadron at Luqa. The flights from the UK to Gibraltar, and then via Fez and Algiers, to Malta were by far the longest and most exacting he had made. He felt he deserved a pat on the back but all attention was riveted on the beautiful new Spitfire he had brought.

Next morning he bummed a ride to Luqa and pumped the intelligence officer about the squadron. Earlier he had his hopes dashed when advised by the adjutant that 'he doubted he would be staying long.' He writes:

> The intelligence officer advised that if I wanted to see the CO about staying with 683, I had better go down to dispersal where I would most likely find him 'shooting the breeze with the "erks" (airmen).' I did so and in revetment shack, found a person without rank badges stretched out on a table surrounded by airmen drinking tea. This was the CO. He asked me about the Spit and why I had come to the airfield that day when I could have stayed in the sack.

Bill Carr doesn't remember what answers he gave but the strange officer, to the amusement of the groundcrew, simply said: 'You can stay.' As Bill Carr also writes:

> I later discovered that all that I had heard about this fabulous character was true. Wing Commander Warburton with all his medals was already a legend. 683 was Warby's squadron and everyone was there only because he accepted them. His ground crew worshipped him. Individuals who didn't impress him, and there was many, were sent packing. I can recall that this practice, and others such as Warby's disdain for rank badges, spit and polish, ID Cards and 'dog tags', on occasion greatly annoyed the RAF Station Commander, Group Captain Willy Merton … The poor man try as he might, couldn't do much about it. Warby was far too valuable a 'One-man Air Force' to be disciplined in the normal way for such prosaic violations. Air Vice-Marshal Park too had his troubles with Wing Commander Warburton, not the least of which was Warby's habit of taking off into the blue without even bothering to tell people where he was going.
>
> Cairo, for example, had its attractions for him and on one solo R and R flight in a borrowed Mark IX Spitfire, Warby was attacked by a group of Me109's. He shot down two of them but neglected to report the incident until five days later when he returned from Cairo and was asked to explain the bullet holes in

the rear of the borrowed plane.

The ladies saw Warby as a charming handsome man and were universally attracted to him. His obvious unique talent in the air against the enemy seems to add to his success in dealing with this problem. He was greatly envied by us, his young pilots, and not just in the air.

On one occasion Warby's father, a salty naval commander, visited his Air Force son in the Sliema Mess. I remember that he, too, wore the ribbons of the DSO and other decorations. On this occasion it was interesting to see that the Senior Service representative was not only a great story teller but could also handle his grog better than most. The evening ended with the famous son and his father happily weaving their way out of the Mess arm in arm, and arguing simultaneously about who had drunk too much to drive the vehicle.

The build-up for the invasion of Southern Europe via Sicily gathered pace. The whole atmosphere in Malta was changing. Air raids were rare and of little consequence. The emphasis was on the build up and construction of the existing and additional airfields so that the large force of fighter planes required to protect the invading troops could be based there. Safi strip, for long just the graveyard for burnt and battered planes, was brought back to life and provision made for three Spitfire squadrons to be based there. A similar graveyard strip at Qrendi was also turned into a similar sized operational fighter base. The Americans, with their vast construction machines and thirst for action, hastily constructed an airfield on Gozo, capable of housing more Spitfire squadrons. Including 683, there were soon to be seven Spitfire squadrons at Luqa alone with another four at Haifa and five at Ta Kali. By the time that Operation Husky, the code name for the invasion of Sicily, was ready for launching in July, Malta, once defended only by three obsolete biplanes, was home base for 22 Spitfire squadrons, numbering between 400–500 of these excellent planes, as well as seven other squadrons including Mosquitos and Beaufighters. The Americans chipped in with three more squadrons of fighters at Pantellaria as well as providing the pilots for the three Spitfire squadrons based in Gozo.

Warby was flying across to North Africa fairly frequently: for conferences no doubt. His flights took him to Algiers, to La Marsa, an airfield just outside Tunis, to Tripoli, to Constantine. He was becoming a well known figure in that part of the world too. He met the American General Spaatz. He had become quite close to Elliott Roosevelt who had the ear of General Eisenhower. His old mentor, Hugh Pughe Lloyd now knighted, may have helped to introduce him to the other Allied top brass. Warby had never been shy of venting his opinions in the highest of places. The Allied chiefs could scent victory in the air and were not averse to hearing from someone who knew the area to be invaded better than anyone else and who was always prepared both to risk his neck and to air his views for the common cause. Warby in neat uniform and with hair cut even looked the part.

For the American 4 July festivities being held at La Marsa near Tunis which by then had become an important Air HQ for both British and American Air Forces, Warby was invited over from Malta, he flew himself there in Spitfire MB774. Freddie Ball CO of 682, the NW African PR Spitfire squadron – and one who had earlier established such splendid rapport between the RAF and the American Air Forces, was likewise invited. Doubtless Elliot also attended and that a splendid party was enjoyed by all.

For the return on 6 July, Warby's Spitfire seems to have been unserviceable and he was lent a rather clapped out P38 PR machine that was being used more as a personal plane than an operational one. Thanks to having several first hand accounts of what followed, the events can be accurately described. First Captain Howard Vestal of USAF, one of the US pilots who had enjoyed the earlier spell in Malta with 683:

> I was operations officer of 5 Squadron and it was I who let Warby 'borrow' the plane. It was a stripped war-weary kind that we just flew for fun ... I told him, with emphasis that, since this was an old plane, he should be sure to hold the brakes on until he made sure the turbo supercharger had cut-in and stabilized, because one would run away sometimes on take-off and could flip you over with dire consequences. Warby nodded agreement but I could tell he was eager to go. When he got towards the end of the strip, he pushed everything to the firewall as he was turning onto the strip and away he went. A few hundred feet down the strip, sure enough, the left engine supercharger ran away and the plane started veering right, ran off the strip and started bouncing on the rough ground. Apparently he had put the gear lever to the up position (which you could do with the weight still on the wheels and when you became airborne, the gear would retract automatically), so that one of the big bounces took the plane off the ground enough for the gear to collapse. The plane started skidding along the ground.
>
> By then I was jumping into my Jeep, along with a couple of pilots one of whom was Johnny Hoover, I think, and we started chasing out after the plane. When we got there there was calm and chaos. The plane was burning with Warby sitting on the end of the wing smoking a cigarette calm as could be. The chaos was caused by the fact that near the end of its uncontrolled run, the plane on fire had gone through a flock of sheep shepherded by a lone Arab. Some sheep had their wool on fire and the Arab was absolutely

berserk. It was an alarming but hilarious event. We were concerned about Warby until we saw he was unhurt and unperturbed.

Wing Commander Freddy Ball, the CO of 682 Squadron, also witnessed the 'prang'. His account is similar. Freddy Ball describes the strip at La Marsa as little more than a dried up salt lake. It was, no doubt, one that had been hastily levelled in the stress of war. Freddy also dashed up to see what was left of Warby. By then, he had left the plane and was sitting on a nearby ant-hill smoking a cigarette as if nothing had happened. Meanwhile a huge pall of black smoke from the plane was spiralling upwards. Upon recognizing Freddy Ball, Warby's first reaction was to try to borrow from him, one of 682 Squadron's Spitfires as he was anxious to get back to Malta! Not unnaturally, Freddy, having seen what he had done to the Lightning, a plane which almost uniquely *didn't* normally swing on take-off, was quite definite in his refusal.

Major Johnny Hoover, one of the very best of the US recce pilots and one who had hit it off well with Freddy Ball, also witnessed the abortive take-off. Somehow, Warby almost as soon as they had rushed up in their jeep had persuaded Howard and Johnny to lend him another Lightning. While efforts were being made to quench the flames, Warby, meanwhile had taken off and was on his way back to Malta in the other P38. When, as ever, a crowd appeared alongside the burning plane, anxious enquiries were being made:

'What happened to the pilot ?'someone asked Johnny in an awed voice, fearing the worst. 'Did he get out?' 'Where have they taken him?'

Johnny Hoover pointed to a fast disappearing speck in the sky. 'That's him up there!'

Warby escaped injury because he was still ignoring the advice that Ken Rogers and Jack Meadows had so often given him. He had not strapped himself in and, when the Lightning crashed down on the strip, its wheels having automatically retracted, he was thrown clear from his seat. Apparently, he had not bothered at that stage of the flight (and the heat of North Africa in July) to close the cockpit hood. He was simply jerked clear and out of the aircraft completely unhurt. Being Warby, he was also completely unshaken. Its an old maxim among flyers that if you have a crash and survive unhurt, it is desirable to get into the air again quickly before you start to dwell about what might have happened but few could have ever got themselves airborne before even the fire of the crash had been put out.

Warby returned to La Marsa in the Lightning the same day and on the following one picked up his Spitfire and flew it back to Malta on the 7th.

Three days later the invasion of Sicily was launched and Warby, who had played such a leading part in its preparation, recorded the event in bold capitals across his log book. At the same time he has recorded his total score of enemy aircraft as: '9 confirmed, 1 probable and 2 damaged.' Elsewhere on the open page he registered his '379th Operational trip and over 1,300 hours of operational flying.' It was almost as if he sensed that he was coming to the end of his time and wanted to record his feats.

On the very day of the invasion, Warby had been briefed to accompany the landings and to record with his cameras their initial progress. It was regarded as a highly dangerous mission at a time when the sky would be filled with enemy planes and AA barrages. Warby's Spitfire would be unarmed, as usual. Warby recognized the danger. Phil Kelley, by then one of his flight commanders in 683 Squadron, remembers it well:

> Although at times, labelled 'Mad Warby', he had a highly professional attitude to tasks which were themselves dangerous and demanding. When given the vital assignment to photograph the coastline as the troops were actually going ashore, Warby, knowing all too well how trigger-happy the Americans could be, (they had even shot at him when their Liberators were bombing Tobruk) went to the trouble of sorting out the Americans most likely to be involved and telling them where he would be and what he would be doing. He even took down a photograph of his (unusually coloured) PR Spitfire, so that they would know exactly what he would look like.
>
> In spite of these sensible precautions, almost as soon as he arrived over the beachhead, US Navy gunners from ships off-shore promptly riddled his aircraft with good and accurate shooting. The Warburton luck held. The plane was severely damaged but Warby just managed to get it back to Malta. One aileron was hanging in shreds and there was a hole in one wing which has been described by Cyril Wood, as 'big enough to pass a bucket through'.

This was the occasion, which has several times appeared in print, when, Warby, on arriving back with the plane in tatters (but still, miraculously, just controllable) replied to the flood of questions from his aghast ground crew with: 'You had better check it out. The R/T seems to be U/S.' It was in all probability his closest run with death. Phil Kelley goes on to explain:

> Warby was so hopping mad inside – 'Those bastard Yanks shot me up – ' that straightaway he went off to Ta Kali and persuaded some of his friends there to organize a fighter sweep over Sicily to lure Me 109s up so that he could let off steam by 'having a go at someone'. The fighter squadron commanders were all his friends and they arranged a high powered Sweep with no less than three Flight or Squadron Commanders flying in the same formation. Warby flew as No 2. The ruse was successful and the Messerschmitts responded to

the challenge. The Spitfires were in the hands of perhaps one of the most experienced flights ever to fly together and they ran rings around the opposition. Not until Warby had personally accounted for his '1 Probable and 1 Damaged' did they return home. There was later one Hell of a row about it because it was a serious breach of orders for three flight commanders to fly together in the same formation. Such men of value had to be preserved. In this case it was three plus Warby, 'The most valuable pilot in the RAF', as Tedder is reputed to have called him.

Warby's Log Book, on this occasion, records the unofficial sortie. He identifies his Spitfire – an armed one for once, as 'V-G', obviously some squadron identification and adds: 'Fighter sweep Syracuse, 15,000 feet. Jumped 6 Me 109. 2 of Section shot down.'

One of the several changes which others were noting about Warby as 1943 reached full summer, was that he was becoming far more of a party boy, a heavier drinker and much less a loner. He was also prone to be casting an eye at others as well as his faithful Christina. Promotion and medals were having their effect upon him. He had always been attractive to the ladies. Quite apart from the glamour attached to his exploits his promotions, medals and enhanced salary, his splendid figure and good looks drew them to him like a magnet.

The signs were, however, that Warby was becoming edgy and dog weary but he was not the man to give in. Another growing annoyance was that by sheer weight of numbers, as well as their ability to learn quick, the Americans were bit by bit taking over the tasks which 683 Squadron had earlier carried out so excellently during the past months. This naturally irked the RAF operational pilots who had showed the way and shouldered the extra burden when the going had been much rougher.

Reading between the lines of many correspondents who have written about that period, the general impression is that many in Malta didn't altogether relish the beneficial change which had come about with the lifting of the siege of Malta. Food was still very scarce but the air raids were fast becoming only a memory. Those who had found that they could take all that the Luftwaffe could throw at them and still flourish, were no longer the outstanding persons, who almost as of right, could more or less do as they pleased provided it was helping Malta to stand firm. Now that the daily danger had receded, they no longer stood out. New units were continually pouring in. Malta's Luqa was fast becoming a normal RAF station with rules and regulations to be observed. Saluting, kit inspections, parades were becoming realities. Those who had been at their best when under fire, no longer were prominent. It saddened them.

The photographs of Warby emphasise some of the changes that were taking place during this period. They show a neatly dressed Warby with hair short and trimmed. The famous battered cap was replaced by a new round top. Warby was undoubtably doing his best to change with the times but, as the occasional irresponsible incidents indicate, the effort might have been gnawing at him: that and the frustration at knowing that his 683 was no longer the squadron that symbolised Malta's resistance. His sense of fun still prevailed in other less dramatic ways. When Phil Kelley's DFC came through (on Warby's recommendation), it was at a time when beer was almost as valuable as gold dust. Warby assembled the officers in the Mess to announce and congratulate Phil and solemnly anointed him with a full bottle poured over his head. Likewise when Keith Durbidge's commission came through, Warby introduced him formally into the Mess and bought him a drink. He then informed Keith that since he had been drinking, he (Warby) would be flying his detail instead of him. When Pilot Officer Durbidge accused him of using his rank and called him a cheat, Warby took umbrage so Keith, respectful of his CO, called him, 'Sir cheat' and Warby perked up again. As Keith says: 'He was like that.'

Keith is another who can recall Warby having been caught by marauding 'intruder' Me109's on his return and having to fly tight turns inside the enemy until they were short of fuel. No less than six persons have recalled such incidents to the author.

Before July was out, Warby and the other pilots of 683 were landing their aircraft on captured Sicilian soil. The enemy airfields which Warby had photographed almost ad infinitum for years were by then in Allied hands. Earlier some of the strips they first used in Sicily had been hastily hacked out amidst the vineyards and melon fields.

Keith Durbidge recalls how wonderful it was, when spending a night at such a strip (this one was called Francesca), to put out your hand under the side of the tent on waking up, feel around and grasp a bunch of grapes off the vine or to walk ten yards along the strip and pick up a melon from a pile which had been put aside when bull-dozing the strip. After the monotonous rations of Malta, it was sheer delight. By the time Keith left Malta in August (with a DFM presented to him by the very popular Governor, Lord Gort), he was 'vaguely aware that the Mediterranean theatre was closing down and control was passing to the Americans.' He felt that he had to get back to the UK and Benson, the home of the PRU but 'In many ways, with hindsight, I wish I had stayed [as Warby had requested] because there was nobody like Warby as a CO.'

On 26 July 1943, Warby flew himself direct from Malta to Heliopolis in a Mark V Spitfire No BR 665, a PR version. In his log book he records '5 attempted interceptions' but no claims of damage either way. On that occasion he was away until 4 August and he spent 1-3 August at Haifa, undoubtedly visiting his father. Throughout he was flying BR

665 and returned in this plane direct from Palestine (Lydda) to Malta via Dikalla to refuel.

Time was running out for Warburton in Malta. His unique ability to get his pictures at almost any height and under almost any circumstances, commented upon in his many official citations, was no longer urgently required. He managed quite a few flights to Heliopolis, to Haifa, to La Marsa where he appears to have become friendly with General Spaatz†. He continued to be chased all over the skies by Me109s on many occasions while persistently out-manoeuvrering them: 'No holes,' he records. He also went on fighting again alongside Wing Commander Duncan-Smith in an armed Spitfire 'FX-T'; clearly a sign that he was becoming bored but he recorded no results. He also suffered on a PR flight an engine failure at 29,000 feet near Salerno but managed to get it going again at 6,000 feet but, on the whole, compared with his 'vintage' flying at 200 feet along beaches with everything firing at him, it was relatively routine: almost dull.

Les Colquhoun writes: 'Rumour had it that Warby was angling to get the Photographic Wing – a North African Photo Recce Wing that was being formed to operate under the American led MAPRW (Med Allied PR Wing).' Les remarks that he was 'flipping between Malta and Tunisia quite a lot.' Christina confirms that this was a difficult time for him. Occasional quarrels between them took place although they were followed by reconciliations. Both must have been all but worn out mentally and physically. Both had been in Malta and suffered from the spartan rationing for too long. Christina had never once had a single break and for the best part of two tortuous years at a time when the bombing had been intense, had managed to keep two demanding jobs going simultaneously: the 'Whizz Bangs' and Captain of D Watch in Fighter Ops. Also she must have worried more about her Warby than he had ever worried about his own safety. Those missing six days of November 1942, could scarcely not have left their mark. His new role of an outgoing more boozy, would-be womaniser must have been hard to take by the one who, in all probability, had first enabled him to be at ease with the opposite sex.

Curiously, the story about Sergeant Pilot Tardif 'I don't want to have to write to your widow' is almost contradicted by one which Warrant Officer Cole relates. He was a crew member of another unit at Luqa but one which shared the crewroom with 69 and 683 Squadrons. He recalls:

> One of the NCO lads of 683 came into the crewroom looking decidedly dejected. When he had arrived over the target, there was a welcoming committee of Me109's ... he belted away as fast as he could and came back without his pictures; much to the disgust

†Under the 1943 re-organisation, Major-General Carl Spaatz was CO of all Allied Air Forces (US and RAF) in NW Africa, answerable only to Tedder himself.

of Warby, who told him off and promptly went and took them himself; successfully, too.

Warrant Officer Cole is another who believes that Warby put a Me109 into the sea by out-manoeuvering it at low level. Warrant Officer Cole adds that 'He was the only pilot on the island with the ability to outfly anything the Germans could put up in order to photograph the enemy airfields ... in consequence when the Americans arrived, their task was made that much easier by having the knowledge presented to them.' He also adds: 'If any man was worth a whole squadron, it must surely be Adrian Warburton ... he enjoyed the greatest respect from every flyer with whom he came in contact. *What a man.*'

All on the island knew Wing Commander Adrian Warburton by name and reputation. He was truly 'The uncrowned king of the island' in its bleakest days, or 'King of the Mediterranean' as Air Marshal Hugh Pughe Lloyd had called him.

Another young pilot who came to know this charismatic CO well was Sergeant Bill Gabbutt, yet another to be awarded the DFM. In part this is because, after the Canadian Gold Dust twins had departed, along with a Flight Lieutenant Sharpe, Sergeant Lewis was killed, the big Australian Snowden was sent elsewhere and Les Colquhoun was, at last, given a well deserved break, Sergeant Pilot Bill Gabbutt then became about the most senior pilot in terms of operational experience. In true Warby fashion, Bill used to be invited into the officers' Mess and he recalls how on one occasion he was left chatting to the Group Captain. No questions were asked. For one reason there still was no officers' RAF uniform material in Malta and it was not unusual for newly created officers to still be wearing their rougher sergeants' material. Bill went on quite a few parties with Warby and remembers one which ended up with midnight bathing in the sea, WAAF's were involved too despite Malta's total lack of swimsuits. During the larking about in the water, Warby got a foot in the eye and appeared next morning with a real 'shiner'. Next morning he accused Bill without any wrathful intent. As Bill says:

He was like that: an exceptional man. He took everything in his stride and made a lasting impression on all. He was almost absurdly courageous.

Bill Gabbutt recalls that on one PR sortie he 'did a Warby' in really bad weather and came back with pictures of Taranto taken from 50 feet. Later he flashed by Messina at the same height. He felt rather dashing about this as Messina was an area near where the Me 109's at Calabria were based. A few days later Warby sent for Bill and asked 'What do you think of these pictures –?'

They were all of Calabria airfield taken from about 50 feet as Warby had not just flashed by but had circled around this Me109 stronghold.

Warby allowed Bill to take part in some of the pre-invasion Sicilian beach photography but in his case the orders were for him to fly at 20,000 feet not the 200 feet that he chose. Bill rates Warby as a 'very good CO. He was strong on operational discipline and got rid of any pilot who showed the slightest sign of the twitch.' In contrast to earlier times, Bill always found Warby correctly dressed. He was changing!

As the photographs show, the Warby of late summer 1943 was as smartly dressed and had his hair cropped as closely as any. He is even wearing a tie in some pictures. Responsibility was having its effects. However when the outbursts came, they were as outrageous as any: possibly due to having been suppressed for so long? No group of pilots thought more highly of Adrian Warburton than the American PR pilots. They echoed the thoughts of the ground crews such as Ken Rogers, Cyril Wood, Jim McNeil etc. Of the small group which arrived on detachment in the spring of 1943, the author, thanks largely to the help of Johnny Hoover and Bill Jackson, has been able to get in touch with four of them. All seem to remember their brief association with Warby (as they also called him) as if it were yesterday.

Sandy Arkin writes: 'He was a charismatic character whose modesty cloaked the outstanding flyer and leader of PR pilots that he was.'

Leon Gray, who became a great American hero thanks to his excellent subsequent PR work over Europe, writes:

He was first and foremost a bona fides hero, a chap who knew his trade, exuded confidence and, by his examples, was able to impart that same confidence to others. My professional and sociable experience with him was most enjoyable. His sense of humour was of my liking. Elliott Roosevelt, my boss, his brother Franklin, Warby, Colonel Frank Dunn and I, after cocktails, wine, more wine and dinner, were leaving a bar in Tunis ... as Franklin Roosevelt (Jnr) fell and slipped, face down in the mud. Warby very quietly said: 'Don't turn the bastard over, someone might recognise him'... Our paths met most often on social events! I flew a sortie or two from Malta and I most assuredly recall the briefings from Warby ... It was a sure quick way of learning in a hurry.

In all Leon Gray flew 104 sorties and ended up with a DSC, Silver Star, a DFC with 4 bars (all American, of course), the Air Medal with 22 bars, a British DFC and a French Croix de Guerre with Palms. Bearing in mind that Warby flew over 360 sorties from Malta alone, it is almost impossible to imagine what his tunic would have looked like if he had flown 360 sorties for the US Air Force, let alone his total of approximately 400.

Lieutenant Joseph Terrett writes:

I did not know him well. I remember him while we were in Malta. There was one incident I remember very vividly. A B-24 returning from a mission over Italy was making an emergency landing at La Marsa. They were on two engines (the other two had failed) when we first spotted the plane then on only one before they began a long final approach. The engine died and the plane bellied in about a quarter of a mile before it got to the runway, skidded and came to rest. By the time that several of us from 15 Recce Squadron arrived some of the crew were lifting the pilot out of the airplane. His left leg was severed and hanging on by a tendon. It was a gruesome sight. I was standing beside Warby and turned to him and asked him if he had seen it belly in, since he had not come over with the rest of us. He told me that he had been on the mission, in that plane, to observe the USAAF bombing tactics. I remember how calm, cool and collected he was to have been through that emergency and later several of us remarked upon this.

There is no mention of the flight nor the crash in Warby's log book. Howard Vestal, he who authorised Warby to depart from La Marsa in the clapped-out P38 on 6 July 1943 also recalls:

I have very pleasant memories of Warburton; mostly humorous, though he obviously was a deep and serious person in many ways. He was a live-wire, energetic and fun loving but he had a profound, even sad, side to his personality also … he might have been a bit war weary but I never saw him depressed. He was always ready to fly another sortie or ready for a party.

Even if Wing Commander Warburton had never once flown a successful sortie, the camaraderie he established with the Americans whom he helped to train was obviously nothing but good for Anglo-American relations†. He was a great ambassador for the RAF. Like Winston Churchill himself, his particular style and qualities went down better with our principal ally than with some of his own countrymen. Also like Churchill, his greatest British admirers came from the so-called 'men of the street' and not from the strata around him.

John Hoover was not on the Malta detachment but, being such a close friend of Freddy Ball, he met Warby from time to time at La Marsa and possibly even in Malta, when landing there at a later stage of the war. He writes:

†He often flew their planes wearing the uniform of an American lieutenant-colonel.

My personal opinion of Warby, other than being an outstanding pilot, was that he was a warm person, somewhat reserved for a RAF type and a very caring person. I got the impression that he really cared about people.

Quite apart from the airmen who personally serviced his planes or developed his films, there were others less directly connected with Warburton who shared their view of him. An airman fitter O.M. Howell (he was one of those who billeted in the Poor House among the lepers still living there) recalls that:

'Our maintenance unit (one which principally serviced other planes) was given a party by Wing Commander Warburton before he left. It was held in a large tent and was much appreciated by all fellow airmen.'

Several airmen make the point that Warby's tasks in his unarmed planes were as difficult and dangerous as any of the war and that, unlike other RAF heroes who are renowned for just one or two headline incidents, such as Gibson and his Dam Busters, Warby went out day after day for a period of three years. Many fully expected him to be awarded the VC.

For reasons which are not known, the personal log books of Wing Commander Warburton contain no entries after August 1943, although there is space for more. The squadron records are no great help either. It is known that 683 Squadron rather pushed out of the limelight by the Americans, was assigned the rather mundane task of mapping and photographing the Adriatic and that Warby took at least a small part in this. He did for instance complete a photo-recce of Scutaria and Dubrovnik on 6 September, his last from Malta. Otherwise during September 1943 he may have been flying back and forth between Malta and the various HQ in North Africa possibly looking after his future. He might even have been ill. It would have been completely out of character to have sat idly by and done nothing. He was due leave but he took this in October.

Meanwhile Malta was full of rejoicing. The Italians surrendered to the Allies on 8 September 1943. Christina has written movingly about this event. In her own words:

All Malta went delirious with joy, I couldn't have cared less. I remember that evening so vividly – the church bells ringing out all over the Island, the streets of Valletta festooned with flags and bunting, the crowds surging to and fro, singing happily. But for me it was an empty victory. For the best part of an hour I wandered aimlessly about the streets, brooding. After all that Warby and I had gone through together, this was how I was celebrating the end of the Malta war – miserable and alone. There was only one thing to do – go and get sloshed.

With this in mind I walked along to the 'Monico'. And then suddenly I saw him coming towards me, running down the street, his arms outstretched:

'Chris. I've been looking all over the bloody place for you.'

It was the first time I'd heard Warby swear and I loved it. Right there in the middle of South Street he went down on his knees and pleaded forgiveness. I wept buckets of tears. Passers-by must have thought we were nuts.†

Within a few days the Italian fleet steamed slowly into Malta as part of the agreed armistice. The Germans, of course fought on. They might have been relieved to have got rid of, at best, a luke warm ally; at worst a nuisance.

On 17 September, 683 Squadron paraded in full and had the splendid squadron photo taken with their famous wing commander in his rightful place. The squadron record states: 'October 1943, Wing Commander Warburton left the squadron on posting travelling by air to the UK via North Africa.' Warby had for the last time, officially, left the island of his unusual christening and the island with which he will always be associated. As Ken Rogers so sagely remarks: 'From then on his career seemed to go into reverse.'

---

†This is but an example of her colourful writing. The author has been privileged to read nearly all her autobiography entitled *Stepping Stones to Malta* or *Carve Malta on my Heart*, but has sadly failed to persuade her either to complete it or to allow it to be published in book form. Extracts have appeared in the *Times of Malta*.

WARBURTON COMMANDS A WING

Adrian did not stay long in Africa on his way to the UK as he appears to have been active during much of the next three weeks in England. Although the official records of 683 Squadron refer to Warburton being posted to the UK via North Africa, in fact almost exactly the reverse happened. He spent time in the UK before being posted to La Marsa in North Africa. What of the future for this highly decorated 'star'?

The Americans in particular wanted Warby to photograph the results of their bombing raids, to carry out PR sorties of future landing beaches further north and to continue to 'deliver the goods', in his own unique fashion. They didn't seem to mind in the least that he flew their planes when he felt like it and that he had acquired for his personal use a US Colonel's uniform. On the other hand, the UK PRU hierarchy clearly did not know what to do with Warby. They had things well buttoned up in the air. They now had a large establishment of squadrons, wings, etc. By 1943 they had also their own 'star'. They also now operated their Operational Training Unit through which all new intakes were put and trained. Warby, by contrast, had never officially been given any PR training. Moreover the PR squadrons and wings in the UK were under the command of officers who did not play cards on hangar floors with the airmen and who did not blaze off at random with revolvers.

Now that the Italians had surrendered the Germans had strengthened their forces there to hold the country. The Allies were not to fight their way through to Rome till June 1944, the same time as the Normandy landings. The Italian campaign was vital to the strategy behind the planning for Normandy and La Marsa had become an HQ of the Allied Air Forces in NW Africa. Reorganizations and amalgamations of the British and American Air Forces were still taking place as the battle on the ground moved steadily upwards through Southern Italy. It was decided to establish a British PR Wing, part of a greater Mediterranean Allied (MAPRW) PR Wing. The British PR Wing would be based in North Africa (for the moment) and would comprise Warby's own 683 Squadron, 682 Squadron, now led by Jimmy Morgan, the South African Air Force 60 PR Squadron, which unlike the other two, flew Mosquitoes. The Wing, No 336 PR Wing, would later also exercise operational control, over the ex-Heliopolis 680 Squadron, (formerly Macphail's 2 PRU). Wing Commander Adrian Warburton was appointed the wing's first commanding officer and the unit was to come into being at La Marsa on

1 November or a few days before if it could be so arranged.

This solved all difficulties for the time being. It kept Warby in the area where he was known and respected. It kept him close to Colonel Roosevelt who was in charge of the overall MAPRW and it left Benson to plan, without any Warby interference, the PR work that had to be done in preparation for the forthcoming invasion of Europe which almost everyone now assumed would be bound to take place, sometime during 1944.

His October leave in the UK seems to have had a profound effect upon Warburton. He had achieved more than perhaps even he could have hoped for. He was aged 25 and was about to take charge of three full squadrons. He had moved for months among the Great and High. It seems possible that he was reviewing his life and thinking of becoming more regular in his approach to it. Les Colquhoun and Phil Kelley both speculate upon the change in him: as does also the observant Ken Rogers, his devoted airman. Some think that big Mac Brown, an older man and a more solid type than Warby, had had a beneficial influence upon the one time maverick: Ed Maloney, too. Neither had been ever far away from his side during the early part of his period as CO of 683. Later Harry Smith took over as his friend and assistant: another efficient Aussie type. Whatever was going on inside Warburton's head that October 1943, the curious thing is that from that time onwards, Warby was apt to tell the tale (which Moren, and probably Paddy alone, had first heard in 1940–41), that he had returned to the UK only to find his wife with a naval man. The tale was however a complete fabrication. He had had no contact with his 'Betty of the Bush' since that one meeting in Blackpool during the late summer of 1940. It was only thanks to having been overseas so long that he had managed to dodge having divorce papers served. As Syd Collins confirms, Warby persisted in nominating his father as next of kin while in Malta and the telegrams sent to his parents at the time when he was missing for five days in November 1942 confirms this.

For the rest of his war, Warby was apt to repeat the story about his wife even to persons whom he scarcely knew.

As during his previous leave, Warby also made contact with his former mentor Tich Whiteley. Also, as before, Warby was terminating his leave in the UK by ferrying a Spitfire out to the Med via Gibraltar. This time, by a coincidence, Tich was also on the point of operating a similar flight. In his case, he was ferrying a Beaufighter out to the Far East, landing initially at Gibraltar. Not unnaturally, they arranged their flights to take place on the same day. They would not be flying in company since Tich's Beau would have enough fuel for the safe and easy way to Gib, i.e. over the sea around the coast of Portugal and Spain, whereas Warby would have to take an overland direct route across Spain – theoretically neutral but still pro-German.

The two had met on 23 October and Tich has written about their meeting with the affection that he clearly held for Warby and which Warby warmly reciprocated. The weather on the 24th when they planned to depart from Portreath, was terrible. Also the Met Office was forecasting headwinds that made it seem unlikely that Warby's Spitfire could reach Gibraltar, even by the direct route. Tony Powner was Dispatch Officer and was not prepared to sanction Warby's departure until the weather and winds would make it a safer operation. Warby wasn't having this and Tich also put in a word explaining that Warby was a very experienced pilot and that he should be allowed to act on his own discretion. The flight plan called for a 4-hour flight. The fuel endurance was also exactly four hours: as Tich recalls 'What's wrong with that? asked Warby!' (no reserve of course). Warby's insistence led to 44 Group being phoned and in the end, Warby was allowed to depart 'at his own risk'.

Another difficulty arose about the need to drop the huge overload tank, in order to reduce drag, after it had been emptied. The Group were not happy about such a 'weapon' being dropped over neutral Spain. It might they pointed out even hit and kill someone. It was eventually agreed that Warby could drop this over Spain 'provided he dropped it behind a hedge or something similar': from all of 30,000 feet! Both pilots eventually departed, probably the only two to do so on a day when even the birds were walking.

By the time Tich, with the slower plane and longer route, arrived in Gibraltar 'on a wing and a prayer' with one engine failed and the other giving trouble, the talk at Gib was already about the Spitfire which Warby had delivered earlier with a dead engine having run out of fuel when about 40–60 miles away and having glided the rest of the way. Moreover Warby, apparently never one to dwell overlong about close calls with death, had by the time Tich arrived, already refuelled and was on his way to take up his new appointment at La Marsa.

Much later Tony Powner heard the full story about the flight. The weather had been truly horrible throughout and Warby had few clues as to where he was. When running short of fuel, he drifted down through the clouds and imagining himself to be east of Gibraltar, was heading west awaiting for the towering rock to show up when he spied, through a gap in the clouds a town which he swiftly recognized as Cadiz well *west* of Gib. As he was gliding towards America with no fuel left, he hastily reversed course and, by the skin of his teeth, managed to scrape into that long welcoming Gibraltar runway built out over the sea. The Warby luck and survival instincts were still holding.

One interesting event that occurred at Portreath during 24 October was a conversation which took place between Warby and Tony's navigation officer Jack Sands: presumably they were discussing the route to be taken and the paucity of fuel available for it in the light of the Met forecast of adverse winds. To this relative stranger, Jack, Warby once more produced the fiction that he was unconcerned about the outcome of the flight and his own safety because he had discovered that his wife had left him for another man.

He was on his way to La Marsa for a new challenge and a prestigious appointment: one that was much to his liking. Yet was being almost suicidally mournful about life and inventing a tale to account for it. Could it be that through all the many close shaves with death, the years of inadequate rations and the exceptional number of operations he had flown, he was losing touch with reality?

In *any* circumstances, 390 or more operational trips would have reduced any pilot to a bag of nerves but in Warby's case, a good 95% of these had been carried out from Malta: under fire, under strafing even: always with inadequate rations, horrific living conditions and for the first two years, with the great fear of capture and invasion daily hanging overhead. Malta destroyed some men within weeks. The less strong wanted to cave in at once. Only Warby and the wonderful ground crews – those who found they could take it and never sought the shelters, remained throughout: never forgetting exceptional persons like Christina and the stout civilian population to whom the island's unique George Cross was rightly directed.

In Floriana, there stands a memorial tothe 2,301 aircrew who have no known grave in that theatre of war. Buried in Malta are the bodies of over 400 RAF personnel including 107 pilots but far more were lost in the drink or over enemy territory. Over 300 AA gunners were killed. The statistics are almost never ending. 3,340 air-raids alone. Warby lived through it all: ever in the heat of it and generally, except when flying in the Marylands, operating unarmed planes; forever being chased by the Macchi and Messerschmitt fighters right up to touch-down. The stress was enormous on all personnel. The author admits to being a physical wreck after only six months of such pressure.

Had Warby been asked to do too much? All attempts to persuade him to ease up in operational flights had failed. As Catch 22 so adroitly explains: the last person to know accurately how operationally tired he is, must be the pilot himself.

Warby having hastened to La Marsa got down to the job in all seriousness. He immediately made himself known to 60 SAAF, and rapidly re-established good relations with 682 Squadron.

For a short while these two squadrons were all that comprised 336 Wing. 683, Warby's old squadron, was still in Malta although not being given much to do other than mapping or 'Army demands' over the Adriatic Greek and Yugoslav area. For instance the 683 Squadron operational records states, as far back as 26 August, 'We ceased to do the Naples and Foggia sorties and there was a temporary feeling of disappointment that we were being crowded out by the Yanks ...'

At La Marsa Warby was busy selecting officers, and persuading the good types he had worked with before to join his new wing. Most of those who had been holed up in Malta for years resisted his blandishments to 'come and join me'. They knew of no finer officer but they had girlfriends and families at home whom they hadn't seen for years and had put their names down for repatriation as soon as shipping could be spared.

In much the same manner as Warby had charmed the Americans who had come under his command at Malta (and since), Warby also had the same effect upon the South Africans of 60 SAAF Squadron. In a way this was an even greater accomplishment as not all South Africans felt the same about the war, and the war aims, as did the British and Americans. Their country had not been touched: they had suffered no London Blitz or Pearl Harbour attack, and there was always the Afrikaans British historical friction to overcome.

Although their association with the CO of 336 Wing was about to be cut short, it is quite remarkable how many 60 SAAF Squadron personnel speak and write about Warby in almost identical glowing terms as do the American PR pilots. There is no doubt that 60 SAAF Squadron was more than happy to become part of 336 Wing under Warburton. Once again he was proving to be an excellent ambassador between the RAF and an allied Air Force.

By 26 October Warby was holding inaugural meetings of his senior staff. Usher Brierley was the commanding officer of 60 SAAF. He writes:

> Warburton was called the uncrowned King of Malta by his many admirers. He was a great friend of 60 [SAAF] Squadron and spent much of his spare time in the Mess where he was very popular with both senior and junior officers.

From a junior officer's point of view this is how he appeared to Robin Pittard, also of 60 SAAF:

> I found Warby a quiet and charming, and almost shy, person. He escaped to mufti with no gongs showing before letting his hair down at a party. He was charming to me, a relative 'sprog' of a lieutenant in SAAF uniform.

Robin adds: 'I only met him in the officers' club and more frequently in a night club in Tunis.' The once off-hand loner seems to have almost entirely shed that guise. Charles Barry, another 60 SAAF pilot, tells a story which shows another new side of Warby's character. Charles was giving an American a lift to a Tunisian 'drome near Ariana where 60 SAAF were based. As he came in to land, the Mosquito he was flying, as Charles tells it, unexpectedly:

> fell out of my hands like a brick and I bounced like a lunatic. After I had gained control, I began taxiing to dispersal and noticed a jeep

following. I accelerated. He accelerated. I accelerated. He accelerated by which time the tail was nearly coming up. At dispersal a fair-haired debonair bloke in the jeep pulled up and yelled at me: 'What the hell do you think you are doing taxiing like that?' I was about to tell him to shove off, when something warned me. This little bloke just might be somebody? He was. He was Wing Co Adrian Warburton with DSOs and DFCs galore. He gave me a helluva lashing and said that he would report me to Usher Brierley, the CO. That night I went to the British Consul's home in Carthage for a party and who should be there but Warby. He recognized me and immediately came over in a different frame of mind. Clearly he wasn't going to hold my indiscretion against me.

Warby's notorious take-offs seem to have been unchanged. Another 60 SAAF pilot Peter Daphne recalls hearing descriptions of his take-off at La Marsa: 'Hell, he went down the runway first to one side then to the other practically sideways and then disappeared in a cloud of spray and was airborne and away.' This confirms what others have said about La Marsa being 'a sea of mud'. Peter Daphne remembers Warby visiting his unit, later (in Italy):

I watched him hold court. He was already a living legend and an immensely popular one: fair hair over a pair of animated blue eyes, tunic awry and scarf flapping, down to a pair of flying booted feet that were, I can only imagine, applying full rudder alternatively to both pedals in a nightmarish aerial manoeuvre.

Warby was known to the South Africans even outside 60 SAAF. Ken Hunter who belonged to another unit writes:

'I never met him personally, but of course, I knew of his exploits (and who didn't?).'

Warby was doing well as commander of a wing and in all probability, perked up even more when in early November, his old 683 Squadron flew in to become the third squadron of 336 Wing. 683 had been taken over by the very able Harry Smith and according to Ken Rogers and others, nothing much had changed. Harry appears to have been a first class and popular CO and was carrying on in the Warby tradition. It was a proud and happy unit, delighted to be part of Warby's 336 Wing.

Meanwhile on the 'gong' front, Warby had again kept to his alleged six month schedule. This time it was the Americans who decided to recognise the part which he had played in enabling the Pantellaria and Sicily landings to go smoothly. On Elliott's recommendation, Wing

Commander Adrian Warburton was awarded the US DFC (same nomenclature as the British: Distinguished Flying Cross).

It was a few days after Warby had officially received this that Ken Rogers arrived at La Marsa. It was known that 683 would be based in Italy as soon as the ground was cleared of Germans but that, as a temporary measure, the squadron would join the other components of 336 Wing at La Marsa (or nearby). Ken had been persuaded by Warby to stay on. Jack Meadows, who had a wife in Lancashire, was however staying in Malta with his name on the UK-bound list.

Ken ran into Warby as soon as he arrived. One of the first things Warby did was to toss a box at him. It contained his American DFC, a miniature medal and the ribbon. It was not something for Ken to keep but Warby had always made it clear that his groundcrews had earned part of his medals. Warby told Ken to grab himself a decent billet of La Goullette – the harbour area of Tunis, and that later they would get out together at a party, to celebrate the new gong.

Actually Ken grabbed himself a too decent billet in La Goullette. Almost before he could get settled, it was bagged by some officers. One pilot who knew Warby well during his period as CO of 336 Wing was Norman Jackson-Smith, usually known as 'Jacko Smith'. He shared a room with Warby in the convent where they were billeted. They had camp beds on the verandah. The nuns had (sensibly!) retreated to some other distant part of the building. Jacko too, had been a witness of the La Marsa prang of the Lightning on 6 July. He saw Warby step out laughing and asking for another aircraft.

Jacko had also been stationed at Thorney Island when 22 Squadron had been there early in 1940 but had not then got to know young Pilot Officer Warburton. However their paths had continued to cross. In September 1943, just before Warby left Malta, Jacko had delivered a Mosquito to Malta for 60 SAAF and the two of them had enjoyed a meal and drinks together in a restaurant or pub in Sliema. By October 1943 Jacko was a pilot of 682 Squadron at La Marsa. Jackson-Smith sums up Warby neatly:

'He was not a brilliant pilot but would fly anywhere when asked.
He had a wild streak in him but was also fearless.'

Les Colquhoun, now a flight commander with 682 Squadron, based at El Aouina, near La Marsa, also knew Jacko Smith quite well and reports on some frightful 'dos' that they had together. Once in Italy, Jacko, according to Les, managed to put out the lights of San Severo from their bedroom window. He was aiming at the bell of the church opposite but instead put his bullet into an insulator of the electricity pylon. Judged by such incidents, the idea of Jacko Smith referring to Warby as being 'wild' takes on another dimension, Jacko now pursues a much more peaceful mode of life. He is a Jesuit friar!

It would seem that Warby, on the same day as when he had earlier bumped into Ken Rogers, wanted company that evening but for a number of reasons, neither Jacko Smith, Charles Barry nor Usher Brierly were in the mood, or in the position, to be with him. If they had perhaps the events of that disastrous 26 November 1943 might have been different.

A WAAF officer, Section Officer Hazel Furney (now Mrs Scott), recalls seeing Warby that evening. She was at a party at the house of the British Consul where. Warby seems to have spent part of the evening. She recalls that they had a rather splendid dance. With only a handful of WAAF officers to match dozens of male officers, it is easy to imagine the girls were never short of dancing partners. Warby, as we know, was no dancer and, no doubt, left when this activity began.

Charles Barry, another SAAF pilot, recalls that, after meeting Warby for the second time that day in the house of British Consul where: 'We were drinking like animals for a short while,' Warby had asked him, and a friend, Shorty Miller, to accompany him on a jaunt to Tunis. Both declined.

Usher Brierly, CO of 60 SAAF, recalls parting from Warby about 11 o'clock that evening when Warby said that he wanted to visit a friend. The two had been together in the hotel which the officers were using as an officers' club. They had a few drinks. The next morning the Wing Adjutant phoned Usher to find out if Warby was with him. This was normal. Warby spent so much time with his new friends of 60 SAAF that he could usually be found there. Shortly afterwards Usher heard from one of his officers who said that: 'As he was coming back late, he had seen Warby's jeep† upside down on the other side of the road.' Usher then rang the Wing Adjutant but by then Warby had been located in hospital.

Jackson-Smith was with Warby at La Marsa during the early evening of 26 November 1943. The two pilots had gone, in Warby's jeep to the officers club in Tunis:

> I told him that I was flying the next day so would not be staying late. He was drinking with a lot of his friends and I knew it would be a long night so I told him I was going back with some of the boys of my squadron.
>
> The next morning I didn't see Warby in his bed so asked where he was. They told me he had run off the road in his jeep on the way back and that he was badly hurt. He had crawled back on to the

†The vehicle in which the crash took place is generally called a 'Jeep' but others maintain that it was Warby's Humber staff car. Others still refer to a Ford Station Waggon. The point is not of any significance and to avoid confusion, the term 'Jeep' is retained.

centre of the road hoping someone would spot him. He was picked up and taken to the British Hospital at Carthage. I went to see him there. He was badly injured with a broken pelvis and other damage. He was not pleased to see me and told me it would never have happened if I had come back with him. I told him I was very sorry but I don't think he forgave me.

Jackson-Smith adds that, 'We knew him as the King of Malta and heard that he was a very brave man. He was wild sometimes but all his friends loved him.' The fact that he later blamed Jackson-Smith for his accident, could perhaps be construed that he had wanted human company and had rather gone haywire when not finding any? The official 336 Wing records state: 'Wing Commander A. Warburton DSO, DFC was admitted at 23.45 hours to RAF General Hospital suffering from a broken pelvis occasioned in an M I accident in which he was involved this evening.'

The official records later mention that Flight Lieutenant J T Morgan (who had replaced Freddy Ball as CO of 682 Squadron) became acting Wing CO. The wing records also confirm that prior to the jeep accident, Warby had been busy getting the new wing into the shape he desired: to quote again the official records: 'During the period 26 October-25 November, *W/Cdr* Warburton had been constantly in touch with Posting staff N W African Air Forces on the subject of posting in of officers to fill the establishment.'

With regards for how long Warby was in hospital, the wing records, in a note dated 7 December. 'Between 27 November and 7 December, *W/Cdr* Warburton was frequently visited in No 1 General Hospital (which was thought to be in Carthage). He is now much more comfortable and hopes to be out of hospital in February 1944.' Thanks to Usher Brierley (CO 60 SAAF) we know that 'his French popsy visited him several times in hospital. She was so glamorous that in that all male ward, the other patients asked, in jest, that whenever she visited, to have screens placed around their beds as just the sight of her was enough to give them ideas.'

Usher also visited Warby in hospital. The lower part of his body then being encased in plaster. Even then Warby was expressing anxiety about whether or not he would be able to 'perform' properly in future.

Adrian mentions his accident in the letter to his father written from No 2 RAF General Hospital, Algiers. Christina also remembers receiving a letter from him in hospital at Algiers and believes that it was called the 'Maison Carré'. According to Jacko Smith, the move from the hospital in Carthage to the one at Algiers took place at least three weeks after the accident. Adrian begins the undated letter to his father with: 'I have been in bed now for just over seven weeks …' That dates the letter as having been written about mid January 1944. He goes on to write: 'I have another three or four (weeks) to go.' In the letter he maintains that when he rolled his vehicle he was sober. He makes no reference to any party and diplomatically states that he was 'leaving one of his squadrons about 10pm after fixing operations for the next day ...' Hardly likely! Few of us are prepared to admit that accidents are our own faults and, after a serious accident, do the victims really have a clear knowledge of what happened?

The real tragedy is that it did happen and that it happened when it did. The timing was especially unfortunate. About 8 December, the entire wing, which now comprised three squadrons, was moved to San Severo in the Foggia plain of Southern Italy. Warby was thus left badly injured and horribly alone in NW Africa. To make matters worse for him, he was relieved of his command. An acting wing commander, by name Gordon Hughes (sic) was sent out from England to take command of 336 Wing and thus as from 27 December 1943, Wing Commander Warburton had no command of any sort. It must have been a most wretched Christmas time.

An account of how Warby eventually discharged himself from hospital has come from Bill Carr, the young 19 year old Spitfire pilot who is now a retired Canadian General, who writes:

> Growing tired of being bed-ridden, he climbed out of the window, 'borrowed' a vehicle and made his way to the airport. There he located some old friends and had them cut off his cast. He borrowed shorts and a shirt and a Mark IX Spit from a friendly squadron commander and flew to see us of his old squadron, now located in Italy. While he had a parachute he had no maps and the aircraft had no oxygen. In due course he found us, and among other things en route had flown over a weather front that topped out at 25,000 ft. Lesser mortals in the best of health would likely not have survived such a flight, yet, the following day, he visited us at dispersal in San Severo and allowed that he must be getting old because he felt too tired to share a few noggins with us that evening.

> W/Cdr Warburton's charisma was unlike any I had ever experienced. While none of us ever hoped to achieve his level of competence as a pilot or his prowess against the enemy, we sincerely hoped for his approval. And this he was wont to give generously when it was justified. How hard we young pilots tried to achieve this may be reflected in the unique achievements of 683 during his tenure as CO. The ground crew too worked like slaves, indeed, I believe they loved the man.

> Warby was a unique officer in a great many ways. Not only was he a very brave person, braver than any I have ever met, but also he was a warm and sensitive human being who tried to hide these facets in his make-up.

> He had the mark of a great leader. He inspired his colleagues

and his subordinates to achieve goals most would not have thought themselves capable of achieving. His disappearance brought disbelief and sadness and generated such a sense of loss and regret in wartime as to be remembered. We lost a great leader … the RAF and the Allies: one of its very best.

The accomplishments of 683 Squadron when judged by the number of pilots who received decoration is truly remarkable. All three of Warby's 'Canadian troops', Mac Brown, Ed Maloney and Phil Philpotts received the DFC : as did Harry Coldbeck and Harry Smith who took over from Warby as CO and carried on in his tradition. Likewise Phil Kelley received this decoration. Keith Durbidge and Les Colquhoun were recipients of the DFM; as were Bill Gabbutt and Fred Simpson. Earlier, of course, all who flew with Warby as crew members had also received the DFM: Paddy Moren, Frank Bastard, Cpl Norman Shirley and LAC Hadden. Nor is Christina omitted. She rightly earned her British Empire Medal. Warby had the gift to inspire all around him. He had no time for those who shirked or couldn't take the incessant raids. One pilot who showed just a tiny bit of 'twitch' was quietly got rid of within 48 hours. The list of those who excelled alongside him is almost endless. Johnny Walker and Johnny Bloxam were also awarded the DFC but in their case the award was not gained under Warby's leadership. It is difficult to find a pilot of 683 Squadron who has contacted the author, who was *not* decorated for his flying achievements. This is by no means the regular pattern: not even in Malta where heroes abounded. If one outstanding man fell, another miraculously appeared from nowhere. It required leadership and inspiration and Warby provided the first and generated the second in abundance.

Although never under the direct command of Warby, H E W McDonald of 682 Squadron writes:

I met Warby (Spark Plug) at La Marsa. I was on 682 Squadron PRU. He was a man: daring and scary. When it was nice weather, quite often out of the blue he would zoom down and beat us up: full of life and pranks. 683 met up with us at San Severo …

This shows that Warby, although attached to no particular squadron did not confine his activities when CO of 336 Wing to purely ground duties. Usher Brierley does not recall his ever flying their SAAF Mosquitos but it seems out of character for him not to have done so. It was a type of aircraft as highly regarded, and as much loved, as the Spitfire. For instance Elliott Roosevelt once borrowed a couple of Mosquitos for one of his PR (US) squadrons and, in spite of many requests, the RAF never seemed able to get them back! There were reports of Warby flying the type when in Malta (via the MT driver Waters) but there is nothing in his log books to substantiate him having done so.

The evidence points to Warby leaving hospital in late January 1944. One drawback to quitting a hospital in a cast via a bedroom window, is that such an 'escaper' leaves without an official medical discharge. Some seem to remember that he did call in at Malta, seeking a clean bill of health and that there he may have persuaded a friendly Doc to write the necessary certificate. But Christina has no recollection of him having returned: and she would have been a most likely person to have known about such a visit, however brief.

Some correspondents consider that Warby did persuade someone to declare him fit to fly. It was certainly a bizarre situation: Warby flying himself around the Mediterranean in either a borrowed Spitfire or a borrowed US Lightning, trying to persuade an authority that he was fit to fly again! Johnny Bloxam recalls that Warby told him about one particular medical problem which had been worrying him ever since the jeep accident. Warby, conscious of the broken pelvis he had suffered, and that for weeks thereafter 'nothing had worked' was concerned about his ability to 'perform' in a truly masculine way. As Johnny Bloxam nicely put it: 'He spoke to one of the nursing sisters, or it might have been a female doctor, about his worry. The person concerned was quite prepared to dispel his worries ... and did!'

The same story comes from Mac Brown and others. Gil Catton attributes his dispeller as being a lady doctor at Tabarka who paid him a pre-dawn call.

LAST POSTING AND BACK TO THE UK

A very significant part of the letter which Adrian wrote to his father when in hospital in Algiers (see Appendix III) is: 'I can't get any sympathy out of the Air Staff. General opinion seems to be "That will keep the b... quiet for a bit, about time too ..."' This implies that Warby had been making enquiries about his future and had been told that he would not be given any Allied Wing or similar responsible job in the plans being made for the reconquest of Europe commencing with the Normandy landings. This had been his hope. As Colonel Roosevelt wrote to the author:

> In January 1944, General Dwight D Eisenhower, who commanded the victorious Allied Forces in the Mediterranean, was transferred to command the Allied Forces being prepared for the invasion of Europe ... He requested the transfer of Air Chief Marshal Tedder, General Doolittle ... and General Spaatz. He also requested the transfer of Colonel Elliott Roosevelt (myself), Wing Commander Warburton and Colonel Leon Gray.

The idea was for Roosevelt, Warburton and Gray, and others who had served with them on PR work in the Mediterranean area to set up a newly created Allied Reconnaissance Wing to be known as 325 Reconnaissance Wing. It would comprise two RAF Wings and three US Groups.

In brief, Warby was to be Elliott's deputy (keeping to the policy that if an American was in charge than a Britisher would be deputy) of a massive Photo-Recce Wing to prepare for the most momentous event of the war: the invasion of Europe. Warby's many visits to HQ in Algiers, Tripoli, La Marsa and elsewhere paid off handsomely. To Elliott, Eisenhower, Spaatz etc it made excellent sense to transfer the winning team which had done so well prior to the Sicilian invasion up to Europe to do likewise for the Big One.

The long letter from Elliott Roosevelt to the author traces his friendship with Warby back to early 1943 when Elliott visited Malta in connection with establishing an emergency landing field for his PR aircraft. There he met Warby and learned from his fellow officers many stories regarding his remarkable exploits. Roosevelt confirms that Warby had expressed interest (probably later) in becoming Deputy Commander of the 90th US Wing. This appears to have been an earlier Mediterranean Allied PR Wing before the establishment of Tedder's MAPRW. More will be seen later about the part that Elliott played in 1944 when attempting to get Warby back into his normal groove. But Roosevelt also wrote: 'He (Warby) was regarded by us all as probably being the best pilot that ever flew an airplane.' High praise indeed but had Elliott ever seen Warby take-off or land? However it was clear that Elliott Roosevelt's wish to have Warby as his righthand man, and as part of General Eisenhower's team, was not being granted: at least not in any way acceptable to Warby. Although it is possible that the hierarchy at PRU at Benson might not have wished to give the maverick Warburton the kind of prestigious position in their HQ that he held in NW Africa, Warby's self-imposed injuries were reason enough not to do so. Warby's own dramatic discharge from hospital probably didn't help his case. An unfit Warburton clearly could not be given a flying appointment until he was officially medically discharged. And you can be sure that Warby wanted an active role not just a desk at HQ. The treatment given Warburton after his car accident and after he was deprived of his 336 Wing has caused a few adverse comments from those who knew him, had served under him and who had been inspired by his leadership.

Les Colquhoun writes: 'His unorthodox approach to the task and his flamboyant ways made him a persona non grata.' Les served a stint at PR Benson as well as his long tour in Malta so knew both places well. He also writes:

> As the PRU hierarchy at Benson took a grip of Middle East photographic affairs throughout 1943, so it became more difficult to fit Warby in: particularly after his accident. I am sure that back in the UK, Warby expected to be greeted as a great pilot who had made a significant contribution to aerial reconnaissance and, in my opinion, this was his just due … it appears that nobody knew what to do with him.

Syd Collins, the former adjutant at Luqa who had been a kind of father confessor to Warby, was at Algiers when Warby was in hospital there. He writes: 'I knew he was worrying about flying again.' Syd seems to have known and understood him well. In one passage he describes him as: 'The very good, the nice and the would-be-bad!'

Henry Sowerbutts, the navigator who had arrived with Phil Kelley in Malta literally 'with a bang', recalls seeing Warby at Benson 'once or twice' but whether Warby was there on a visit or to plead his case or on a posting, he didn't know.

However on 1 April 1944 he was posted to the American Air Base at Mount Farm, a companion aerodrome to Benson and the one from which most USAAF PR flights from the UK departed: his position was a Liaison Officer with the US 7th Photo-Recce Group (part of the 8th PR Wing or 325 US Wing).

Syd Collins' affirmation that Warby wanted to fly again is significant.

Many in his position might have regarded themselves as being on 'easy street'. After all, he was being posted to live with the Americans who so greatly admired him. He was based with them too. This meant that he could enjoy their higher standard of wartime living which in part stemmed from their wonderful PX organization which somehow always ensured that their men serving overseas were seldom short of any of the luxuries – drinks, cigarettes, chocolates etc, which they were accustomed to at home. Many pilots who had miraculously survived as many close calls with death in the air as had Wing Commander Warburton, would have thanked their lucky stars that the liaison job involved no more flying risks. Essentially liaison jobs were office jobs with social connotations: one that could almost be done in the Mess or on the end of a phone. In the parlance of the day: 'It was a piece of cake' and could have been regarded as a fitting reward for one who had risked so much in the air for the common cause. Although only aged 25 or 26, W/Cdr Warburton was a worthy veteran who might have welcomed being 'put out to grass': and in a luscious field, too.

But Warby was not an ordinary mortal. For one thing, he had lived on praise and adulation for years. He thrived on it. He responded to it. He probably resented being 'put out to grass'. He was like a tired and battered gladiator who wanted again to re-enter the area where he had once known fame and glory and where he had once responded so well to the acclaim. Even if it meant facing death again, that's where he wanted to be. Moreover he had mixed with the likes of Hugh Pughe Lloyd, Carl Spaatz, Elliott Roosevelt, Arthur Tedder, 'Mary' Coningham and the President's other son. He was accustomed to being 'in the picture' at the highest command conferences.

Warby also knew that he had put all he had into building up a successful RAF Wing at La Marsa. In the brief months he had been in charge, he had got it off the ground and flying well. In all probability, he resented having it taken away from him (as his letter to his father implies).

Above all he was a pilot who wanted again to fly. To be able again to operate where he had once excelled.

As Ken Rogers had predicted, 'In the UK he would have been smothered … too many rules and such' but was the Warby of 1940–43, the so called 'Mad Warby', the same as the Wing Commander of 1944 who had built up and commanded 336 Wing with such dedication? Had Warby, lingering in hospital in North Africa with all his friends having moved to Italy, once more been reviewing his life? Had his new determination been not recognized?

Johnny Bloxam whom he happened to meet at North Camp, Gibraltar, when passing through flying a P38 northbound about March 1944, remarks that he appeared then to have been fully recovered physically and to have been both rational and normal in his manner and conversation. Yet there are stories, repeated from a number of sources that for much of his time in the UK, Warby was depressed. In that letter to his father written from hospital, there is a sentence: 'If I do move [away from Africa] then maybe I shall be able to settle with my friend once and for all.' The friend was most probably Christina, since a reference in the same letter to a 'Cairo bint' shows no other serious involvement.

The Americans to whom Warburton became attached from at least 1 April 1944 officially (and possibly unofficially earlier ?), noticed a change in the man. They no longer remember him as a happy-go-lucky devil-may-care pilot. Elliott Roosevelt writes about him in the following terms:

> When Warburton was transferred, along with his Allied fellow officers to England in January 1944, he assumed the post of Deputy Commander of 325 Reconnaissance Wing. Shortly after he arrived in England he exhibited extreme depression to his fellow officers. He confided to a few that he had lost his wife to another man while serving overseas in Malta, Africa and Italy and had not seen his wife for a considerable length of time. After this he became more and more morose ...

Some of the details and dates of this long letter are not quite correct. Ignoring this, the essential point seems to be Warby's very noticeable depression and the statements which he was still making about his wife.

Major John Hoover of the USAAF confirms his state of mind: 'I do vaguely recall Warby being grounded about the time Leon Gray and I met him in the Wings Club in London in March or April 1944...' In a later letter John Hoover writes: 'My view was then, and is now, that he was very depressed and despondent because of his marital problems, being grounded and not in action any more; just sort of fed up with the war and everything in general ...'

Since the marital problems were a complete fiction, something else must have lain at the heart of what was gnawing at Warby. Paddy Moren reckons that what was really causing Warby to be so depressed was that he had been taken out of the spotlight and denigrated (as Warby saw it) to a minor role. In Moren's considered opinion, Warby was a man who had to live in an aura of praise *or*, if that was being denied, then he acted so as to elicit human sympathy. Many have commented upon the sensitivity of the man, his warmth and care for human life. At heart he seems to have been a man who genuinely like to 'smell the flowers by the wayside'. The letter he wrote to his mother† from Haifa is but an example. In that letter he was far removed from the public's adoring gaze. For once he could allow himself to display characteristics other than bravery, flippancy and his 'couldn't care less' surface attitude.

†See Appendix III.

In short, Paddy Moren believes that Warby was hiding his anger and disappointment at not being allowed again to command a Wing and so play a leading and dramatic part in the preparations for the great Normandy invasion, behind a smoke screen of disappointment at having his marriage come unstuck. There is much to support this theory. Denied the chance to shine in the air and the glory attached to it, Warby, so Paddy Moren believes, was falling back on his reserve attention-getter: sympathy. He describes it quite brilliantly: 'We are all actors from Puck to the melancholy Dane but few of us ever become leading actors like Adrian Warburton who, akin to many others who achieve notoriety on the stage of life, doted on applause, recognition and praise.'

It might help to understand better the state of his mind to know how he spent his time between the end of January when he borrowed that Spitfire and flew himself to San Severo and the end of March when Johnny Bloxam happened to run into him at Gibraltar in an American P38 heading north for the UK. Where had he been? From where had he come? His appointment as liaison officer to the Recce Group of the USAAF is, according to the Air Historical Branch, dated from 1 April. Unfortunately his log book contains no entries beyond the end of August 1943: not even for September when he was still flying operationally from Luqa. Commander Geoffrey Warburton is long since dead. It would seem likely however that if Warby had the use of either a P38 or a modern Spitfire (the Mark IX had a range of 1360 miles), then he would have arranged another visit to Haifa where his father still was. The two of them appear to have become the best of friends, and once even played that old joke where they meet in a bar deliberately fail to recognise one another until Adrian insults his father, the Senior Service Commander. Whereupon Geoffrey Warburton dresses down the young RAF officer and ends up demanding to know his name, number and address. When the last is given, Commander Geoffrey Warburton then says: 'Then you must be my son', and the two collapse with laughter with their arms around one another.

There is as much mystery about the missing two months of February and March 1944, as there is about his last, allegedly final, flight although the author has unearthed a lot more detail about this than has been previously published. All that can be said with certainty is that by the time he was back with the Americans in the UK he was not always the same fun-loving Warburton that they had known had come to love earlier. Something was gnawing at him. Something that indirectly was to lead to his last known flight.

THE LAST FLIGHT

Just as had happened many years before when Lawrence of Arabia – the man to whom Warburton has been likened – met his end under rather strange circumstances and so led to a spate of rumours that still persist today that he wasn't really dead but was being made out to be so, much the same occurred when Adrian Warburton, and the aircraft he was flying, disappeared from the face of the earth on 12 April 1944.

The circumstances of the origin of the flight were largely unknown but have been well explained by several of the Americans involved. Wing Commander Adrian Warburton, whether or not still officially grounded for medical reasons, departed from Mount Farm, the airbase used by the squadrons of the 7th Recce Group, USAAF, in a P38F5B No:42–67325 on the morning of 12 April 1944. The flight was one that Elliott Roosevelt had specially arranged for Warby. As Elliott writes:

> ... he exhibited extreme depression ... he became more and more morose and when he expressed an interest of flying a mission with Colonel Hoover ... over a target and photograph it then fly south over Switzerland to our old airport of San Severo, he was granted the permission to make this flight on the morning of 12 April 1944.

However Elliott Roosevelt's memory misled him here since John Hoover wrote in a letter to Constance Babington Smith (for her book *Evidence in Camera*):

> I believe that Elliott's memory is worse than mine because I do not remember flying with Warby (sic) on this sortie ... the best I can recall about Warby's last flight is that I believe that he had four Mustang P51 fighters with him as escort as far as Lake Constance ... At this point fighters left him as briefed and returned to the UK ... nothing was heard from Warby from this point onwards.

However the CO of the recce group concerned, Colonel George Lawson, has a clear recollection (as would be expected) of the details. He recalls that Warby had been with the base for several months (thus suggesting that Warby had attached himself to the Americans at Mount Farm long before being officially posted there) but had seldom flown. In George's opinion, Warby should never have been allowed to fly the P38 over Europe. It was a plane which lacked the speed, height and general performance of either the

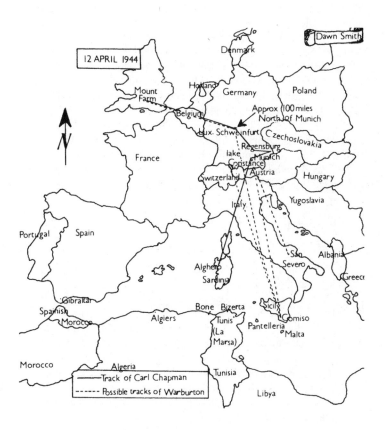

12 APRIL 1944

Dawn Smith

Denmark

Holland

Germany

Poland

Mount Farm

Belgium

Approx 100 miles
North of Munich

Lux. Schweinfurt

Czechoslovakia

France

Regensburg

lake
Munich
Constance)

Switzerland

Austria

Hungary

Italy

Yugoslavia

Portugal

Spain

San
Severo

Albania

Alghero

Sardinia

Greece

Gibraltar

Bone Bizerta

Sicily

Spanish
Morocco

Algiers

Tunis
(La
Marsa)

Pantelleria

Comiso

Malta

Morocco

Algeria

Tunisia

Libya

Track of Carl Chapman
----- Possible tracks of Warburton

latest Spitfires (of which George had managed to get some for his unit) or the Mosquito. He was opposed to the proposed operation but was over-ruled. He knew Warby was a Spitfire expert but was far less experienced on P38's. George Lawson, who had not known Warby in Malta or at La Marsa, had not the intimate knowledge about Warby and the operational reputation that he had acquired from the Mediterranean theatre of war. George Lawson believes that one reason why Elliott Roosevelt considered that the operation would be OK was that an experienced P38 pilot, Captain Carl Chapman (and not John Hoover as Roosevelt recalled) was designated to accompany Warby. Elliott had a high opinion of Carl too. All three had become friends – with Carl and Adrian 'real buddies'. The plan was for the two P38's to fly together for part of the way and then, when 100 or so miles north of Munich, for them to diverge in order to photograph different targets. Later they would rendezvous and continue together.

A search for Carl Chapman ensued. Although the search ended with sad news that Carl had died quite recently, the author had the good fortune to to receive from Claude Murray (who had been alerted by George Lawson of the matter) a copy of a letter written by Carl Chapman on 3 July 1983 which gives Carl's personal recollections of the flight that he and Warby made that morning. Mac Brown also spoke to Carl Chapman about the flight and confirms almost every small detail. In a document headed: 'Warby 7PG (Photorecce Group) Hist 1 Misc. Comments about Wing Commander Warburton (RAF)', Carl Chapman wrote:

Here are the facts as I remember them, keeping in mind that I didn't remember the dates.

After the bombing of the ball bearing plants at Regensburg and Schweinfurt, we had outstanding requirements to obtain D/A† photos of them ... they were deep in Germany and they were real sensitive about them (with) considerable protection. Since most of our interception problems came over the target or on the way home on long missions, I declared that on this one it would be a good idea to continue south and land and refuel at Alghero on the island of Sardinia where I knew a squadron of F5s were stationed. Then return to Mount Farm directly through France.

The flight plan called for (our) two planes flying together to a point about 100 miles north of Munich and then splitting up; one flying due east and the other south east ... I got Regensburg [implying that Warby got Schweinfurt?]. We were to continue to the Czech border and photo other targets and meet over Munich at

†Presumably Damage Assessment.

a predetermined time and fly together to Sardinia. (I don't know where San Severo came into the picture because it was never considered in any way).

When I returned to Munich at the appointed time, I called Warburton many times but he simply didn't show up. We were not so far apart that if he was in trouble I could have heard him had he called. After waiting around and calling for a while I flew on to Sardinia. I waited there until there was no hope of his making it then I returned to England the same day.

It should be noted that I had to get personal approval from Elliott Roosevelt (the USAAF Wing Commander) for Warburton to accompany me on this mission ... It might be pertinent to point out that we were nowhere near Lake Constance.

After Warburton was lost I had many visitors from the RAF and RCAF (who were personal friends) (Mac Brown and co.) who wanted to know the details of the mission. I also know for a fact that Wing [presumably the USAAF 8th Recce Wing] HQ took a lot of heat over it.

On the copy of the report a person, who is identified as 'Pat Keen'† by annotation in ink, has added:

This does not jibe with the record of either of the Association of RAF Photography Officers or with Group Mission records: 12 April 1944 in MEWD†† ... Schweinfurt, Zwickau, Oschersleben, Halle and Leipzig ... all planes turned back due to clouds and dense contrails. Only one group from 3BD penetrated to the German border.

MEWD ... 357FG (Fighter Group?) sent 8 P51's to escort two P38's in Munich area but only two were able to keep up with the recce planes.

Yet it does seem to jibe. Even the names of the two P51 pilots who kept up with the P39s are known, Lt 'Kit' Carson and Lt Ollie Harris.

Regarding the policy of sending fighters with P38's over Europe, John Hoover writes: 'It was about this time (April 1944) that we experimented with using fighter escort but for several reasons we soon abandoned the idea: the fighter escort was not always available; the rendezvous always seemed to get screwed up. Also a single recce plane drew less attention than did one with a flight of fighters escorting it.'

---

†A USAAF PR Wing historian.
††The Mighty Eighth War Diary – the book about 8th USAF by Roger Freeman.

Reading between the lines, it would appear that in the first place it might have been Carl Chapman who first considered flying a sortie alongside Warby. Both were Roosevelt favourites. When it was put to Elliott, he approved the idea as a means of helping Warby get back to his former cheerful self. He also seems to have arranged (perhaps privately with Warby) that Warby should head for San Severo after the official reconnaissance had been completed. However, neither Elliott nor Warby seem to have put Carl in the picture regarding this. It was the kind of addition that would have raised no eyebrows in the Mediterranean but being a private arrangement of a personal nature might have caused a few more formal comments in the more regular European sphere of operations.

Following upon the earlier advice that Lake Constance in Switzerland figured large in Elliott Roosevelt's recollections (he declared that the rendezvous was to be over Lake Constance, not Munich), contact was made with the Swiss authorities to ascertain if any P38 had been known to have come to grief in that country on that day. Thanks to a most helpful Swiss Air Force historian Florian Davatz, who sent details of all the *hundreds* of Allied aircraft which sought refuge or crashed in Switzerland during the entire war, it was learnt that 12 April 1944 was one of the rare days during that year when no aircraft of any kind was known to have ended up in that neutral country.

In part this exploded the theory which at one time was held by Elliott Roosevelt. Many years ago, he mentioned in a radio broadcast that he considered it possible, even likely, that Warby had become so depressed and war weary, that he might have deliberately slammed his P38 into a Swiss glacier just to 'end it all' without trace or the need of a funeral. But his 1986 letter to the author shows that he no longer considers this a possibility. Mac Brown agrees. He admits that this might just be so but that the odds against it are very large.

Johnny Hoover had advanced his personal opinion that since Warby was an outstanding pilot and he was, on 12 April 1944 when he went missing, flying a reliable twin-engined aircraft with a good single engined performance, he rules out Warby failing to return from this last flight due to either pilot error or mechanical malfunction. He thinks it possible that because Warby was depressed due to his marital problems, being grounded and not being in action any more, he either bailed out or landed near some remote village in Spain, Switzerland or Italy. He believes that he may have been fed up with the war and everything in general. On the other hand he also considers that Warby's injuries caused by the jeep accident, could have incapacitated him (black-out etc) causing him to crash.

Howard Vestal, at La Marsa recalls:

Some of my friends said that he made some statements (probably in jest) about spending the rest of the war in Switzerland ... and there was some speculation that he may have done that when he didn't return from the mission of 12 April (his final flight). I personally don't think anything like that happened. There is some mystery connected to his disappearance, however, in that there was not a trace of him or the plane.

The number of correspondents who have suggested to the author that Warby just might still be alive, 43 years after having been regarded as 'missing believed killed', is quite remarkable but there appears to be no single thread of evidence other than unsubstantiated rumour. Warby, like Lawrence, was unique and the rumours could have been fuelled by the memories of his previous disappearance without trace in Greece for one night and those five days in November 1942 as well as by his occasional unannounced flights 'into the blue' during his period when CO of 69 and 683 Squadrons at Malta.

As a consequence, the news of his disappearance was first greeted by disbelief. The RAF, as soon as they heard that he was missing, promptly sent signals asking if the plane was with them to a number of RAF bases in Italy and the Mediterranean (not only to Malta). Signals were even sent to Haifa to see if he had ended up there. All to no avail.

The Americans also believed that Warby and their plane would turn up somewhere. Not until 6 May was P38F5B no: 42–67325 officially reported as 'missing in action'. However, as time went on, the loss was eventually officially recognised by the RAF.

The stories, as related by Johnny Hoover, that Warby had deliberately made his own exit from the war must have reached the ears of the British authorities. Apart from sending signals to a number of RAF stations throughout the Mediterranean to see if he was there, as has been reported by Phil Kelley, they omitted to advise his parents – Warby's declared Next of Kin – that anything was amiss, *until over two weeks had passed*. In November 1942, when he had been shot down over Bizerta, they took this action next day.

When eventually they did send Muriel Warburton the dreaded telegram that every mother always feared, it was a most unusual one. In the first place it was not sent until 1 May, 17 days after Warby had disappeared without trace. Also it contained an unusual final request: 'Should news of him reach you from any other source please advise this department.'

It seems that the Air Ministry was still at least half convinced that Warby had gone away on some private venture not associated with the RAF and that he might have contacted his parents, or would be doing so. It is also significant that they again contacted his parents and not any wife. They then still seem to have been in ignorance about Betty of the Bush.

The Americans seem to have been equally uncertain about what Warby might have had in mind, and where he might have ended up. For a plane to fail to return from an operational trip on 12 April and to have not been declared 'missing in action' until 6 May must surely be unique.

A further fact that might have persuaded the authorities to regard Warburton's disappearance as no more than a personal venture, may have resulted from information submitted by Colonel George Lawson, of 7th Recce Group, which was operationally responsible for the missions flown by Carl and Warby. It was he who had opposed Warby operating over Europe in a P38 but had been over-ruled by his superior General Elliott Roosevelt. George had the job of collecting Warby's personal effects and forwarding them to his mother. He recalls that they amounted to so little that they could all be 'tied up in a towel or pillow-case. Not even a spare uniform'. Some may have interpreted this as some sort of 'proof' that Warby had departed along with most of his spare clothes and other personal things, with deliberate intention of never returning. If indeed this was so (and the author does *not* rule it out) then it belies any suggestion that Warby had deliberately slammed his P38 into a Swiss glacier.

Many have their own theories about Warby's last flight. Some think that, after having completed whatever mission he had to do, he was heading for San Severo and was either shot down or crashed with the aircraft falling into a lake (Lake Constance is often mentioned but this is only because Elliott Roosevelt mentions it, as the rendezvous point) or into the sea with the body trapped in the plane. Others refer to the likelihood of Warby suffering oxygen system failure and quote how insidiously that kind of failure creeps up on the unwary pilot. Others think that he simply got lost and ended up in the sea. Running short of petrol, as had happened on the flight from Portreath to Gibraltar, is another possibility. The weather was known to have been poor that day which is why most USAAF operations were cancelled. This introduces a thought that the plane might have become iced-up or even have been broken up by severe turbulence.

George Lawson suspects engine trouble. As he writes:

> I was of the opinion that Warby had no business in flying missions in a F5 (P38). Since we had numerous Spitfire IX's and he was highly qualified in that airplane. Also we had been having terrible engine problems with the F5: sometimes as many as 50% came back with engine failures: thrown rods and the like.

George adds:

> I remember him personally … He was liked by all Americans and he liked the Americans. He could not gamble or play poker with us

because he had very little money … although he was a young Wing Commander his salary was very small compared with the Americans but he was in on most everything in a very quiet way … Although he wore the RAF uniform he was just like one of the American pilots and was treated that way … he was someone to look up to.

Thanks to research carried out by Robin Higham, it is known that by flying at reduced speed and at lower altitudes a P38 could extend its range to over 1,800 miles: also more significantly that if the starboard engine failed the aircraft lost its electric power and thus its R/T.

It can be argued that, after Carl and Warby parted 100 miles from as he says Munich, Warby, without even photographing any target, at once set course for San Severo. It could also be that one reason why the two never met at the rendezvous was that they were given different rendezvous areas. Carl to Munich, Warby to Lake Constance. Somewhere they had got their lines crossed. Lake Constance made far better sense. Why hang about over Munich which was ringed with AA guns and fighter bases when nearby neutral Lake Constance offered a much safer rendezvous area? Lawson, in particular, thinks that Carl's memory here is at fault. Also Mac Brown recalls Carl mentioning Lake Geneva as the rendezvous. This might have put him out of R/T range from Carl by the time that Carl had arrived over Munich. If Carl was going to Sardinia and Warby to San Severo any rendezvous was pointless. San Severo might have been beyond the range of the aircraft if, despite its theoretical range of almost 2,000 miles (in 10? hours), it had been fuelled to fly only as far as Sardinia and then be refuelled there as Carl had planned. If Carl didn't know about San Severo, how could have the men who fuelled the plane at Mount Farm know? The speculations are endless. If shot down by the Germans, the P38 could yet have staggered as far as Switzerland and then crashed into glacier or uninhabited mountain top, leaving no recoverable remains.

Major Usher Brierley of SAAF recalls that Warby had already visited them earlier at San Severo after having been given the liaison officer's appointment with the Americans. He then had exhibited no signs of depression and told Usher that he had a lovely job. He later let it be known to Usher that he would again be visiting them about 12 April 1944, at San Severo in a Mosquito† for them to use and asked him to lay on a party on the 12th, which, says Usher: 'We were only too pleased to do.' That sounds like the charismatic Warby of old. It seems strange that only when in the UK did he seem to be upset or depressed or be moaning about an alleged unfaithful wife. As Usher writes: 'Warby never arrived, we were expecting

†Usher might have mixed the types Lightnings and Mosquitoes, both were twin engined fighter types. Usher's 60 SAAF flew Mosquitoes.

him to by Gibraltar' but 'he flew direct and was presumably shot down over enemy territory.' Charles Barry, another 60 SAAF pilot, has no recollection of seeing Warby at San Severo. Others also recall that Warby was expected at San Severo but never showed up: instead he was reported missing. Signals enquiring about him were received.

Les Colquhoun submits a story which he heard at the time and in one respect it has a surprising ring of truth to it. He recalls:

> The story we heard was that he took off in the PR P38 Lightning to record a Fortress strike. We never knew what happened on that ill-fated sortie except that neither he nor his two escorting Mustangs returned.

Les was at Benson and close to where the flight was planned. He has got it absolutely right that Warby had been sent to take photos of a Fortress strike (on those ball-bearings works) and absolutely correct that he was being-escorted by two fighter planes and that they were P51's, which the RAF called Mustangs. His is a story which has much truth to it but it still doesn't offer any explanation of why Warby (and the Mustangs) didn't come back: unless all three were shot down but if so, then wreckage and bodies should have been discovered.

During the war, the author heard a rumour that Warby had flown back to Malta, that the devoted ground crews had hidden his plane and that he was quietly living there with Christina: this is known to be at least partially untrue. Christina although still in Malta could not possibly have concealed him for long. Also she has assured the author that she never saw him again after he departed at the end of September 1943. Warby might well have been trying to fly direct to Malta and then have come to grief on the way and ended up in the Mediterranean or Adriatic due to enemy action, ice, engine failure, lack of oxygen, weather, inadequate fuel or navigation error etc. If this is what he was trying to do, that would account for the paucity of possessions he left behind at Mount Farm, the rest being with him.

After the war great efforts were made to identify those planes, and the pilots flying them, which had crashed or been shot down over Europe. Italy was scoured. With regards to Warby, no information was discovered. The matter might in this case have been complicated by Warby being in an American plane, and operating an 'off-beat' sortie. The RAF investigation team which searched Italy for lost flyers took no particular note of crashed American planes: only British ones. The most valuable clue concerning what may have happened that 12 April 1944, of any likely credence, comes from a most unexpected quarter.

After the war, although the RAF made no great hero out of Warby; nor St Edward's School either: (at least not in the same manner as they lauded

Guy Gibson or Douglas Bader) nevertheless the Borough and County of the town of Poole near Bournemouth decided to name a street after him. It was part of a decision to name a small number of new streets after the great RAF and FAA heroes of the war. Along with Bader, Gibson and many other popular names, they named a street 'Warburton'. He was the only 'Aerial Reconnaissance' pilot as they called him to be so honoured. This prompted a Mr Norman Prowting of Wimborne to try to find out more about all the aircrew selected for this honour. In Warburton's case he got in touch with Alison, Warby's sister who has since died. She told him about the Roy Nash articles which had appeared in the London *Star* a few years earlier. Norman Prowting then contacted a Battle of Britain RAF sergeant pilot friend of his who did not know Warby but knew of him. This pilot made exhaustive enquiries both in England and in USA where fortunately he had excellent connections because after the war he had worked for the USAF. Although he unearthed nothing conclusive he did remark in a letter to Prowting that: 'The remains of a burnt out P38F5B (the *exact* type which Warby was flying on 12 April 1944) had been discovered outside Comiso, West Sicily, in August 1944: a burnt-out wreck that nobody claimed at the time.' Not just a 'Lightning' or a P38 but a P38F5B.

It is quite a co-incidence. Especially as there were elements about Warby's last flight which might have led to it not having been officially recorded† due to the fact that an RAF pilot was flying a US aircraft under unusual circumstances, i.e. Warby might still even have been officially grounded medically: Warby was only a liaison officer with 7th Recce Group USAAF, not an operational pilot.

If one draws a line from north of Munich where Warby was last seen by Carl, to Malta it passes right over Sicily and if Lake Constance really was involved as Elliott thinks and as Lawson considers far more likely, the line between there and Malta *passes directly over Comiso* likewise if Warby was flying direct from Schweinfurt to Malta. Johnny Hoover has confirmed that a F5B could just reach Malta non-stop.

Was Warby, when taking that last flight, trying to get back to Malta where all his great triumphs had been recorded and where he had known love and where he was regarded as the 'Uncrowned King'? If so there are a host of reasons to suggest why he ended up in a crumpled burnt-out heap near Comiso and only some 80 or so miles from Malta: shortage of fuel and engine trouble are two obvious possibilities.

It seems doubtful that the full circumstances of the last flight taken by Adrian Warburton, pilot extraordinary, the pilot who knew no fear, will ever be known. Time has probably obliterated what traces might at one

---

†The departure form of 7th Recce Group *does* list Chapman's departure but *not* Warby's, nor was 42–67325 a 7th Recce Group aircraft.

time have been available to prove, or disprove, that the aircraft which crashed near Comiso was the one in which he had left Mount Farm.

It would however in some ways have been a fitting, if sad end, to this courageous but unconventional character if he was indeed trying to get back to the island where he had been so strangely christened and where his name will always be remembered and where also, in all probability, he found true love.

Indisputably while in Malta Warby had earned and found the love of his flight commanders and devoted airmen. He had also found in Christina a different kind of warming love. Almost for sure he had found his true self there: the bold inspiring leader with the caring man within as described by some of his more observant companions of war. Yet for all this he emerges at times as a man with a 'mirror personality'. He seems so often to have been whatever others expected him to be. At school, he seems almost determined to be the very antithesis to the traditional fit healthy minded team-spirited boy. In his early days in the RAF, where his flying skills were found to be wanting, he seemed to delight in being regarded as a 'one-off', an unusual type. It was as if, unable to attract attention to himself by merit he resorted to notoriety. Throughout the entire period of his life, until perhaps the last year or so, all describe him as a loner. His mother said he seemed to be content with his own company but was this his nature or was it the refuge he had adopted to conceal the fact that he was really a sensitive and caring person at heart? Those early childhood days when his parents were abroad and he was being farmed out in boarding schools and grandparents, could also have left its mark on him.

Once he had won the respect of his understanding and talented flight commander Tich Whiteley, Warby fell naturally into a different mirror role. Tich saw a potential hero in Warby and Warby seemed determined to prove Tich right here, fortunately, he found himself in company with a most unusually brilliant air gunner, Moren, who was akin to Warby in spirits and guts. From then on Warburton would dare anything rather than let down those who showed the trust and admiration for him. For Tich and Paddy, and to sustain their continued approbation, Warby would have walked on fire. Fortune took a hand when, as Tich left, so did AVM Hugh Pughe Lloyd appear on the Warburton horizon. Warby was now in favour with the Top Brass of the island and there was no way that he would ever let any of them down either. Malta demanded a supreme effort. Warburton gave it without a thought to his own survival, which he had always doubted right from October 1939 onwards.

What part did the vivacious, equally determined, Christina play? This will never be known in detail but gradually she seems to have unwound another side of his withdrawn personality. In Malta it seems doubtful that a man of almost feminine, if deliberately hidden, sensitivity could possibly have survived the conditions of that blasted besieged all-male society for long without the care of solicitude that only a loving woman can provide. Did she smooth the raw edges of his character and later pay the penalty by having him casually play the field as in Cairo and Tunisia?

Fate was again kind when, with Paddy Moren departed from his orbit, Warby in his Beaufighter found crew men of the worth and deep understanding of Norman Shirley and Ron Hadden. By then also he had already captured the imagination and devotion of many of the humble and hard working 'erks', the real heroes of Malta. Once he had their wholehearted approval he saw to it that he would live up to their expectations of him.

His discovery that Corporal Shirley and LAC Hadden possessed the highest qualities of manhood, further reinforced his belief that uniforms and ranks meant little when the 'chips were down'.

When alone in his Spitfire with no chance of developing a similar rapport with aircrew, Warby then established a close liaison with Ken Rogers and the Lancashire Lad, Jack Meadows, 'Con' Rutter, Ken Fielder, Jim McNeil and scores of other airmen. Warby attracted devotion from far afield and somehow had the nose to sense from where it was likely to be forthcoming.

For as long as Warburton was in Malta, the formula worked. Men, and Christina, devoted themselves to him. In return he gave himself generously to them. He mirrored the devotion of others. Airmen even wrote poetry about him.† Warby was almost necessary to the morale of those who had showed that they could take the appalling bombing and shortages. He became the emblem of the island's resistance. He was also the island's eyes.

The relief of Malta by 1943 was, in a way, the first soundings of the death knell of the Warby legend. The island no longer needed a hero or an emblem of its resistance. It no longer called for daily desperate measures. There was no longer a need for someone to stand, and be seen, on the parapet brandishing a defiant sword. The preparations for the landings at Pantellaria and Sicily brought back a temporary need for daring adventures. This and the admiration of his new found American friends brought back a resurgence of the Warby spirit. With it came opportunities again to mix with the High and Mighty in command: all stimulants to the Warby ego. Again his response was of the highest order. For his new American devotees, for especially Top Brass like Spaatz and Roosevelt, Warby would continue to dare anything: likewise for the South African pilots he met shortly afterwards in North Africa who also fell under his spell.

That jeep accident at the very time when the war was fast moving away from the Mediterranean as a whole and Malta in particular left its mark. His subsequent lack of a key job at Benson and his difficulty in finding another flying job or even official medical clearance was a bitter pill for

†See Appendix II

Warby to swallow. No longer would he have opportunities to shine: no longer could he play the role of the defiant hero in an almost lost cause. While he lingered for months in hospitals the opportunities to win the acclaim of others, or to keep up his six monthly gong schedule no longer existed. No extra medal could be won in hospital. There was no parapet on which to stand. The troops needed no rallying cry. Indeed they and the war was being won far away from where he lay. By December 1943 the war was being won by overwhelming weight of arms, by American logistics and there was no leading role for the likes of individuals like Adrian Warburton. Vast Allied plans involving thousands of units and enormous interlocking complexities were being made. Plans in which there was no part for a brilliant Maverick.

And now forty years later Malta alone, and the colleagues who knew him, give him the place of honour he deserves. In the Malta War Museum, they have created a special Warburton corner.

For as long as there are people on that island who can remember the terrible days and nights of that long siege when, so it seemed, the whole might of the Luftwaffe was descending continuously on this small rocky outpost, Malta will remember its 'Uncrowned King', Adrian Warburton DSO and Bar, DFC and two Bars, American DFC, all won in Malta.

As David Beaty has wisely said: 'Malta wasn't real' but it did happen and it is to be hoped that this tribute to the man who above everyone else on the island helped to see that it survived in spirit as well as deed, will remind others that in a country's hour of need, men arise from virtually nowhere to respond.

It is fitting to let an airman, one of the humble 'erks', sum it up. John Tanker, when writing to the author, mentions: 'When people speak of Malta, we can say with pride, "I was there. Wonderful memories of wonderful men: thanks for knowing them."'

Malta and Warby, whose name will always be linked with it, are also a reminder that, no matter who we are, or where we are, we all need the balming influence of love to bring forth that which lies best and deepest within us.

May it always be so.

CHAPTER ELEVEN

POSTSCRIPT

BY
CHRIS GOSS

It was thought that the terse signal received by the Air Ministry could well be one of the last things referring to the loss in action of Wing Commander Adrian Warburton. Dated 25 April 1944, it read:

> The following message was received from Commanding Officer 7th Photogroup [sic] quote W/C A Warburton is missing in action from 12 April 1944 while on an operational shuttle run mission to Italy. Officer was flying an F-5-B airplane number 42-67325. He was last contacted by a P-51 fighter pilot near Lake Constance headed south. Officer was supposed to land at Algehro or San Severo…

Warby had simply disappeared and for years afterwards, unsubstantiated rumours sprung up that he had crashed in Sicily or was lying in the wreckage of his aircraft in the sea off Venice. However, this was not the case and in fact the pieces of the jigsaw were all out there, waiting for someone to put them all together. That person was Frank Dorber.

Frank's imagination had been fired by reading an earlier edition of this book back in 1993. He found it sad that such a distinguished and highly decorated RAF hero had no known grave and as a result, he became determined to try and find out what happened, where he had possibly crashed and, if at all possible, to recover his remains so that he could get a proper Christian burial.

Initially, Frank contacted Tony Spooner who had no further information to share but typical of Tony, gave him encouragement. However, Tony himself was very busy with a roll of honour to all those who had died during the Second World War serving with Coastal Command and together with his other writing projects, had precious little time to help Frank.

Undeterred, Frank continued with his quest. As Warby was flying with an American unit, RAF records were sparse to say the least; 'last contacted by P-51 by Lake Constance, Switzerland' was all that was written on the Casualty Card written at the time and now held by the Air Historical Branch. Furthermore, a year's worth of records of the 7th Photo Reconnaissance Group, 325th Reconnaissance Wing had got lost which included the entries for 12 April 1944. As a result, Frank could not determine the precise flight route whilst the details of the aircraft he was flying could not be confirmed for certain. Additionally, and of further irritation, it was normal for the United States Army Air Force to file a

Missing Air Crew Report (MACR) for aircraft and aircrew missing on operations-they failed to file an MACR for Warby's loss, presumably assuming that the RAF would do this; however, as the RAF records show, the RAF failed to do this, presumably assuming that the Americans would do this! The jigsaw looked even more jumbled.

Most would have given up by now but Frank continued, exploring all possibilities.

After contacting numerous aviation researchers on the Continent, eventually in 1999, Frank seemed to have discovered something. Hans Grimminger, an amateur historian from Augsburg in southern Germany , managed to obtain a copy of a contemporary report which, albeit very brief, confirmed that at 1145 hours (local) on 12 April 1944, an 'American Lightning' crashed at Egling near Dünzelbach, having been shot down by anti-aircraft fire from Heimatbatterie 211/VII, and that the pilot was apparently killed. Hans also stated that after the war, a team of Americans visited the crash site, recovered an engine, but failed to excavate further, probably not having the time or equipment to do so and it was therefore believed therefore that the body of the pilot was still in the wreckage. Parish records for Egling could add nothing further but Herr Braumüller, the current owner of the field where the aircraft crashed, confirmed that they were still ploughing up small bits of aircraft wreckage.

However, there was still no firm evidence that this was Warby's plane so Frank continued looking for proof. In 2001, he contacted the Rector of Egling who managed to find witnesses to the crash whilst at the same time re-confirming that there was no documentary evidence referring to the crash held in the town archives. He stated that at the time of the crash, Herr Siegfried Klingl was on the road 150 metres from where 'a twin tailed aircraft' crashed. Herr Willibald Maxhofer remembers American personnel arriving at the crash site in Spring 1945 and that they attempted to excavate the site but gave up as the remains were too deep. However, they appeared satisfied that they had apparently identified the aircraft and that they had recovered some human remains. Curiously, another eyewitness, Herr Paul Berchtold, confirmed that human remains had been found and that his late father had been convinced that the pilot was British.

Frank now believed that there was sufficient evidence to organise the recovery of the wreckage but this was not as easy as it would seem. The authority for the recovery of the wreckage could only come from the Federal German Government and it was normal policy that, as there were still so many crash sites on the Continent, such recoveries would only occur if there was a danger to the local community from unexploded ordnance or if the land was about to be built upon.

By the Summer 2002, Frank had contacted the Volksbund Deutsche Kriegsgräbefürsorge (the German War Graves Commission) who, thanks particularly to the efforts of Herr Hermann Laage, had agreed to excavate the crash site. The Air Historical Branch also confirmed that should human remains be discovered, the Ministry of Defence would meet the costs for a proper burial at the nearest Commonwealth War Graves cemetery and would pay for the immediate surviving next of kin plus a companion to attend the ceremony.

Thanks to the efforts of local professor Dr Panratz Fried, responsibility for the excavation was given to Dr Anton Huber, the respected District of Landsberg am Lech's Custodian of Local Historical and Cultural Interests and after a number of delays, the excavation commenced on 19 August 2002. After two days of digging, an Allison engine, as used by Lockheed Lightnings, was recovered together with a makers plate indicating the aircraft was an F-5 version†. A propeller was found to have two bullets holes in it whilst a burnt length of film further confirmed that this aircraft was a photo-reconnaissance aircraft. It was inevitable that some human remains would be found and these were handed over to American military authorities, specifically David Roath, Mortuary Affairs Director of US 21st Theatre Support Command based at Katzweiler whose unit was responsible for investigating American crash sites in southern Germany. David Roath was not one to speculate as to the identity of the remains but stated he would only do so when and if American authorities had matched the engine to Warburton's aircraft. As a result, he anticipated a delay of five weeks or so before he could say if it was Warburton or not; Frank still had to wait to see if his quest to find Warby's remains was at an end.

Meanwhile, the RAF's Casualty Branch, who like the Air Historical Branch and British Embassy in Berlin had been involved with this since Frank's first approach in 1999, also had to wait. Sue Raftree, one of the Casualty Branch members, explained what they would have to do once confirmation that it was Warby had been received:

> Once a World War Two aircraft is discovered with human remains, the embassy in country will advise us of the find. It is then our job to investigate, try to identify the remains and to trace the next of kin.
>
> When relatives are traced, the team will make contact and organise a proper burial in the country in question. This is done with appropriate honours at Ministry of Defence expense. Two next of kin from each family are invited to attend the ceremonies.
>
> When a downed aircraft is discovered and its crew buried with dignity, it helps to close a chapter of British military history and enables relatives to come to terms with their loss. This is important for all those who served during two world wars including those who survived and the families of all those who did not.

---

† Dr Huber's account of the excavation can be found in Appendix V

On 21 November 2002, the Air Attaché in Berlin, Gp Capt John Moloney, received a phone call from David Roath. David believed that he now had enough evidence to draw a sensible conclusion that the remains were Warby's. All that now was needed was to trace the next of kin and arrange the burial. However, the former was not as easy as it appeared.

Frank Dorber had managed to find out that Warby's sister Alison's married name was Gethen but she had passed away. However, she had two sons and a daughter and that he was in contact with Charles Gethen, Warby's nephew and probably his next of kin.

However, before this could be confirmed, it had to be ascertained what had happened to Warby's wife Eileen (or as she was more commonly known, Betty). It was known that Warby had married Eileen Mitchell in October 1939 at Portsmouth Registry Office, that she had been married before and that she had a daughter, Sheila, at the time of her second marriage. However, Eileen stopped claiming her War Widow's Pension in 1966, possibly as she had remarried, and that after 1973, her whereabouts or, for that matter her new married name, could not be ascertained. It appeared fairly certain as if Charles Gethin would represent the Warburton family at the funeral.

Understandably, the discovery of a war hero's remains generated great media interest and as a result of this, a final twist to the Warburton story would occur. A Mrs Sheila Hunt read one of the articles, totally unaware until then that she was reading about her stepfather. Sheila quickly contacted Sue Raftree to state that her mother, Eileen, had married a Leonard Westcott in 1976 and the two of them had then moved to Australia. In 2001, Leonard had died and contrary to rumour, Eileen was alive and well and would be returning to live in the United Kingdom in May 2003; her expected arrival back in the United Kingdom would be 5 May 2003, nine days before the planned memorial service and burial at Durnbach. The final piece of the jigsaw had fitted into place.

All that now remained was to allow Warby to rest in peace. Sue Raftree and the British Embassy now had to work tirelessly to ensure that things would go to plan. Eileen Wescott, well into her 90s, returned to the United Kingdom as planned and on the evening of 13 May 2003, she and her daughter Sheila were flown to Munich and driven to their hotel at Tegernsee where they joined many of the others responsible for the following day's events.

At 1100 hours on 14 May 2003, Sqn Ldr The Reverend Alan Coates conducted the Memorial Service for Wg Cdr Adrian Warburton DSO and Bar, DFC and Two Bars, DFC (USA) at the St Agidius Church, Gmund. A reading was given by Air Marshall Sir Roderick Goodall RAF (who represented the Chief of the Air Staff) and at 1145 hours, exactly the same time that Warby's plane crashed, Warby's coffin and mourners departed for

Durnbach War Cemetery. There, in a hailstorm of biblical proportions, a bearer party from The Queen's Colour Squadron of the Royal Air Force, lowered Warby into the ground for the final time whilst a trumpeter from The Central Band of the Royal Air Force played the last post and a lone piper played 'Lament'. Warby could at last rest in peace, his wife Eileen commenting how beautiful the area was and how fitting it was that her husband would be buried near to where he was killed.

It is appropriate that the final word on this 58 year-old mystery comes from Frank Dorber:

> If it were not for Reverend Kahnert, the local priest, Professor Pankraz Fried and his friend Dr Huber, all of whom collectively rallied the local community to aid me, it is highly likely that Warby would still be in that field now. With the German War Graves Commission offering full cooperation and David Roath and his US Memorial Affairs team pulling out all the stops when they understood whom I believed the airman was in that field, they enabled success to be achieved…. It is appropriate that the entire region of Bavaria and specifically those communities around the River Paar do get recognition in glowing terms for their grace and goodwill; they 'did us proud' so that we could recover him.

Thanks mainly to Frank Dorber, 'Warburton's War' had finally ended.

APPENDIX I

CITATIONS

Flying Officer Adrian WARBURTON (41635) No. 431 Flight.
DISTINGUISHED FLYING CROSS
London Gazette, 11 February, 1941, p.832.
'This officer has carried out numerous long distance reconnaissance flights and has taken part in night† air combats. In October, 1940, he destroyed an aircraft and again, in December, he shot down an enemy bomber in flames. Flying Officer Warburton has at all times displayed a fine sense of devotion to duty.'

Flying Officer Adrian WARBURTON, DFC (41635) No. 69 Squadron.
BAR TO DISTINGUISHED FLYING CROSS
London Gazette, 9 September, 1941, p.5217.
'This officer is a most determined and skilful pilot and has carried out 125 operational missions. Flying Officer Warburton has never failed to complete the missions he has undertaken, and in the actions fought, he has destroyed at least three hostile aircraft in combat and another three on the ground.'

Acting Squadron Leader Adrian WARBURTON, DSO, DFC, & BAR, (41635), No 69 Squadron.
SECOND BAR TO DISTINGUISHED FLYING CROSS
London Gazette 3 November, 1942, p.4753.
'Since August, 1942, this officer has completed numerous operational photographic sorties, many of them at low altitudes and often in the face of opposition from enemy fighters. His work has been of the utmost value. In October 1942, his gallantry was well illustrated when he directed an enemy destroyer to a dinghy in which were the crew of one of our aircraft, which had been shot down. Although he was fired upon by the destroyer and engaged by Italian aircraft, he remained over the area until he observed the drifting crew were picked up by the destroyer.'

---

† A misprint "eight" was probably intended.

Flight Lieutenant Adrian WARBURTON, DFC & Bar (41635).
DISTINGUISHED SERVICE ORDER

London Gazette, 20 March, 1942, p.1275.

'This officer has carried out many missions each of which has demanded the highest degree of courage and skill: On one occasion whilst carrying out a reconnaissance of Taranto, Flight Lieutenant Warburton made 2 attempts to penetrate the harbour, although as there was much low cloud this entailed flying at a height of 50 feet over an enemy battleship. In spite of the failure of his port engine and repeated attacks from enemy aircraft he completed his mission and made a safe return. On another occasion he obtained photographs of Tripoli in spite of enemy fighter controls over the harbour. In March, 1942, Flight Lieutenant Warburton carried out a reconnaissance of Palermo and obtained photographs revealing the damage caused by our attacks. This officer has never failed to obtain photographs from a very low altitude, regardless of enemy opposition. His work has been most valuable and he has displayed great skill and tenacity.'

RECOMMENDATION FOR HONOURS AND AWARDS

BAR to DISTINGUISHED SERVICE ORDER

London Gazette 6 August 1943

Wing Commander Warburton has commanded No.683 Photographic Reconnaissance Squadron since its formation on 8th February, 1943 and prior to the formation of this squadron he commanded No. 69 Squadron.

This officer has flown a total of 375 operational sorties involving 1,300 hours flying. From Malta he has completed 360 sorties with a total of 1,240 hours. During his tour of duty in Malta, he has covered all the Italian and Sicilian targets continuously, invariably obtaining 100% cover with his photography.

In recent months, since he has commanded No. 683 Squadron, he has continued to operate on all the routine sorties required from pilots of the squadron, selecting for himself the sorties which have been considered of a more dangerous nature.

On a recent operation, one camera became unserviceable. In order to ensure that full photographic cover would be obtained, he covered every target, including Taranto, three times being continuously chased by M. E. 109s.

On 15th November, 1942, Wing Commander Warburton was despatched on a photographic reconnaissance of Bizerta. He was attacked by M.E. 109s and his aircraft being damaged he force landed at Bone. From there he went to Gibraltar, returning to Malta a few days later in a fighter aircraft. He encountered two J.U. 88s on his return journey which he engaged, destroying one and damaging the other.

On December 5th, this officer carried out a photographic reconnaissance of Naples. In spite of intense flak and enemy fighter opposition he covered the whole of the target area at 4,000 feet.

On May 18th, he took low level obliques of the whole of the Pantellaria coastline from a height of 200 feet. He was fired on continuously by the A.A. coastal batteries but succeeded in obtaining results which proved extremely valuable in the eventual invasion of the Island.

Wing Commander Warburton has destroyed a total of nine enemy aircraft when flying armed reconnaissance aircraft and three on the ground.

The importance of the results obtained by this officer in spite of intense enemy opposition and in all weathers cannot be too highly estimated. The success of operations carried out from this Island, the safe arrival and departures of convoys are largely dependent on the accuracy of photographic reconnaissance.

Wing Commander Warburton is to a great extent responsible for this successful reconnaissance. His personal enthusiasm for operations, his courage and devotion to duty have set the highest example to all with whom he has associated.

CONFERRED BY THE PRESIDENT OF THE UNITED STATES OF AMERICA

DISTINGUISHED FLYING CROSS

Acting Wing Commander Adrian WARBURTON, DSO & Bar,
DFC & 2 Bars, (83267), Royal Air Force Volunteer Reserve.

London Gazette, 18 January, 1944, p.359.

'While on a mission to obtain urgently needed photographs of the coast-line of Pantelleria on June 3rd, he distinguished himself through his resolute courage and calm efficiency under fire. Flying over the island at two hundred feet, within easy range of every type of anti-aircraft battery and drawing fire of even the large coastal guns, Warburton photographed virtually the entire shore line, gaining information of inestimable value to the Allied Forces which later invaded the island. His proficiency as pilot and photographer, and his selfless devotion to duty reflect great credit upon him and the armed Forces of the United Nations.'

Letters of Appreciation from General Alexander and Air Marshal Coningham

TAG H.Q.,
15 ARMY
GROUP.
10th July, 1943.

I should like to express personally how much I appreciate the photographic work which the R.A.F. have done in preparation for operation HUSKY and I should like to pay particular tribute to W/Cdr WARBURTON, who I believe, himself, took the most valuable low oblique photographs of the landing beaches.

These obliques have been extremely useful both to the planning staffs and to the assaulting troops to whom they have been distributed.

I fully realize the danger involved in making these sorties at very low heights and very close to any enemy coast, and they are as technically perfect and complete as if flown on a peacetime exercise.

If you think fit, I would be grateful if you would convey to W/Cdr WARBURTON my personal thanks.

(Signed) H.R. ALEXANDER.
General,
G.O.C.-in-C,
15 Army Group.
Air Marshal Sir Arthur Coningham, KCB, Etc.,
A. C.O., NATAF

FROM: Air Officer Commanding, Northwest African Tactical Air Forces.

TO: Headquarters, Northwest African Photographic Reconaissance Wing, La Marsa.

Date: 23rd July, 1943

The attached letter of appreciation from General Alexander is forwarded with a request that the duplicate copy which is enclosed may be given to Wing Commander Warburton.

I shall be grateful if you will also accept my personal congratulations on the magnificent work which is being done. Before the recent operations commenced there was a period when we were having difficulty with photographic work, but it has now become one of our strongest branches and I am sure that it will go on from strength to strength.

/s/ A. Coningham
Air Marshal,
Air Officer Commanding,
NORTHWEST AFRICAN TACTICAL AIR FORCE.

Outside Pfarrkirche St Agidius, Gmund an Tegernseee. Left to right: Frank Dorber, Hermann Laage, Herr Laage's assistant, Dr and Frau Huber. *(Frank Dorber)*

Queen's Colour Squadron Personnel Royal Air Force Regiment stand vigil over the hearse and coffin during the service. (*MOD Crown Copyright 2003*)

Queen's Colour Squadron Bearer Party carry the coffin into the Durnbach War Cemetery. (*MOD Crown Copyright 2003*)

Betty Westcott (formerly Warburton) looks on as her daughter Sheila lays flowers by the graveside. (*MOD Crown Copyright 2003*)

Jack Vowles, who served with Wing Commander Warburtin in Malta lays flowers at the graveside. (*MOD Crown Copyright 2003*)

Queen's Colour Squadron Bearer Party prepare to lower the coffin.
(*MOD Crown Copyright 2003*)

Wing Commander Adrian Warburton's headstone.
(*MOD Crown Copyright 2003*)

APPENDIX II

The Great Luqa Harrier

Salute the man since no praise is too high
For Adrian Warburton's deeds in the sky.

From nineteen forty and ever since then
This sixty nine squadron man amongst men
Has bravely flown o'er the bluest of seas
Piloting Maryland aircraft with ease.
Flying from Malta to spy from the air,
Probing reconnaissance flights everywhere
Enemy forces are grouped to wage war
From Southern Europe to Africa's shore.

Cast in the role of a far seeing eye
His acts have plagued Rommel's lines of supply:
In three years flying from Luqa airfield
Bringing home pictures of harbours that shield
Italian battleships anchored in port,
Dead scared to sail as a convoy escort:
Fearing that Malta's great Luqa harrier
Would dog their course despite any barrier.

Indeed this all purpose man of air space
Must surely rank as a super air ace.
Soaring to film war from high altitude,
Gliding through cloudbanks when hotly pursued,
Evading Luftwaffe fighter attacks,
Shooting down planes over Appenine tracks,
Obtaining strategic intelligence
Considered vital for Malta's defence.
Salute the man since no praise is too high
For Adrian Warburton's deeds in the sky.

JOHN SNOOK 1943 (then a 19 years old LAC).

APPENDIX III

Warburton's Letters to his Parents

R. N.
Haifa
10 Oct. 1941

Dear Mum,

Rather a shock, but here I am. I had one foot on the boat from Malta, only waiting permission, and instead posted to Egypt. What a shock! So to compensate they allowed me some leave – ten days – and considered it a favour, crew were not impressed as it is the first leave in about two years, but it is better than nothing. You will be happy to know that I have retired from operations for a bit and am going somewhere as an instructor, but I don't know where, I will let Pop know where I am going to be. I spent a few days near Cairo but was not very keen, too many 'Pongos' for the R.A.F, all were very serious types trying to win the war from their offices in the most comfortable manner possible. So I hitch hiked up here and arrived in father's office, 'much amazement'. He seemed quite pleased to see me and has been showing me the town, very bon. He lent us the car and we visited Nazareth etc, but not much catch as I think Madame Toussards made most of the antiques. We tried to walk on to Gallilee but no success so [unreadable]

My leave is up very soon so I shall have to leave soon but with a bit of luck may be able to hike up here for Xmas, incidently hiking is quite a pastime up here, all the family hide behind a hedge while best looking girl stops a car, then out come family and pile in as well, all very cunning. You probably have seen that we have been doing plenty of work, but the Wop does not seem very keen, he usually throws his bombs into the sea and runs home, next day Italian papers claims that all targets have been flattened. I saw Target for Tonight very impressive, our Wellington boys stood us a party on the strength of it.

Incidently you seem to be having a rough time, and here I am living in the lap of luxury, the food is very fine over here, even in the desert. Everybody gets all they want and no rationing, so it suits me. I lost a bit of weight in my last job but am regaining it rapidly. Pop's looks extremely fit, brown as a berry and only a very little rounder, he knows everybody and seems very cheerful, I have been to nothing but parties, since I arrived. The bathing is grand and can the Jews cook, there are a lot of Austrian and German Jews here, and they certainly know how to be comfortable.

Father took some photos on the beach the other day so you will probably get some soon, cheerio for the present, give my love to all,

All my love

Adrian

Haifa
2 April (1942)

Dear Mum,

Just finished my leave and how exhausting it was, am now going south for a rest. Father as young as ever, gave me the time of my life, riding etc, we went to Jerusalem and looked round, weather lousey. Then we went and saw some Roman ruins a very nice run, the countryside magnificent, baby Iris and lupins, rock plants galore, you would never have stopped digging. I flew father up to Beirut for a night he was very thrilled and never stopped telling everyone.

Your greetings card was very sweet and arrived at a most appropriate time, I hope you got a Christmas card from me. I met up with a lot of boys the other day do you remember Norman Ramseyer from Winchmore Hill, I used to belong to the Territorials with him, we had a very good party on the strength of the meeting.

I am sorry I could not get home, they pulled a fast one on me, I was all set one foot on the boat, and then they sent me the wrong way, I was very upset as I had hoped to get home for Xmas, never mind I shall keep trying and maybe anything will happen.

Father put a most amazing good show here, so that you may be congratulating him soon. I expect he told you he had some fun. He seems to want to come home, but as he can't, he does very well, of course he knows everybody and we have had a party nearly everynight. I seem to have been introduced to everybody in Haifa, it's been great fun. I got about 14 days and am leaving today, I hope to be up here again soon, or may be home, who knows.

I hope you are not working too hard. Father tells me you have been doing all sorts of odd jobs, perhaps life is easier now that things seem to have eased off. I have been doing the same sort of job, but am getting a rest at the moment. Perhaps I can wangle a passage, it seems such ages since I saw you, well who knows?

Give my love to Alison and Granny etc.

All my love

Adrian

No 2. R.A.F.
General Hospital
Algiers

Dear Dad,

Many thanks for the health enquiries, they caught up with me at last, and I have been in bed now for just over seven weeks, I have another three or four to do. I can't get any sympathy out of the Air Staff, general opinion seems to be 'that will keep the b- quiet for a bit, about time too', not very satisfactory. I had just got my own Wing started, quite a game, still it started working and has been running smoothly ever since, a little consolation. As regards injuries, a bit shaking to begin with, but O.K. now, nothing worked for about a fortnight from my waist down, and the Doc's reckoned that I had had it, but we fooled them and everything is now in perfect working order, the spine is completely O. K. and I am just waiting for my pelvis to harden, this is no line. I must admit I am a bit fed up to get pranged in a car smash, believe it or not sober??? I was leaving one of my Squadrons at about 10.00 pm after fixing the operations for the next day, on a dead straight road, when I was blinded by some pretty powerful head lights, so stuck my head down and watched my own gutter, next thing I carried out a perfect slow roll, and the car collapsed, the lorry did not bother to stop and there I lay for a couple of hours, nice type? This story has been proved by the A P M. who inspected the wreckage and car tracks while I was still out in hospital, so no cracks. Something was bound to happen sooner or later. I just got away with it, trying to get photos of the first landings in Sicily, second P38 cut out on me on take off, I hadn't got my straps done up and got chucked out just before it exploded …

As you will have seen there has been a big change round among 'the high paid help' and my boss Elliott Roosevelt is moving so maybe I will go along with him, I hope so, as he is very nice to work with. If I do move then maybe I shall be able to settle with my friend once and for all.

I nearly managed a trip to the States but got caught by Tedder for the wing, now that I have got into hospital anything may happen, perhaps Tokio here we come, you seem brassed off so come and join us. Your prospects don't seem so good, but Haifa is certainly a lot better than any of the central MED ports that I have seen, they are mostly dead as door nails.

Best of luck anyway and keep a bottle, I may get down to you.

Cheerio

Adrian

P.S. The Cairo BINT is only relaxation, needed sometimes.

APPENDIX IV

Note and Telegram to Christina

A hastily scribbled note from Adrian to Christina

Dear Christina

Am with Marko. Please come and join us. Mara says you are coming to supper. If you don't come soon, I will come and look for you.

Tout mon amour, pour que to me n'oublie pas completement.

Adrian

Telegram from Muriel Warburton to Christina 5 June 1943

GLAD AND PROUD TO HEAR OF YOUR DECORATION EVERYBODY THRILLED

MURIEL WARBURTON

APPENDIX V

Translation of Dr Anton Huber's Account of the Excavation †

On 12 April 12 1944, a Lockheed P-38 Lightning crashed on a field about 400 metres south of the village of Egling a.d. Paar, west of Munich/Bavaria. Despite the fact that the scene of the crash had been cordoned off, pieces of wreckage were collected and removed over the following days.

An inhabitant of Egling, who was 17 years old at the time, reported that in July 1945 he and about 20-25 Romanians used shovels and pickaxes to excavate the remains of the aircraft. One day an American arrived in a Jeep, went to the excavation site and made a list of the letters and numbers on some of the metal plates [from the wreckage]. The workers did not dig very deep and soon abandoned the excavation work. At that time there was a rumour that the Americans had dug up one of the aircraft's engines. It was also reported that during the time of the reallocation of agricultural land, another engine was dug up. This tale passed down by word of mouth was definitely proved by the recent excavation.

Military historian Frank Dorber had been dealing with the case of the missing Wing Commander for about 10 years and was looking for the crash site all over southern Europe. Two years ago he wrote to the archdiocese München-Freising and requested a check by the parish/vicarage of Egling to see if an aircraft had crashed at that time and where the remains of the pilot had been buried. His letter was forwarded to the Catholic Military Bishopric in Bonn and to the vicarage of Egling a.d. Paar. There the request was passed to Professor Pankraz Fried who carried out initial investigations of the circumstances of the crash. He contacted several authorities and collected extensive material. Pankraz Fried also involved and encouraged myself, an experienced archaeologist and regional conservationist for local geography and history.

The search for the actual spot of the crash where the Lightning had vanished in a field some 59 years ago proved to be very difficult. There were no written documents and eyewitness statements from children or young persons at that time, were contradictory. The main reason for these contradictions was the reallocation of agricultural land which had been carried out in the district of Egling in 1951-52. The field borders and very often the owners of the properties had also changed. After such a long time

---

† I am, as always, indebted to Bernd Rauchbach for the translation.

and many changes it was very difficult to pinpoint the situation in 1944.

The Landsberg police were also investigating the case. They questioned property owners and took aerial photos of the area south of Egling which soon indicated a possible crash site. Pankraz Fried also questioned property owners and tenants and, eventually, we applied for the permission to dig. The field had already been planted that Spring 2002, so the excavation was delayed until the first half of August, when the grain had been harvested.

In the meantime we made preparations. It was clear that the basic work of the excavation had to be done by a powerful mechanical excavator. We used a local building contractor for the work together with two young men who also offered their help and we hoped to carry out the excavation very quickly. The programme for the excavation of the aircraft and the pilot was discussed with the property owner, the Mayor and the members of the team.

Work was scheduled to begin on 10 August 2002 but wet weather caused a delay and it was agreed that there had to be at least three dry days after the heavy rain before it was possible to dig into the clay soil. Three rainy days were followed by three sunny days and the work was planned to start on 16 August.

The day before 16 August was Assumption Day, a Bank Holiday. After church, farmers and other men met in the village pub and, naturally talk turned to a discussion of the crashed airman. Suddenly, one of the men taking part in the discussion mentioned another completely new crash site. This man, 17 years old in 1944, thought that our spot was the wrong one. He particularly remembered that he, together with a group of Romanians, had unearthed parts of the plane but this was about 70-100 metres south-east of the spot we had assumed was the right one. We met at the new spot, found the property owner and talked with him. He readily gave some information but he also said that he knew from his late father that the plane had not crashed on one of their fields, but in a field which was further to the west.

On a reconnaissance photo, taken of this area by the Americans in July 1944, you could see a small spot, which we interpreted as being the crater of the crash. It roughly matched with the statement of the property owner. The aerial photo was transferred to a map on a scale 1:5000 and we were finally able to pinpoint the crash site.

On 19 August 2002, the excavator dug a ditch in an east-west direction, two metres wide and 35-40 centimetres deep. After a short time the colour of the soil changed and became darker. This was the eastern edge of the crater. After 2-4 metres, this change of colour vanished again. We had found the western edge of the crater. Next we widened the ditch to the north and south to find the perimeter revealing the oval line of the crater.

We took particular notice of the consistency and colour of the sub-soil as a change of colour could indicate possible finds and erected a measuring scale so that it was easy to identify the location of any finds.

Our plan was firstly to clear away the northern third in layers then the southern third and finally the middle. The reason for this procedure was to make sure that the important centre-section of the aircraft, the cockpit with the remains of the pilot in it, could be shown in profile from both sides.

In the northern area of the excavation, we soon found the crater which had been dug out at the time when the agricultural land was reallocated and the 3.2 metre deep crater filled with gravel. Photographic records and drawings were made. It was certain that people had searched the ground some 50 years ago and that they had recovered a fuselage/tail boom. They had not left any records.

The excavation was continued in the southern third. Later that afternoon we discovered what we were looking for. We were surprised to find the blade of a propeller and, below it, parts of the engine as it had been said that both engines had already been dug up, one by the Americans in 1945, the other in the early 50s. The propeller blade was salvaged on that first day and to a large extent we had achieved our initial goal, the identification the aircraft.

The next day we dug up a second propeller blade, parts of the engine and the turbo-supercharger which were the parts of the left fuselage of a P-38. Similar ones must have been in the northern part of the crater.

In the southern area we dug down to 3.6 metres. The third propeller blade could not be found. It had probably broken off when the plane crashed, would have been lying on the ground then taken away.

In the afternoon we started to examine the important centre part of the crash site. You could see that the wreckage was not as deep in the ground as the engines which were by far heavier. It covered an area of 40 centimetres deep and 140 to 150 centimetres wide. There were pieces all over the place, some partially burned and others turned to charcoal. The claylike subsoil was a brick-red colour which was a clear indication of a fire. The human remains which were found also showed traces of fire and eyewitnesses unanimously reported that the aircraft had been on fire when it crashed. The fire would also have continued on the ground for some time. A photo taken after the crash proves this and clearly shows smoke rising from the crash site. An eyewitness said he had watched the aircraft burning on the ground from a tree in the southern part of the village, and had heard a noise which could well have been the sound of exploding flare signal ammunition. One of the cases was found in the cockpit area.

On 20 August, the unearthed human remains were handed over to Kriminalhauptkommissar [Detective Superintendent] Rupert Kramer of Kriminalpolizei [Criminal Investigation Department] Fürstenfeldbruck for further investigation. On 22 August, we examined the complete crash site and finished the excavation. Several parts of the wreckage and human remains turned up and were also salvaged. On the same day, all mortal remains, including those which had been found on 21 August, were handed over to David Roath, U.S. Army.

David Roath and his team looked through all the finds, took photos and registered all important objects for the records. Some parts were packed and taken with them and many smaller and larger parts left. These were cleaned and sorted over three days. The rest of the soil was passed through a sieve and many small parts were discovered some of which were handed over to Douglas Baty, U.S. Army, on 21 October 2002.

One propeller blade was given to the property owner, the other to the local museum. Parts of the engine were left at the farm, where all finds had been stored after the excavation. Three pallets with the rest of the wreckage were stored at the military airfield at Penzing and transferred to England in January 2003.

After having looked through all the finds and considering all the facts it was almost certain that this aircraft, which had crashed near Egling a.d. Paar on 12 April 1944, had been a reconnaissance P-38.

Some important facts and eventual proof emerged:

1) There were no weapons on board but there were cameras and a roll/spool of large-format film.
2) Blue paint was applied to some parts of the wreckage which was typical for an F5B Lightning reconnaissance aircraft.
3) The place and time matched Adrian Warburton's mission.

Warburton had taken off from Mount Farm Airbase, England, on 12 April 1944. Captain Carl Chapman had been flying with him in another F5B and their route took them over the Munich area. Chapman reported that he had tried to contact Warburton several times on the radio but did not get any answer. After waiting for some time he flew to Sardinia and stayed there for a while, until there was no hope that Warburton would join him. He then flew back to England.

It is most probable that the aircraft had been fatally hit by an AA-battery of 26th Flak-Division at Lochhausen (Munich) and that it was not able to make it to Switzerland.

On 11 December 2002, Mr David Roath, Director of the United States Army Memorial Affairs Activity - Europe, gave a lengthy presentation at the town hall of Egling. His extensive report concluded:

Based on the evidence of historical reports, on-site investigations, and aircraft artefacts the skeletal remains associated with this crash site are believed to be the remains of Wing Commander Warburton.

This documentation was given to the British Ministry of Defence and the Royal Air Force at the end of November.

Many rumours had developed over the years, but at last, this dramatic

Second World War incident was clarified for both Egling and the Royal Air Force. After so many years of uncertainty it may be a consolation for those relatives who are still living, to know that Adrian Warburton was laid to rest with full military honours at the military cemetery Dürnbach near Gmund/Tegernsee.

This excavation was acknowledged by Professor Dr. Pankraz Fried in a few brief words in his report on 11 December 2002 to the meeting at the Egling town hall:

This compassionate humanitarian act makes a great contribution to international understanding after those two terrible wars.

Postscript (22 Aug 2003):

Currently a memorial is under consideration at the crash site to commemorate the 60th anniversary, 12 April 2004 and it is probable that the former Bishop of Regensburg will hold a commemorative service at the site. The Bishop himself had been a German Flakhelfer [anti-aircraft auxiliary] in the Second World War.

Other Goodall paperbacks from Crécy Publishing

Air Gunner
Mike Henry
The first-hand account of the experiences of an air gunner, lucky enough to survive when so many young air gunners perished.
220 pages, paperback, photograph section
0 907579 42 6 £4.99

Clean Sweep
Tony Spooner DSO, DFC
The remarkable story of Air Marshal Ivor Broom who rose from the rank of Sergeant Pilot to Air Marshal receiving the DSO, three DFCs, an AFC and other decorations along the way.
278 pages, paperback, photograph section
0 907579 18 3 £5.99

Enemy Coast Ahead
Guy Gibson VC, DSO and Bar, DFC and Bar
Wing Commander Guy Gibson gives one of the most brilliant descriptions of the Dambusters raid by the Lancasters of 617 Squadron which he himself led.
256 pages, paperback, photograph section
0 907579 62 0 £5.99

Keeping Watch
Pip Beck
The story of an R/T operator in Bomber Command who talked down bomber crews returning from operations, met them off-duty and, all too often, mourned their loss.
192 pages, paperback, photograph section
0 907579 38 8 £5.99

Lancaster Target
Jack Currie
The classic story of one crew's fight to survive a full tour of operations in the night skies of wartime Europe. Flying Lancaster bombers from RAF Wickenby, Jack Currie chronicles the life and death struggles against flak, night fighters and perilous weather.
192 pages, paperback, photograph section
0 907579 28 0 £6.99

Mosquito Victory
Jack Currie
This sequel to *Lancaster Target* graphically and humorously describes all aspects of life as a WWII RAF bomber pilot on 'rest'. Mess life and antics intermingle with Jack's real task of instructing trainees on the four-engined Halifax bomber and his subsequent return to the élite Pathfinder force flying Mosquitoes of 1409 Weather Flight.
176 pages, paperback, photograph section
0 907579 33 7 £5.99

Night Fighter
C.F.Rawnsley and Robert Wright
With John "Cat's-Eyes" Cunningham, "Jimmy" Rawnsley was half of one of the RAF's leading night fighter crews, destroying over twenty enemy aircraft.
256 pages, paperback, photograph section
0 907579 67 1 £5.99

Night Flyer
Lewis Brandon DSO, DFC and Bar
The exciting story of one of the most successful RAF night fighting partnerships of the war, the book also charts the development of night fighting.
208 pages, paperback, photograph section
0 907579 77 9 £5.99

Nine Lives
Al Deere OBE, DSO, DFC and Bar
The renowned autobiography of New Zealand's most famous RAF pilot who saw action from the Munich Crisis to the invasion of France in 1944.
288 pages, paperback, photograph section
0 907579 82 5 £5.99

No Moon Tonight
Don Charlwood
A Bomber Command classic, this is the breathtaking story of a wartime bomber crew facing the nightly bombing of the most strongly defended targets in Nazi Germany.
224 pages, paperback, photograph section
0 907579 97 3 £5.99

Only Owls and Bloody Fools Fly at Night
Tom Sawyer DFC
Flying Whitleys and Halifaxes, Tom Sawyer became one of World War II's most experienced station commanders and his account provides highly readable anecdotes about squadron life in Bomber Command.
224 pages, paperback, photograph section
0 907579 92 2 £5.99

Pathfinder
Air Vice-Marshal Don Bennett CB, CBE, DSO
The autobiography of the leader of the Pathfinders – the élite force designed to carry out pioneering target-marking and precision-bombing of Nazi-occupied Europe.
272 pages, paperback, photograph section
0 907579 57 4 £5.99

Rear Gunner Pathfinders
Ron Smith DFM
The story of the air war over Germany as seen from the small Perspex bubble of a
'Tail-End Charlie' rear gunner in a Lancaster.
200 pages, paperback
photograph section
0 907579 27 2 £4.99

Uncommon Valour
AG Goulding DFM
A comprehensive account of Bomber Command's part in the Second World War,
together with a personal view of the leadership of the force in those crucial years.
192 pages, paperback
photograph section
0 85979 095 9 £4.99

Wing Leader
Air Vice-Marshal "Johnnie" Johnson CB, CBE, DSO and Two Bars, DFC and Bar
The thrilling story of the top-scoring Allied fighter pilot of World War Two -
'Johnnie' Johnson.
320 pages, paperback, photograph section
0 907579 87 6 £6.99

Wings Aflame
Doug Stokes
The acclaimed biography of Victor Beamish, the legendary Irish station
commander who flew an incredible 126 fighter sorties in the Battle of Britain.
224 pages, paperback , photograph section
0 907579 72 8 £5.99

Wings Over Georgia
Jack Currie
Forerunner to the best-selling *Lancaster Target*, the story of Jack Currie's early
training in the UK, followed by a period with the US Army Air Corps and his
return to England to join Bomber Command.
156 pages, paperback, photograph section
0 907579 11 6 £3.99

Crecy Publishing Ltd,
1a Ringway Trading Estate,
Shadowmoss Road,
Manchester M22 5LH, UK
Tel: 0161 499 0024
Fax: 0161 499 0298
sales@crecy.co.uk
Order online at **www.crecy.co.uk**